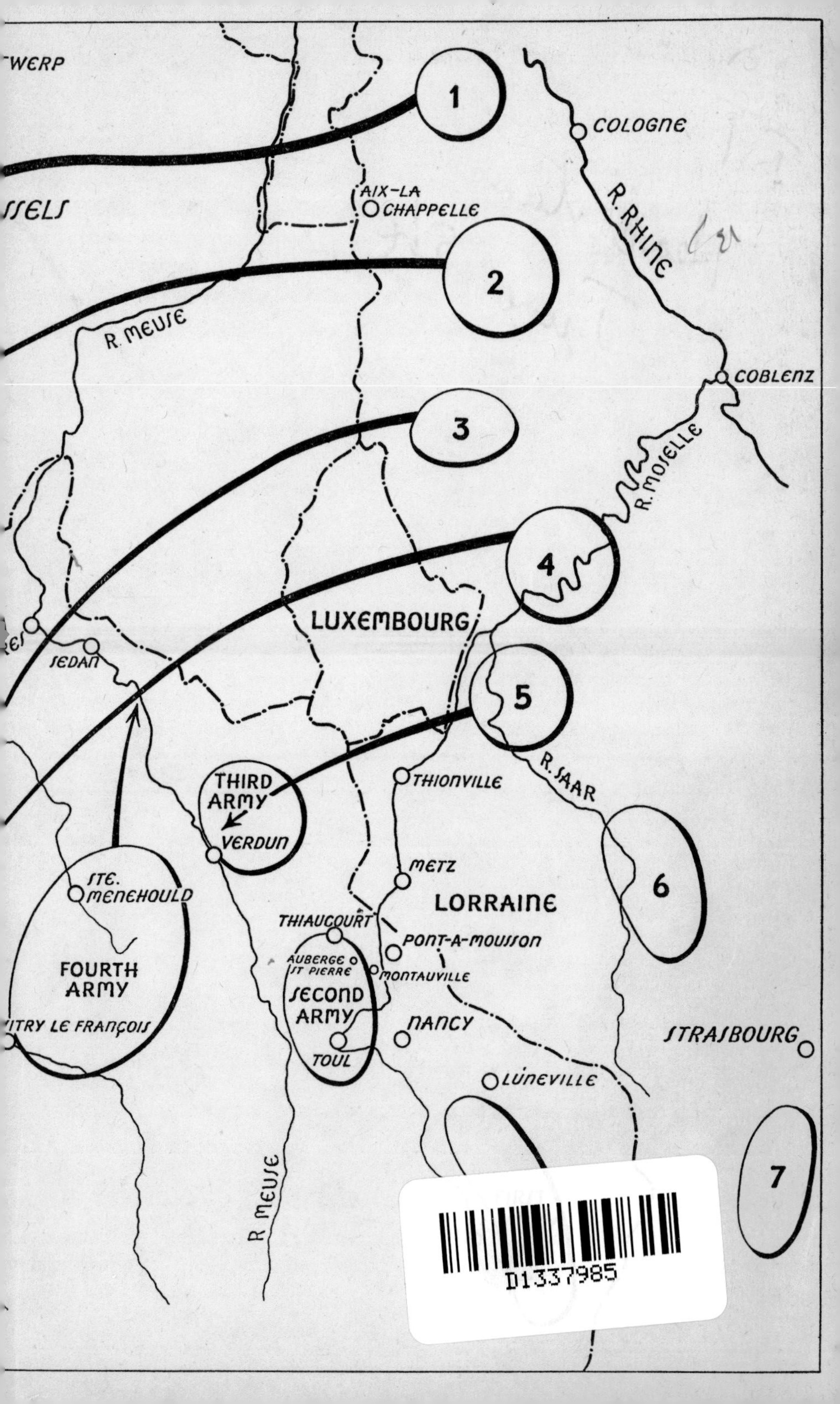
1
2
3
4
5
6
7
COLOGNE
R. RHINE
AIX-LA CHAPPELLE
R. MEUSE
COBLENZ
R. MOSELLE
LUXEMBOURG
SEDAN
R. SAAR
THIONVILLE
THIRD ARMY
VERDUN
METZ
STE. MENEHOULD
LORRAINE
THIAUCOURT
PONT-A-MOUSSON
AUBERGE ST PIERRE
MONTAUVILLE
FOURTH ARMY
SECOND ARMY
NANCY
TOUL
STRASBOURG
LÜNEVILLE
R MEUSE

T.T.
Hearthstones
June 5th

SO FULL A GLORY

De Lattre, 1948

A biography of Marshal de Lattre de Tassigny

SO FULL A GLORY

by Major-General Sir Guy Salisbury-Jones
K.C.V.O., C.M.G., C.B.E., M.C.

'But I will rise there with so full a glory,
That I will dazzle all the eyes of France.'
—*King Henry V*

With a Foreword
by the late Viscount Norwich

Weidenfeld & Nicolson
7 Cork Street London W1

First published in 1954

Made and printed in Great Britain by
William Clowes and Sons, Limited, London and Beccles

CONTENTS

Foreword by Viscount Norwich ix
Introduction xi

PART I: THE CAREFREE YEARS 1889–1914

1 Sure Foundations 1
2 Sailor or Soldier 4
3 Alert 9

PART II: THE FIRST WORLD CRISIS 1914–18

4 Beau Sabreur 12
5 Farewell to the Cavalry 16
6 Infantry Ordeal 18

PART III: THE ILLUSORY PEACE 1919–1939

7 Morocco 33
8 Capricious Fortune 44
9 "Le Régiment de Lattre" 55

PART IV: ADVERSITY 1940–1943

10 Blitzkrieg 62
11 The Giant of Rethel 70
12 The Pause on the Aisne 81
13 The Last Phase 86
14 The Call of Vichy 94
15 The Drama of Montpellier 103

PART V: TRIUMPH 1943–1945

16 Flight to Freedom 114
17 North African Springboard 121
18 "Dragoon" 128
19 Fateful Decision 140
20 Northward 154
21 Bigger Fences 160
22 Unacceptable Orders 168
23 Colmar 177
24 Victory 185
25 Retrospect 200

PART VI: AFTERMATH 1945–1950

26 A Mission Cut Short 207
27 Paris 215
28 Insecure Seat 225
29 The Stage of Western Europe 233

PART VII: THE LAST MISSION 1950–1952

30 Indo-Chinese Background 241
31 Lift up your Hearts 245
32 A Timely Gamble 251
33 Intuition 254
34 Mortal Blow 258
35 Statesman and Diplomat 262
36 Fortitude Sublime 270
37 The Peace of Mouilleron 275

EPILOGUE 278

BIBLIOGRAPHY 279

INDEX 280

LIST OF ILLUSTRATIONS

De Lattre, 1948 *Frontispiece*

1 De Lattre at Auberge Saint-Pierre, 14 September, 1914. Painting by Müller *Facing page* 84

2 De Lattre's forged identity card 85

3 Window of the prison cell at Riom 85

4 Regimental Commander, 1935 100

5 *En route* for France with Bernard, 1944 100

6 De Lattre and Montgomery 101

7 De Lattre in Indo-China 101

LIST OF MAPS

Concentration of the armies, 1914 — *Front Endpaper*
Western Front, 1916 — *Page* 25
Verdun — 25
The German bid for victory, 1918 — 31
Morocco — 32
German offensive, May 1940 — 69
The last phase, 1940 — 93
Rethel, May and June 1940 — *Facing page* 96
Elba — *Page* 133
The advance on Toulon and Marseilles — 153
Northward, 1944 — 159
The forcing of the Belfort Gap and the advance to the Rhine — 167
First attempt to close the Colmar Pocket, December 1944 — 183
German attacks North and South of Strasbourg, January 1945, and the liquidation of Colmar Pocket, January and February 1945 — 187
Indo-China — 240
Crossing of the Rhine and exploitation into the Tyrol — *Back Endpaper*

FOREWORD

IT is a popular figure of speech to refer to a man who belongs to a certain category as being the last of his species. "The Last of the Barons" was the title of a famous novel and "The Last of the Dandies" that of a successful play, and I have heard one of my contemporaries described as "the last of the wits". Such appellations are inaccurate and misleading, but if a film were written round the life of Marshal de Lattre de Tassigny it would probably be entitled "The Last of the Beaux Sabreurs".

There was indeed much in his character and his achievements that would seem to merit the title, but none the less it would be as superficial and deceptive as such titles usually are. *Panache*, that French word which can no more be translated into English than the spirit which inspires it can be fully appreciated by the majority of Englishmen, was not only part of de Lattre's character, an inborn quality, but also belonged to his military philosophy. Experienced French officers know that their men are inspired by brave words and gallant gestures that to Englishmen might seem theatrical. During a French advance in the First World War the captain of a company fell and word began to pass among the men that he was dead. The next moment a lieutenant was mortally wounded and cried out before he fell, "Yes, my children, the Captain is dead and the Lieutenant is dead, but continue the attack."

That was an example of *panache* in its full glory, just as de Lattre's insistence on the impeccable turn-out of his troops in the hour of humiliating defeat in 1940 was an example of *panache* in its steadfast endurance. For *panache* is of little value unless it has to support it unswerving devotion to duty and insatiable appetite for hard work. That de Lattre possessed both these qualities nobody who reads his biography will doubt. Nor will any doubt that he has been fortunate in his biographer.

General Salisbury-Jones knew de Lattre and he also knows France. He has, therefore, been able to supply the background without which it would be very difficult for the British public to form a clear picture of the man. And in supplying that background he has done more. He has shown something of what the French suffered during those tragic years, sufferings which have not yet ended, and wounds which have not yet healed, and which must leave behind them scars that will be borne until the day of judgment. The General writes of these events with calm detachment, but with comprehensive sympathy which cannot be too highly praised and which will probably change or moderate many opinions, formed hastily in the heat of war and not hitherto subjected to the cool review for which a more satisfactory peace might have afforded an opportunity.

The establishment of historical truth is an endless process. This illuminating biography provides an important contribution towards its completion.

22nd December, 1953 NORWICH

INTRODUCTION

IN the summer of 1944, while passing through Algiers on my way to Italy, I met the late Lord Norwich. "If you go to Naples," he said, "you must go and see General de Lattre de Tassigny; he is a most dynamic personality, and I regard him as the future Foch of France."

By taking Lord Norwich's advice, I came to know the Marshal for the first time, and later was to see much of him. It was impossible to be indifferent, either to his charm or to his wrath, which could be equally disarming. From the beginning to the end, his life was a spectacular gallop. With all the splendour of some mediaeval knight he rode fearlessly forward; but it was only on the morrow of the greatest disaster which had ever befallen his country that he reached the pinnacle of fame. At home and abroad, there were those who had lost faith in the grandeur of France, and it is against such a background that his achievements will be most fairly judged and his more unusual actions the better understood.

It is not possible for me to mention by name the many who have helped me, and I trust they will accept this brief expression of my gratitude. But I should like especially to thank Madame de Lattre de Tassigny for her help and encouragement, Monsieur Roger de Lattre de Tassigny, the Marshal's father, who at the age of ninety-seven was kind enough to receive me at Mouilleron, and the Comtesse de Marcé, the Marshal's only sister.

I am deeply indebted to the authors and publishers of those books on the Marshal which have already appeared in France, and to which reference is made in the bibliography. I refer particularly to the following: Louis Chaigne, *Jean de Lattre* (Fernand Lanore, Paris); De Lattre de Tassigny, *Histoire de la Première Armée Française* (Plon, Paris); Michel-Droit, *De Lattre, Maréchal de France* (Pierre Horay, Paris); Robert Garric, *Un Destin Héroique, Bernard de Lattre* (Plon, Paris); Bernard Simiot, *De Lattre* (Flammarion, Paris); Thomasset, *La Vie Exaltante de Jean de Lattre de Tassigny*

(Baudinière, Paris); *Au Maréchal de Lattre de Tassigny, Hommages, Ordres du Jour, Discours* (Alsatia, Colmar).

I should also like to express my thanks to the Historical Section of the French Ministry of War for allowing me to see the War Diary of the 14th French Infantry Division in 1940.

Finally, my thanks are due to Brigadier Fryer, Brigadier Carey, Major Sherwood, and Major Sleep for their invaluable advice over the maps.

PART I

The Carefree Years

1889–1914

1. SURE FOUNDATIONS

AT the turn of the century the inhabitants of Mouilleron-en-Pareds and the surrounding country would often stop and stare with amazement at the exploits of an intrepid young horseman. "There is Monsieur Jean again," they would exclaim, shaking their heads. "One day he'll break his neck."

The young horseman was Jean Marie Gabriel de Lattre de Tassigny. He had been born on the 2nd February, 1889, and was an only son. He had one sister, Anne-Marie, born two years earlier, who was subsequently to become the Comtesse de Marcé. From his earliest youth Jean set out to astound and dazzle the world about him; and so it was to be for the rest of his life. Before he was six he had already begun to display those qualities that later were to make him so bold a horseman. Helped by his father's coachman, Jacques Daniau, he would climb on to the back of his father's Great Dane, generally to fall off on the other side. He never lost his nerve, but acquired in increasing measure that appetite for risk and danger that was to become so marked a trait in his character.

Mouilleron-en-Pareds is a quiet little village in the depths of La Vendée, a remote region of France lying on the Atlantic coast, south of the Loire. There is something unmistakably solid about Mouilleron, with its plain white houses, strongly built, and its robust and massive church, with a roof that is almost flat. Upon a hill, hard by the village, are clustered the ruins of a few old windmills. Majestically they dominate the countryside, with its network of fields and hedges, stretching like a boundless sea of foliage into the distant blue horizon. The windmills of Mouilleron and the splendour of that view made a profound and mystic impression upon the young de Lattre, which he was to retain till the end of his days. The message they brought was of grandeur and peace.

Here and there, in this part of La Vendée, the fields are dotted with hard granite rock, and their cultivation demands patient and laborious toil. It is not surprising, therefore, that this land should have bred generations of robust peasants, whose rock-like strength has been enhanced by the depth of their religious faith. Every Sunday a tuneful carillon calls the faithful to Mass; and upon the heads of the older women may still be seen the trim white head-dress which changing fashions have failed to destroy. When the waves of the French Revolution surged over France, for long they beat in vain against La Vendée, which became a stronghold of royalist resistance. Not until 1793, when Kléber and Marceau were sent against them, did those stubborn peasants succumb. More than twenty years later, when Napoleon escaped from Elba, La Vendée rose again, drawing off appreciable forces that might have strengthened the army of the Emperor on the field of Waterloo.

It was at Mouilleron also, twenty-five years after the battle of Waterloo, that Georges Clemenceau was born. Although he inherited neither the religious nor the royalist traditions of La Vendée, it was the land of his birth which gave him his indomitable will; and in the First World War, when he was seventy-seven and the fortunes of his country were at their lowest ebb, it was he who held it firm. "Père la Victoire" was the name he earned.

The de Lattre family was numerous in the north of France and in Flanders, and it was in 1740 that Jean's forebears affixed to their name that of their property of Tassigny, near Guise. Although most of the de Lattres had been municipal magistrates, here and there a soldier could be traced. In 1848 a de Lattre, who was an infantry officer, prevented Poitiers from rising, and during the troubles of 1873 an uncle of the future Marshal compromised his future by raising the white standard of the Count of Chambord at the military school of Saint-Cyr.

The father of Jean de Lattre was Roger de Lattre de Tassigny. He came from Poitiers and only settled at Mouilleron after marrying Mademoiselle Anne-Marie Hénault, the daughter of the Mayor, whose own father-in-law had been Mayor of the village since 1817.

Roger himself succeeded his father-in-law as Mayor in 1911, and in 1953, at the age of ninety-seven, he was still in office. Thus the father, grandfather, and great-grandfather of Jean de Lattre between them were Mayors of Mouilleron for nearly a hundred and forty years.

It is of interest to record that although the Hénault family were now strong royalists, the great-grandfather of Anne-Marie had been an officer in the Civic Guard under the Revolution. But romance had intervened to soften any antipathy he may have felt towards the nobility, and he fell in love with a lady of noble birth named Mademoiselle Rosalie Duchesne de Denant, who, together with her three sisters, had been imprisoned and condemned to death. The three sisters perished, but Hénault helped Mademoiselle Rosalie to escape and he afterwards married her.

Roger de Lattre de Tassigny was a man with a strong sense of duty, and a character of the highest integrity. He cherished no great ambitions, but remained the conscientious and highly respected citizen of Mouilleron, content year after year to do his duty in the village of his adoption. The conscientious performance of a task was the guiding theme of his life. One day, when his ninety-seventh birthday was already behind him, he was discussing with a stranger the merits of his young secretary. "All that I ask of him," he said, punctuating every word with an expressive motion of the hands, "is that he should do his work thoroughly and conscientiously." The convincing punch behind those words revealed his character. Such was the grand old man who inspired in his son so profound an affection, and who imparted to him that high sense of duty and that insistence on high standards that always remained with him.

The mother of Jean de Lattre was a woman of considerable intelligence, and she, like her father, enjoyed entertaining in their modest home at Mouilleron the notabilities of the neighbourhood. In any company her personality was pre-eminent. "Moreover," in the words of her daughter, "she personified goodness, had no enemies, and everywhere inspired friendship and trust. Together with my father she passed her time in giving service to others." She possessed also in full measure the ardent faith of La Vendée. It was from his mother, therefore, that Jean inherited those human qualities that were so often to disarm his enemies, and that faith that was to support him in so many moments of crisis. The crucifix which she gave him on the occasion of his first Communion was the same one that was placed in his hand at the moment of death. But for all her good influence, she tended to spoil him. Generous and warmhearted, she would often plead with his father to give him what he wanted. "Mon petit Roger," she would say, "let him have it. He deserves it, for one day he is going to be great."

Such were the surroundings amid which de Lattre grew up. In the days to come his impulsive and intensely human nature might sometimes tempt him to stray from the accepted paths. But deep down in the soil of La Vendée the foundations had been surely laid, and through all the squalls and tempests of his full and restless life they would always hold him firm.

2. SAILOR OR SOLDIER

WITH the passing of childhood, Jean's spirit of adventure grew. He ever sought the forbidden fruit of danger. Twice he was nearly drowned; and the handling of this turbulent but likable youth became an increasing problem. In the years to come he was to perplex and baffle the soldiers and statesmen of his own and other lands, but the honour of first trying to control him was to be shared by two German governesses.

The Great Dane no longer provided that spice of danger that he needed, and it was Jacques Daniau again who taught him the elements of horsemanship. The horse became his absorbing passion, and he was determined to acquire an animal of his own. Yielding to that disarming charm which he could exert with such dexterity, his grandmother advanced him the money, and the horse was his. This was the animal that gained for him a reputation for uncommon daring, for in those early days he was a bold rather than an accomplished horseman. With the support of Jacques Daniau, he embarked upon every conceivable adventure, always in search of bigger obstacles and more difficult country. There were hair-breadth escapes both for rider and horse. On one occasion they became hopelessly bogged, and a team of oxen had to come to the rescue. Daniau entered fully into the spirit of these escapades, but at times he was at his wits' end to know how to hide from the father the misadventures of the day.

If Jean was not riding, he would often seat himself on the box of his father's carriage and take over the reins from Daniau. Then, to the discomfiture of the passengers, he would drive like Jehu. The nerves of his unfortunate mother were often severely shaken. One day, when he was driving more furiously than usual, his mother loudly remonstrated. Jean shouted back that it was not he who held the reins, but Daniau, who had been drinking too much! Daniau still delights to recount this story. The holidays would generally end with Jean driving to the station at break-neck speed, for never was enough time allowed. If necessary, the train would be held, and with the utmost goodwill the station staff would ensure that the boy and his belongings were bundled into it. Already he seemed to possess that uncanny power over men which was to make so many his slaves. His love of speed never left him, and in later years a drive with de Lattre in a car was exhilarating or terrifying. As with the horse, so with the car, full gallop was the only pace.

The influence which the horse exercised upon the formation of de Lattre's character cannot be measured. In recent years there has been a tendency to decry equitation as a useful form of military training, but there is little doubt that the horse can endow its master with a feeling of power and a contempt for danger that nothing else can give. Moreover, in the saddle an intelligent mind tends to detach itself from the earth and to soar to higher planes.

Jean's father was determined that his son's education should be of the best. In Mouilleron, under an erudite priest and a retired lady school-teacher of unusual ability, he received a good grounding, particularly in the classics. In 1898, at the age of nine, he went to the College of Saint-Joseph, at Poitiers, where his father had been before him, and where the classics formed the basis of the education. Opinion seems divided as to his conduct there. It would be surprising if, with his zest for life and adventure, he did not occasionally kick over the traces. One of his teachers wrote of him as follows: "If he was inclined to make fun of things, it was never from malice. He was a good worker, he had ambition in the good sense of the word, and was very original. He was always among the top students, and frequently first. But above all, he showed great character and determination, and was already a leader of men."

De Lattre was always highly sensitive, and when the day came for his confirmation, and illness prevented his attendance, he seems to have taken his misfortune badly. The Rector of Saint-Joseph, Father Bardier, a man of outstanding personality and wisdom, who had discovered unusual qualities in this pupil, decided himself to prepare him for confirmation, and began to take a special interest in his development. Father Bardier in turn inspired the highest respect on the part of de Lattre, for he was a man who strove after all those things which were later to be so dear to his own heart. He believed in grandeur and the elevation of the mind, and to achieve his purpose he was always organizing not only religious fêtes but theatrical performances, concerts, and gymnastic displays. Many of the well-known stars of the day were asked to Poitiers, and all was done regardless of expense. But Father Bardier was a great disciplinarian, and a man of the highest ideals. Religion, duty, honour, and country were his articles of faith. The influence which he exercised upon de Lattre was profound, and until Father Bardier's death in 1925 his former pupil continued to visit him in Paris. By the year 1904 his secondary education had been completed with brilliance.

De Lattre had always been fond of the sea, and in 1904, when he was fifteen, he decided to be a sailor, and went to the College of Vaugirard to prepare for the Navy. There he came under Professor Henri de Gaulle, father of General Charles de Gaulle, and a man of great culture. He passed his written examinations with ease, and there is little doubt that he would have passed the oral test also, for his power of speech was not the least of his gifts. But destiny had not intended that he should be a sailor, and when the date arrived for the oral test he was ill. He might have tried later, but in the meantime, he had decided to prepare for Saint-Cyr and to try for the Cavalry. All those gifts with which he had been so plenteously endowed would now be devoted to the service of the Army. But the love of the sea remained with him for ever. In the flat in Paris which he occupied at the end of his life, model ships were proudly arrayed with his trophies of war.

It was to the "Corniche" at Sainte-Geneviève in Versailles that de Lattre went to prepare for Saint-Cyr. Bethouart, afterwards to command a corps in de Lattre's First French Army at the end of the Second World War, was also there, and he described his contemporary as a "big chap, handsome, and smiling, moving about among his fellow students with ease, and without shyness or haughtiness, interested in everything, pleasant with everyone, and already, as always, in search of new contacts". This search for new contacts was a characteristic that followed him through life; he loved to have friends in every circle, and, like his mother, he needed the company of stimulating minds.

When he decided that the effort was worth while, de Lattre's capacity for work was prodigious. Saint-Cyr and the Cavalry were worth-while goals, and of those who passed into Saint-Cyr from the "Corniche", de Lattre was top. But during the same period his boisterous spirit demanded an outlet. Before going to Saint-Cyr his father had sent him to Brighton to improve his English. Although the accounts of his stay there are meagre and conflicting, there seems little doubt that he ran a little wild. His views on money were simple: it was there to be spent; and it seems that at Brighton he spent it in that grand and generous manner that so well befitted him. Whatever may be the truth in regard to his escapades at this time, he was determined to enjoy to the full the fleeting hours of youth. In after life, in his happier moods, he loved to reminisce, and he always spoke of Brighton with unusual warmth and affection. Can it be that there, perhaps for the first time, there was a little romance?

It is difficult to believe that the carefree youth at Brighton was the same de Lattre who a few months later was to accompany his parents on a pilgrimage to Lourdes. There he was to be seen walking barefoot to the Grotto, and helping to carry a stretcher on which lay a dying woman, who was cured. Several years later he again sacrificed his leisure hours to go to Lourdes and help a consumptive girl from La Vendée in whom his family was interested. But with de Lattre everything was unpredictable. There was nothing ostentatious about his acts at Lourdes; they were a true expression of his warm and generous heart.

To pass into Saint-Cyr with a high place gave a cadet the privilege of choosing his arm. De Lattre's first serious ambition had therefore now been realized: the way to the Cavalry, with all its splendour, was now clear. Already at Saint-Cyr, sword and spurs gave to the cavalry cadets an element of *panache* that distinguished them from the others. How well this befitted de Lattre! Throughout that colourful career which was only just starting, *panache* was to be his inseparable companion. Many might mock, but together they were to accomplish great things.

Before going to Saint-Cyr de Lattre served as a trooper in the 28th Dragoons at Provins, just to the south-east of Paris. In those days Saint-Cyr, since destroyed by Allied bombing, was steeped in the traditions of Napoleon. Every corner, inside and out, bore the name of one of his marshals or one of his victories. But susceptible though de Lattre was to atmosphere, Saint-Cyr does not seem to have inspired in him the will to work of which he was capable. The cadet who secured so good a place on his arrival seems to have done little to make a success of his career there. Perhaps, now that he was safely on his way to a commission in the Cavalry, he saw no point in deploying more than the minimum amount of energy necessary to get him through Saint-Cyr and on to the cavalry school at Saumur. He found it irksome to be subjected to a hard discipline by superiors whom he did not always respect. Fools he would never gladly suffer, and there were probably few instructors at Saint-Cyr with the intellectual stature of Father Bardier. One of them incurred his displeasure from the outset: it was not the fact that politically the instructor held extreme left views which put de Lattre against him, but the fact that his instruction was mediocre, and mediocrity he abhorred. On one occasion, recalling the events of 1873, this instructor said to de Lattre: "I hope you are no relation of the de Lattre who raised the white standard at Saint-Cyr at that time." "On the contrary," replied the cadet, "that was my uncle, and I am proud to be his nephew."

De Lattre decided to have nothing more to do with this instructor. To oral questions he made no answer, and if it was written work, he handed in a blank sheet of paper. This attitude was sufficient to ruin his chances of passing out well from Saint-Cyr. In fact, he passed out nearly last, and over-turbulent behaviour at the end of their last term resulted in several cadets being detained for eight days after the rest had started their leave. Among them were de Lattre and Bethouart. On the eve of his military career, therefore, it hardly looked as if a successful future was assured.

3. ALERT

SAUMUR was to prove a happier experience. There de Lattre was surrounded by men after his own heart, and the horse was supreme. In such an atmosphere his qualities were able to develop to the best advantage. Very soon he earned a reputation as a horseman of uncommon skill, and when he passed out at the end of a year and received his commission in the 12th Dragoons, he was already regarded as an officer with qualities above the average.

Physically also de Lattre was above average, and, in the uniform of the day, he was a splendid representative of the French cavalry officer. The officers of the regiment still wore red breeches, a neat black jacket with silver buttons, and a high white collar. The helmet, with its long, flowing plume, completed the dazzling picture. A little vanity was surely permissible, and he was happy.

It was now 1911 and the 12th Dragoons were stationed within a few miles of the German frontier, partly at Pont-à-Mousson (see map on front endpaper), on the Moselle, and partly at Toul. Already relations with Germany were strained, and in that same year there had been the crisis at Agadir in Morocco, when a German cruiser had put into port ostensibly to ensure the safety of German lives. The atmosphere, therefore, that prevailed at that time among young officers in a French cavalry regiment stationed near the frontier may well be imagined. At any moment war might break out, and they would be the first to be in action.

Rarely has the morale of a regiment been as high in peace-time as was the morale of those French cavalry regiments on the frontier in the years that preceded the First World War. Young officers dreamed of the day when they would lead their troops triumphant over the border to recover Alsace and Lorraine, snatched by the victorious Prussians in 1871.

The proximity of the frontier and the constant threat of war kept all at concert pitch. From a hill overlooking Pont-à-Mousson, on the eastern bank of the Moselle, the cathedral of Metz, then a German city, was easily visible. A few miles away there was a broad plain, through the centre of which ran the frontier. Many were the occasions when French and German cavalry regiments would both be exercising on the same plain within a few hundred yards of each other.

It was known that the officers of a German cavalry regiment at Metz had sworn, on the outbreak of war, to capture the officers of the 12th Dragoons in bed, and the latter were equally determined not to be caught napping. The Commanding Officer estimated that German cavalry could reach Pont-à-Mousson within thirty-five minutes of their crossing the frontier and his receiving the warning. By dint of constant practice, the regiment could at all times be ready for action within thirty-five minutes. To ensure that by no trickery would they be captured in their beds, many of the officers had rope ladders down which they could escape from their bedroom windows if the enemy should surreptitiously enter the house.

There were many false alarms. One summer evening the Commanding Officer was giving a party in his garden. Suddenly, a figure in German uniform appeared over the wall. Charming ladies in their evening dresses scattered into the bushes, while the nearest officer went for the enemy. The intruder just raised his hands in time. He was a young French officer; German uniforms were easy to come by, for most regiments had a few specimens to enable the men to recognize the enemy if war should come.

On another occasion there was a more serious alarm, and it so happened that the Commanding Officer's favourite charger was lame. As he left the house, he dramatically handed a revolver to his wife, instructing her to shoot the horse rather than let it fall into the hands of the enemy. Fortunately, again, it was a false alarm.

Such was the atmosphere in which de Lattre soldiered on the eve of the First World War. Peace-time soldiering can rarely have more effectively combined realism with enjoyment, for they were a happy band of officers, and the state of constant readiness by no means precluded amusement. On most Sundays race meetings were organized by the cavalry regiments in the various frontier towns, and de Lattre was as keen as anyone. But there was no officer in the regiment who was more zealous in the performance of his duties. Often he would take his troop up that precipitous hill that overlooked Pont-à-Mousson, and, with his sense of the theatrical, he would point his sword towards Metz and make the men salute the city that once belonged to France. It was a gesture that was intended, in all seriousness, as a vow that not a man in the troop would rest until the lost city should be regained for France. In later years the critics of de Lattre might deplore his sense of the theatrical, but they could never deny that he raised the morale of those who served under him to a pitch that was rare. To him everything that he ever undertook became a mission, and into those who served under him he infused the spirit of crusaders.

It must have been an exhilarating experience to serve under young de Lattre, but for the timid it could provide anxious moments. One day he would lead his troop to the brink of a precipitous quarry. "After me," he shouted, and after their intrepid leader the men would scramble down the slope that had always been regarded as impossible. On other occasions he would organize a boar hunt. Cut-and-dried training programmes he abhorred; his men must ever be prepared for the unexpected. Such methods did not always earn the approval of his superiors, but they produced a troop that was as resilient in mind and as contemptuous of danger as any soldiers have ever been in peace-time. The test was soon to come.

PART II

The First World Crisis

1914–1918

4. BEAU SABREUR

AT the end of June 1914, at Sarajevo in Bosnia, the heir to the throne of the Austro-Hungarian Empire, together with his consort, met sudden death at the hands of an assassin. To many the event had little significance. In France, the 14th July was celebrated with the usual gaiety, and it was followed by the seasonal exodus from Paris. President Poincaré went on a state visit to Russia. In England, too, men's thoughts turned towards the impending holidays. In the minds of a few only were graver thoughts revolving. The public schools dispersed; with some reluctance, the older boys sacrificed a few days of the holidays to undergo in camp—not too seriously—the elements of military training. Within a few months many of them were to meet untimely death on the battlefield, while—all too late—Great Britain armed for the fight.

The closing days of July saw Europe racing headlong to disaster. With unavailing voices, sane and sober statesmen appealed for peace. In memorable language, the British Foreign Secretary portrayed the tragic scene: "The lights of Europe are going out." By the 3rd August France was at war. Meanwhile the invader had swept into Belgium, whose neutrality Britain was pledged to defend. By the 4th August, therefore, Britain too was committed to war.

For most people in England it was difficult to believe that their own future was at stake. But a peace-loving people was not insensitive to the appeal of a great cause, and the plight of Belgium stirred them deeply. There was no conscription, but the best in the land flocked quickly to the colours. For those who hesitated, patriotic songs were composed, such as "We don't want to lose you, but we think you ought to go". Bitter lessons had still to be learnt.

In France, too, patriotism was strong. For nearly fifty years she had mourned Alsace and Lorraine. Now her Army would go forward to recover them. At the Gare de l'Est in Paris, although mothers, wives, and sweethearts might weep for a moment, there were scenes of excitement and fervour as trainload after trainload of reservists moved out of the station and headed eastward.

To the north, between Aix-la-Chapelle and Thionville, the Germans had concentrated five armies which were to pivot on Thionville, sweep through Belgium, and within five or six weeks roll up the whole French Army against the Swiss frontier (see map on front endpaper). To the south of Thionville, in Lorraine and Alsace, two armies only had been concentrated: their rôle was to be purely defensive, and if, as expected, the French were to take the offensive on that front, they were even to be prepared, within limits, to give ground. Such, in outline, was the Schlieffen plan as modified by Von Moltke.

Although the French had foreseen the possibility of a German advance through Belgium, they had not expected it to extend so far north as it did. They had concentrated four armies, therefore, between the Swiss frontier and Mézières, and the British Expeditionary Force was to concentrate on their left near Maubeuge. A reserve French army round Vitry-le François was to be prepared to intervene, to the east or to the north, as circumstances might demand. The main intention of the French was to break up the German advance to the north and themselves to take the offensive on the Alsace-Lorraine front.

When war came the 12th Dragoons were still on the frontier facing Lorraine, and they formed part of the XX Corps under General Foch. The moment for which de Lattre had lived and trained his men had come. But for a while impatience had to be curbed, for initially the regiment had to play its part in covering the concentration of the armies. Moreover, so determined were the French not to appear as the aggressors that on the very eve of war those troops nearest the frontier, including the 12th Dragoons, were ordered to withdraw.

But de Lattre's troop was soon patrolling forward with all the *élan* which its commander had instilled, and as early as the 11th

August de Lattre received the first of the many wounds that were to lay him low. A piece of shell struck him in the knee, but his absence from the regiment was as brief as possible, and by the beginning of September he was back again.

Meanwhile, events had taken a dramatic turn. On the Alsace-Lorraine front initial French successes had been countered with heavy losses; indeed, on that front the Germans had themselves decided to depart from their original plan and to assume the offensive. On the French left, Joffre had ordered forward the Third and Fourth French Armies in a north-easterly direction against the left flank of the Germans moving through Belgium. Unexpected strength was encountered. By the 21st August, when the British Expeditionary Force was in contact with the Germans at Mons, the French Commander-in-Chief had realized the full magnitude of the attempted German envelopment. Coolly, in the face of seeming disaster, he decided to swing back his centre and left, and by the simultaneous transfer of troops from the right of his front to the left, to constitute a new army, the Sixth, north of Paris. Requisitioned taxis helped to speed the move.

It was then that the Germans made a fatal blunder. At Le Cateau, on the 26th August, Von Kluck, commanding the First German Army, had fought a hard battle with the British. Assuming from that moment that they could be ignored, he had decided to swing south-east, avoiding Paris, thereby hoping the more quickly to roll up the French left. By this ill-conceived plan he exposed his right flank to the new Sixth Army, then being constituted. Joffre seized the fleeting moment. The Sixth Army advanced, and the victory of the Marne resulted. To avoid the trap, the Germans withdrew, but by the 9th September they had recovered themselves. On the grim heights that dominated the northern bank of the Aisne they held the Allies, and it was along that line, with occasional fluctuations, that the front remained stabilized for the rest of the war.

Away to the east, too, the Germans abandoned the offensive; and, harassed by the French Cavalry, they withdrew northward. In these operations the 12th Dragoons took their full share. On the 14th September de Lattre was returning with his troop after patrolling for four days between the Moselle and Thiaucourt.

While moving across some open country in the otherwise wooded area west of Pont-à-Mousson, now in no-man's-land, they suddenly ran into a patrol of Bavarian Uhlans near Auberge St. Pierre. In a flash, he was off at the head of his troop and in a few seconds he was well clear, only to find himself single-handed in the face of four Uhlans. He continued straight for the nearest, whom he killed with his sword. He had just killed a second, when one of the others transfixed him in the chest with a lance. De Lattre succeeded in disengaging, and at that moment the rest of his troop came up and drove the Germans off. A few seconds later de Lattre fell from his horse, with the point of the lance still sticking into him. The shaft had broken off; it was a serious wound; the point of the lance had entered the upper part of his chest, reached the shoulder-blade, and perforated the lung. Despite great pain, he found sufficient strength to tell his men to leave him and go back with the information they had acquired. They were only to come back and fetch him if they could. However, while the rest of the troop rode off, his Troop Sergeant Bavidot managed to get him into the saddle again, and led him off in search of help. Reaching a farm near Montauville, just west of Pont-à-Mousson, owned by Monsieur and Madame David, he carried de Lattre inside with their help, and they did their best to dress the wound. Bavidot, after some hesitation, tried to extract the point of the lance. To do so, he had to put one foot on de Lattre's throat.

Meanwhile de Lattre's horse had broken loose, and it found its way back to its old stable at Pont-à-Mousson. Some of the inhabitants were still about, and catching hold of the horse, they found the name of its owner stamped on the saddle in accordance with regulations. Bavidot meanwhile had found two volunteers, and with their help he managed to move de Lattre on a stretcher into Pont-à-Mousson. There was little they could do for him beyond placing him in a cellar, where it was hoped the Germans might not discover him, if they entered the village. But after finding de Lattre's horse, the villagers had already got word back to the nearest French troops, and the 5th Hussars had sent out a patrol under a subaltern named Schmeltz to try to find de Lattre. With them they took an ordinary farm wagon, the wheels of which they covered with straw to deaden the noise. On the outskirts of Pont-à-Mousson the patrol encountered some Uhlans but brushed them aside. More Germans were also found in the town. But these also were driven off, and under cover of night they managed to get de Lattre back to the French lines. De Lattre never forgot Schmeltz, of whom he always spoke as his "saviour".

If it had not been for de Lattre's robust constitution and his iron will, he could hardly have survived the long hours which were to pass before he received attention. More remarkable still was the speed of his recovery. Within a month he was back with his regiment. But there is little doubt that he returned too soon. Throughout the war the wound troubled him, and often he had to fight hard to prevent himself going sick.

If anyone had regarded the flamboyant young cavalier as a mere showman, their doubts had been for ever dispelled. At the end of the year, when he was still only twenty-five, de Lattre was made a Chevalier of the Legion of Honour. This was a rare reward for an officer so young, and no cavalryman could wish for more. He was very human, and he was proud of his Legion of Honour, and proud of his citation; but he derived greater pleasure still from a painting done by Müller, showing him riding down the Uhlan, which was given him by a non-commissioned officer in his troop named Deutch. Under the picture Deutch wrote: "To the leader loved by his men, whom he trained, understood and led in battle."

5. FAREWELL TO THE CAVALRY

DE LATTRE must have been one of the last officers in Europe to be wounded by a lance. On other battlefields the Cavalry still had a glorious rôle to play, but on the Western Front the days of the horse in battle were numbered.

By the end of 1914 the machine-gun had proved supreme.

Against its wall of spurting lead, the assaults of the Infantry had been launched in vain. Both sides went to ground, and, from Switzerland to the North Sea, the labyrinth of trenches grew. Night after night the Infantry working-parties laboured to thicken those endless belts of wire. Digging and wiring became their lot. Sometimes there was a trench raid to relieve the monotony, and an occasional offensive might carry the line forward a few hundred yards; but soon it was digging and wiring again. The newly won ground must be consolidated.

In the early stages, the Cavalry might dismount and take turns with the Infantry; but they kept their horses, awaiting the miracle that would pave the way through those accursed trenches and wire. But they waited in vain, and for men like de Lattre the long deadlock became intolerable; moreover his intelligence alone sufficed to make it clear that the chance of the Cavalry was more than remote. An outlet for his impatience was soon to come. Brought up on the doctrine of "l'offensive à outrance", the officers of the French infantry had led their men forward with supreme bravery, but they had fallen in their hundreds, and, by the end of 1915, the gaps in their ranks had reached such proportions that they could no longer be filled. Such was the situation which led General Joffre to launch an appeal to the Cavalry to find officers for the Infantry.

De Lattre who had again been wounded, was among the first to submit his name. It was a decision that was only made with cruel heart-searching. The horse had been everything to him. Moreover, he had no illusions. He knew what his life as an infantry officer was to be; but anything was preferable to the weary waiting of the Cavalry. If part from the horse he must, at least he could take with him to the Infantry the spirit of the Cavalry. It was the break-up of a happy band of disillusioned officers. All their eager training at Pont-à-Mousson seemed to have been in vain. But the spirit of the 12th Dragoons was not to be suppressed. Some, like de Lattre, took it with them to the Infantry; by others it was taken to the Air Force.

All that de Lattre felt when he volunteered for the Infantry is described in a letter which he wrote to his sister at the time. It clearly reveals the sensitiveness of his nature, and the lofty ideals which already animated him.

"It is a great sacrifice; and for me, now that I have made my decision, these days are like some cruel torture. Any day now, I am expecting to go. I never knew how greatly I loved what I am now about to leave . . . but at this moment we have all got to do our duty, and disdaining suffering and death, to lead our men, no matter where or how. That is the only thing that matters. But my poor men (mes pauvres petits bonhommes) whom I have tried for so many months to train—it is they whom I shall miss. I cannot think how I had the courage to ask to leave them. Why am I going? Almost solely because I have been decorated, and because I regard the appeal of General Joffre to be more pressing than any other. Besides, I feel that it is my simple duty to set the example. I have often said to my men that 'honour obliges': now I am sure that they will believe me. There are three of us in the regiment who are going, and we are all in the same squadron. I am proud to say that we are all doing it without calculating the cost, and without any thought of ambition. God understands our intentions and the depths of our thoughts. May His will be done. More than ever, I place my health, my efforts, and my courage in His hands."

These words were not lightly written. They were a truthful reflection of the character of the writer. In de Lattre there was ingrained that sense of duty that had also been his father's. It was profound beyond measure, and it demanded complete and unquestioning submission to every sacrifice.

In submitting his name for the Infantry, de Lattre felt entitled to make one request. He applied to join a regiment of his beloved Vendée, the 93rd Infantry Regiment. His request was granted, and on joining the Regiment, he was at once given command of a company, with the acting rank of captain.

6. INFANTRY ORDEAL

IT was an exhausted 93rd Infantry Regiment, the 3rd Battalion of which de Lattre now joined. It formed part of the 21st Infantry Division which had already suffered heavy casualties in unavailing attempts to pierce the German lines. Officers and men, who had lived through those gruelling months, and seen so many of their comrades killed, were not likely to look with favour upon this newly joined and impeccably turned-out officer, straight from the Cavalry. Some had heard of his exploits in the opening days of the war, but that did not mean that he was going to prove equal to that drudgery and discomfort which were now to be his lot.

Even in those long periods of stagnation, the worth of a company commander was soon discovered. Rarely have officers lived so close to their men, or more completely shared their hardships. Whether in the mud of some so-called trench, or in the relative comfort of a dug-out, all they did or said, and all their reactions to discomfort or danger, were immediately known to all. The men were not long in doubt about de Lattre. At the time he took over, rations failed to come up regularly, and he set about with a refreshing vigour to put things right. Moreover, whenever it was humanly possible, he contrived to get the cookers almost into the front line, so that under the worst conditions a hot meal was available; he was not one of those to flop into his dug-out and make himself comfortable until the battalion was relieved. He was always going round the lines, getting to know the men, and generally keeping things going. "Captain de Lattre", wrote one who served under him at the time, "was sometimes exacting, but we loved him none the less, and we understood him. Besides, he always set the example. He was far more strict with the N.C.Os, from whom he exacted the very utmost." De Lattre indeed was exacting, and under the most impossible conditions, he would insist on the highest standards being maintained. On occasions, if there was no water available for shaving, he would make the men use a part of their wine ration for the purpose. To the surprise of all, whatever the conditions, he himself remained as impeccably dressed as on the day he joined them.

No one at that time was nearer de Lattre than his soldier-servant, Louis Meriaux. Meriaux was one of those unfortunate young men who in 1914 had been cut off from his parents, when his home was overrun by the Germans. The misfortune of Meriaux stirred a chord of deep sympathy in the warm and sensitive heart of de Lattre. In later years, Meriaux recalled that one day de Lattre had said to him, "My good Meriaux, would you like me to be your adopted father for the war?" Meriaux never forgot it. His devotion to his company commander was complete. At times de Lattre suffered much from his wounds, particularly from the lance-wound, and on such occasions Meriaux looked after him as a mother might look after her child.

Under his constant attention to their welfare, the morale of de Lattre's company had no equal. Indeed, by the beginning of 1916, de Lattre had sufficiently made his mark in the battalion to be appointed second-in-command. In March, the Regiment moved into a new sector near Mourmelon on the Marne (see map on p. 25), where a quarter of a century later, as Commander of the 14th Infantry Division, he was to face for a second time the overwhelming hordes of the invader.

Meanwhile, to the east, in the middle of February, the rumble of gunfire had heralded the opening of the hardest fought battle of the war. At the the end of 1915, the Germans considered that the military effort of France had been spent, and that a hard blow against the French front might pave the way to victory. But they themselves had not the resources to launch an offensive along the whole front. It was necessary, therefore, to select a sector in which limited forces might achieve the desired results. It may seem curious that the fortified zone of Verdun, with its strong belt of forts, should have been chosen as the point of attack. But it was felt that this zone was so important to the French, that even if the Germans failed to reach their objectives they would compel the enemy to use up his strength in its defence.

At the outset of the battle, Verdun itself was nine miles from the front line at its nearest point (see map on p. 25). The town lies in a hollow, and through it from south to north flows the Meuse, with high hills on either bank known as the Côtes de Meuse. At four o'clock on the morning of the 21st February, there fell on the Archbishop's Palace at Verdun a fourteen-inch shell, which had been fired at a range of twenty-two miles. The battle had started. Later, the bombardment started along a front of twenty-five miles, from the Meuse to Etain. Nothing like it had ever been seen before. By a vast concentration of artillery, the Germans had hoped to pulverize the defences, and to create a "zone of death" in which nothing could survive. Such was but a foretaste of the ordeal that was to come. It was not until the evening that the bombardment lifted, and three German army corps went forward to the assault on a front of about ten miles, east of the Meuse. For the first time, highly trained shock troops with special equipment preceded the advance.

By the 25th February the situation had become critical, and at midnight, General Pétain assumed command. For more than four months the battle was to rage. At the outset Verdun had not been badly damaged; only here and there a ruined house reminded one that the town was within range of the heavier guns of the enemy. But in the weeks that were to follow, as the fury of the battle increased and the ground changed hands with the swaying fortunes of the fight, it gradually assumed that grim appearance so familiar in the other battered towns of France. Day by day, too, under the pounding of artillery, both German and French, the green fields disappeared; villages were swallowed up and sank into the ground. Even the ruins were churned to powder, until there was nothing to distinguish them from the vast ocean of dust or mud that surrounded them. The monotony of the scene was only broken by those grim, gaunt skeletons that once were woods. It became virtually impossible to trace the front line accurately on the map at any given moment.

With relentless pressure the enemy redoubled his onslaught and extended the front of attack; and with indomitable courage the French held on. "Ils ne passeront pas" was the spirit that sustained them. Along "La Voie Sacrée", as the road to Verdun came to be called, an endless stream of lorries carried regiment after regiment into that insatiable slaughter-house that lay beyond. In a few months, in those few square miles, the life-blood of France was poured out, and for generations to come, the effects would be felt. From February to June, in that one battle, French casualties reached the appalling total of more than 442,000.*

By the early summer, the 21st Division was engaged in the battle. The forts of Vaux and Douaumont had fallen, and the front had contracted, so that Verdun itself was within a mile or two of the front line. On the 10th June the 137th Regiment of the Division

* 179,000 (apart from officers) were killed, missing, or prisoners, and 263,000 were wounded; with officers, the total was probably 460,000.

took over a part of the line, ironically known as the Ravin de la Dame, to the North of Thiaumont. De Lattre, with his battalion, was in reserve, attempting to enjoy a few days' rest in the Citadel of Verdun, where at least they enjoyed protection against the shelling.

On the 11th June, the Ravin de la Dame was submitted to an intensive bombardment by the enemy. When, on the evening of the second day it lifted, and the Germans came forward to the attack, one battalion had been virtually exterminated. "Those who were not killed," recounted a survivor, "were buried alive. Rifles and machine-guns were buried or clogged with mud, but we had to defend ourselves, so bayonets were fixed, and remained so until death. The few who survived were taken prisoner, and all that marked the position which the vanished battalion had held was a row of bayonets pointing to the sky. Beside each body the Germans had stuck a rifle with the bayonet still fixed." "La tranchée des baïonnettes," it came to be called.

The men who went to that grim death in the Ravin de la Dame were all natives of La Vendée. In the words of a contemporary account, "they were magnificent soldiers, inspired by a profound religious faith. Many were saying their rosaries as they fell; they were determined not to withdraw one inch from the ground that had been entrusted to them to hold; for their leaders had told them that the fate of Verdun and the fate of France demanded their sacrifice."

The attack on the front of the 21st Division was one of many attempts by the Germans to capture the Thiaumont strongpoint, and it was as a result of the threat that developed on the front of the 137th Regiment that, on the afternoon of the 12th, de Lattre's battalion received orders to move up at night to try to close the gap. The critical nature of the situation prevented reconnaissance before the move. No guides could be provided; there were no tracks, few landmarks; and there was no moon. The only solution was to march by compass, and upon de Lattre fell the task of leading up the battalion. It was by no means easy: the only light that illuminated that dreary shell-pocked waste was the intermittent glow of the "Very" lights in front. Some of those who were near de Lattre that night retain vivid memories of his confidence; they recall him, compass in hand, and with steps that never faltered, leading them through the battered outskirts of Verdun, and into the darkness beyond.

Throughout those testing months the maintenance of morale demanded the most stalwart example on the part of the officers. The evidence of all who remember de Lattre in those distant days confirms that he always radiated cheerfulness and encouragement. Years later, a man who served under him at the time recalled a night when the battalion was to carry out a relief and was caught by one of those infernal bombardments that so often greeted a relieving unit. There were no communication trenches, and the men sought cover in the nearest shell-holes. Many of the guides were killed or lost; there was inevitable confusion and there seemed every likelihood that daylight would come before the relief could be completed. The moment the shelling ceased, it was de Lattre who came up. In no time he had taken hold of the situation, and, almost single-handed, he succeeded in completing the relief before dawn. The writer of that letter had said to a man near him at the time: "If that officer is not killed, he will go a long way."

Meanwhile, plans had matured to relieve the pressure on Verdun by an Anglo-French attack on the Somme. On the 1st July the assault was launched. Limited success only was achieved, and, during the months that followed, the flower of Britain's manhood perished too. Early in September, behind the British front, in "Happy Valley" and other familiar areas near Albert, mysterious little dumps began to appear. They were a new form of water tank, so men said. But the secret soon was out. They were in fact the first tanks ever to be seen on the battlefield; and so, on the 15th September, supported by these new weapons and with hopes renewed once again, the infantry went forward to the attack. But over that shell-tattered ground only a few of the "tanks" could make much progress, and once again the infantry were mowed down. The deadlock continued.

At the end of July, de Lattre had again been wounded and had to be evacuated. But he was not happy away from his unit, and to a friend in the battalion he wrote: "I have been given a month's convalescence, but I hope I shall not have to complete it before joining you again. Already I am feeling better. Come then! we'll pass the winter together. Remember me to the 'petits poilus' in the liaison section." These were no vain words, for although he went to spend a few weeks convalescing with his parents at Mouilleron he was determined to get back to the battalion at the earliest moment. A few weeks later he wrote to the same friend: "I shall be with you in a few days now, before my convalescence is finished. . . . I hate feeling inactive here, knowing what all those wretched people are suffering on the Somme. . . . Every day I keep hearing of more people who have been bereaved. Yesterday I went with my father to a near-by village to break the news to a poor family that their second son had been killed. The grief of the mother was terribly painful to see."

De Lattre was back with the battalion in October in the Verdun sector near Fort Douaumont. Although the battle had now died down, the advent of the winter rains had converted the battlefield into a sea of slimy mud. A few well-worn paths led forward to the various sectors, but even these were so muddy that going was impossible unless the sappers put down wooden "duckboard" tracks or the men attached contraptions to their boots to prevent them from sinking. To stray from these paths might well mean drowning. In the front line, men remained in the mud throughout their tour of duty. The hardships of that winter were beyond description, and again men in the battalion recall de Lattre, after four wounds, still "spending himself without counting the cost, with no thought for himself, thinking only of his men and every night, going round his mud-sodden posts, bringing comfort to all. As at Thiaumont, so at Douaumont, he was the very soul of the battalion."

But his wounds began seriously to trouble him, and he was ordered a rest. The Verdun drama was over. It must have been difficult for de Lattre to associate those grim and ugly scenes which he had just witnessed with that grandeur and glory which he liked to see in everything. And yet he wrote to his sister at the time: "In this war, there is no other glory than the heroism of the men, and their complete submission to duty and resignation to the most atrocious sufferings."

He had now had two years in the front line, with the occasional break necessitated by wounds. Already he had survived beyond the normal span allotted to an infantry officer, and well might he have been excused if he had sought employment on the staff, but

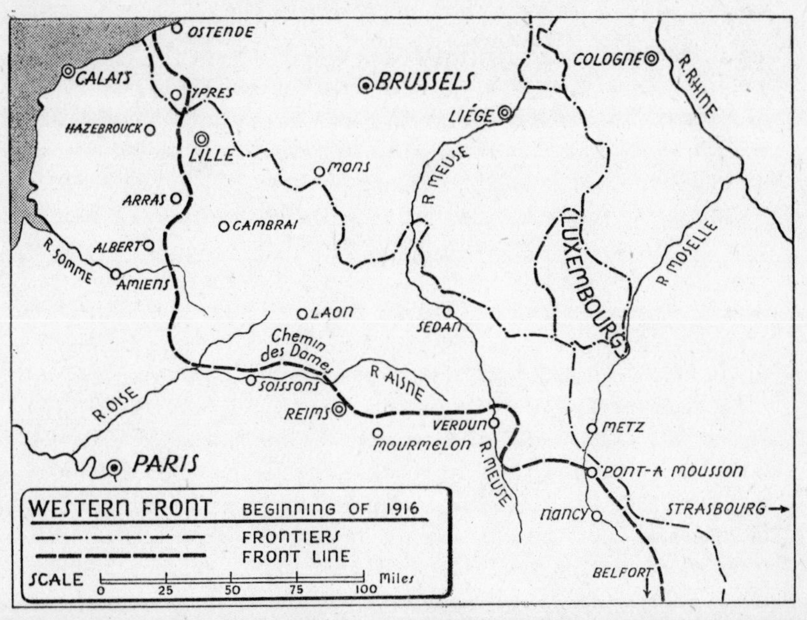
OSTENDE
CALAIS
YPRES
BRUSSELS
COLOGNE
R. RHINE
HAZEBROUCK
LIÉGE
LILLE
MONS
R MEUSE
ARRAS
CAMBRAI
LUXEMBOURG
R MOSELLE
ALBERT
R. SOMME
AMIENS
LAON
SEDAN
Chemin des Dames
R AISNE
SOISSONS
R. OISE
REIMS
VERDUN
METZ
MOURMELON
R. MEUSE
PARIS
PONT-A MOUSSON
WESTERN FRONT BEGINNING OF 1916
FRONTIERS
FRONT LINE
NANCY
STRASBOURG
SCALE
0 25 50 75 100 Miles
BELFORT

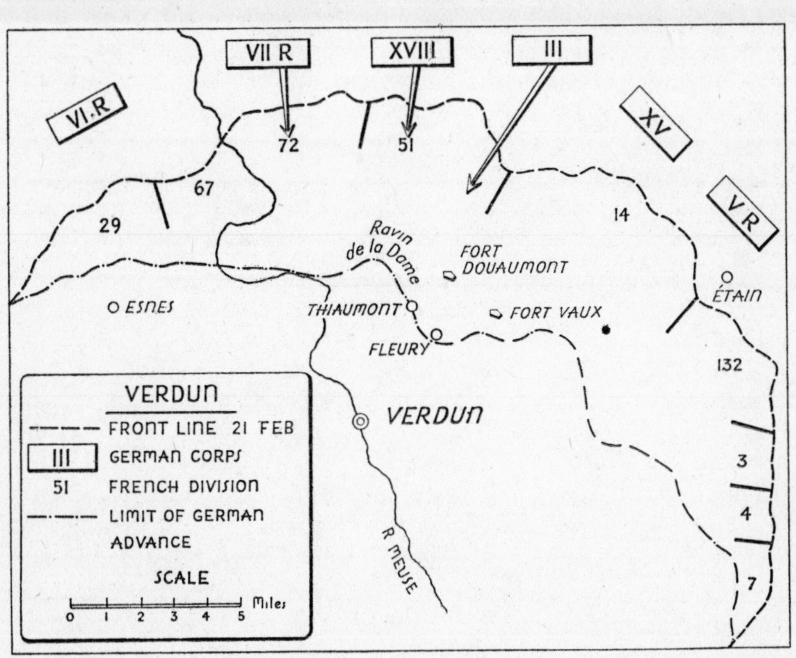
VII R
XVIII
III
VI.R
XV
72
51
67
V R
29
14
Ravin de la Dame
FORT DOUAUMONT
ESNES
THIAUMONT
FORT VAUX
ÉTAIN
FLEURY
132
VERDUN
VERDUN
FRONT LINE 21 FEB
III GERMAN CORPS
51 FRENCH DIVISION
LIMIT OF GERMAN ADVANCE
3
4
R MEUSE
SCALE
7
0 1 2 3 4 5 Miles

no such thought entered his head. Whether with the battalion, on leave, or convalescing, his overriding thought was for the welfare of his men. By the spring of 1917 he was back again, ready to command his battalion in the disastrous offensive that was about to be launched by General Nivelle.

The sector allotted to de Lattre's battalion was on the Chemin des Dames, that ill-named ridge north of the Aisne, and east of Soissons, which was soon in turn to become another slaughter-house. After a few weeks' training, the battalion moved up to the vicinity of Soissons. It was then ordered to relieve a colonial unit, which had suffered heavy casualties in the first days of the offensive.

Hardly had the battalion taken over the line when it was heavily attacked; but by an immediate counter-attack it regained an important trench in which it reorganized for a further attack against a labyrinth of underground works near Cerny. In this attack, which took place on the 5th May, de Lattre was able to achieve a measure of surprise, and he reaped his reward. Although the battalion sustained three hundred casualties, it took five hundred prisoners. Much material also was captured, and more than one counter-attack was driven off. Although the casualties had been heavy, compared with the disastrous operations taking place on the rest of the front, this operation was regarded as highly successful. The 93rd Infantry Regiment was cited in Army Orders, and de Lattre received his eighth mention in despatches.

The days which followed the launching of the Nivelle offensive, in the early part of 1917, were to impose upon infantry commanding officers a yet heavier strain than that which they had already been called upon to endure. The casualties at Verdun in 1916, and on the Somme, had reached appalling levels. Hardly had the French Army had time to recover, when it was again to receive cruel punishment. It was not surprising, therefore, that its morale was threatened; there were even murmurs of mutiny. De Lattre was as able as most to meet such a crisis, but he turned also to the chaplain for support. "I want you to gather together your friends every evening," said de Lattre, "and to address a few words to them. I, myself, will be present." There was no trouble in his battalion. Throughout his ordeal with the Infantry, de Lattre was always aware of that immeasurable rôle, which the chaplains could, and did so often, play. One day in 1920, he was ecalling his experiences in the First World War: "I was always orried," he said, "on the eve of an attack, to think of those of r men who upon a word from us would have to go forward, risk their lives and perhaps to appear before God. It was im- sible to discuss such a subject with them; and yet I felt that I some responsibility in the matter. I often, therefore, asked haplain to be present, without being seen, while the battalion forming up for the attack, and, as they went forward, to pronounce absolution."

During these operations, one of de Lattre's best young officers was seriously wounded, and had to undergo a dangerous operation at the casualty clearing station. Despite his suffering, he contrived to write a letter to his commanding officer. When the letter arrived the 93rd Infantry Regiment was still in the forward area, and on the morrow de Lattre's battalion was due once again to move into the front line. De Lattre himself, apart from the strain and fatigue of protracted operations, was feeling continued discomfort from his own wounds: but it was typical that he should find time to reply at length to his wounded subordinate:

> "Yesterday the letter arrived which you were kind enough to write to me. We were very worried about you . . . but the disability which will result from your operation will be much less serious than we feared, and we have all been greatly relieved to learn this. You were deeply loved in the battalion, 'mon pauvre petit', and I personally had a very special affection for you, based on your uprightness of character and nobility of thought. Unfortunately, during this war you will not be able to come back to us, but you may be sure that the memory which you leave with us is very lasting . . . it will give me real pleasure to come and talk to you about the battalion and all its little worries which you shared so helpfully with me, with that delicacy of feeling that you always showed in everything that you did. Regard your Legion of Honour with pride. For you, it was not intended merely as compensation for a serious wound: it is what you have deserved. It is the highest mark of honour that can be given you, to reward that modest and resolute bravery, with which you have for so long inspired the battalion. Your last deed on the battlefield led to the success of the operation, and the material, but above all the moral, conse-

quences of our success, in so far as the whole regiment is concerned, have been far greater than you imagine. Tomorrow we go back into the line to continue our good work. May the memory of your valour help and encourage us. Have confidence in life and in the future. . . . For the rest of your life, honour will always be with you. Let me often have your news. I embrace you affectionately. . . ."

Whatever the critics might say, de Lattre never forgot those who had served him well. To those who failed him he could be ruthless, but even then, except in extreme cases, more than once he was known subsequently to look after their interests.

De Lattre himself was very soon to leave his Regiment. Apart from the effect of his wounds, he continually had a temperature and was rarely without a cough. Yet, so long as the operations in Champagne continued, he refused to go sick. At last, when the battle died down he was ordered a rest, and was evacuated to hospital in Versailles. His ordeal as an infantryman was over. It had been severe and long; for to few front-line soldiers, in those days, was it given to survive for three years.

At the end of 1917, de Lattre left hospital, and was appointed Intelligence Officer to his old division, which was still on the Chemin des Dames. In his new appointment, there was much to compensate for the sorrow of leaving his regiment. He was brought into touch with the intelligence staffs both of neighbouring and superior headquarters. Moreover, there were three American divisions now in the area, and with his horizon so greatly broadened, his mind was stimulated, and he gained a wealth of new experience. It seems that it was during this period that he acquired the habit of working late into the night. For hours he would pour over a map, and few could read one better than he: when he expounded a situation on the map, the hills would rise before the eyes, and rivers almost seemed to flow.

Meanwhile, the Revolution in Russia had allowed the Germans to transfer vast forces to the West in a final bid for victory. By the 20th March, all was ready, and shortly after midnight, on a fifty-mile front, between Arras and La Fère, the guns struck up their deafening prelude (see map on p. 31). For four hours the British defences were drenched with shells, and at dawn, sixty-two enemy divisions went forward to the attack. Penetrating to depths hitherto unheard of, they almost divided the Anglo-French armies.

In April the enemy drove deeply again into the British front south of Ypres, but was checked before Hazebrouck. Then in May, as a diversion, he flung fifteen divisions against the four French and three British divisions holding the Chemin des Dames front. The 21st French Division was among those attacked. Although he had been warned of the impending attack, the Army Commander had refused to thin out his forward positions. When, therefore, the initial bombardment of the enemy crashed down upon the Chemin des Dames, it inflicted stupendous casualties among the tightly packed infantry of the defenders. Now for the first time de Lattre experienced the intensity of the mental, as opposed to the physical, strain that a hard-fought battle can impose upon the staff of a division. Moreover, those last days of May were to bring him much sorrow. When the attack started, his beloved 93rd Infantry Regiment was holding the front line. By the evening of the first day of the attack the three battalions of the regiment had been reduced to sixteen officers and 150 other ranks, and by the evening of the 30th the numbers were still further reduced to about 100. De Lattre felt the blow deeply. Yet bitter though these events were, they provided him with that invaluable experience that can only be learnt in a hard school. The tactical blunders which in May 1918 led to the destruction on the Chemin des Dames of his old regiment, left a deep imprint upon his mind. Twenty-two years later, he himself was to be a divisional commander fighting a defensive battle against overwhelming odds. There is little doubt that he was able to draw with profit upon the lessons which had remained stored in his mind over the intervening years.

There were now three ugly bulges in the Allied line, and in July the enemy made his final attempt to break through against Gouraud's Army in the Rheims sector. Gouraud had been warned, and, thinning out his forward positions, he completely baffled the Germans. The attack broke down. The enemy had shot his bolt, and in the middle of July the Allies went over to the offensive. In words attributed to Marshal Foch, it was now "Tout le monde à la bataille."

Gradually, along the whole front every allied army took up the strain and went forward to the attack. At long last that strong impenetrable wall, which had defied the onslaughts of so many brave men, began to give. The trenches, mud, and wire, the grim familiar landscape of shell-torn ground and ruined villages, and the distorted and derelict trees would soon be left behind. In a few weeks, green fields and woods began to take their place: real villages were entered. At first they were deserted, but, as the advance continued, civilians again began to appear, and here and there a charming smile would gladden the hearts of the victorious armies.

After its mauling on the Chemin des Dames, the 21st French Division had been withdrawn to rest and refit: but it was back again there in time to participate in the final advance. With uncanny swiftness, the drama was now drawing to its close. On the 11th November, when weary guns boomed forth their final blast, the 21st Division was advancing between Rethel on the Aisne and Mézières. In that same area, twenty-two years later, de Lattre was to taste the bitterness of impending defeat.

When the war ended, although only twenty-nine, de Lattre had already been promoted from "Chevalier" to "Officier" of the Legion of Honour, and he had been mentioned in despatches eight times. In later life he was to make many enemies, and to become the target of the most ruthless criticism, but none could deny that in the First World War his conduct had been beyond reproach, and that his courage, both physical and moral, had been second to none. But the price of such a record was heavy. To quote his old father, "In that First World War he never spared himself, and he finished it riddled with wounds." Upon a character already difficult, those years of strain left a permanent mark, and they did not tend to dispel those outbursts of temper that were to become so proverbial.

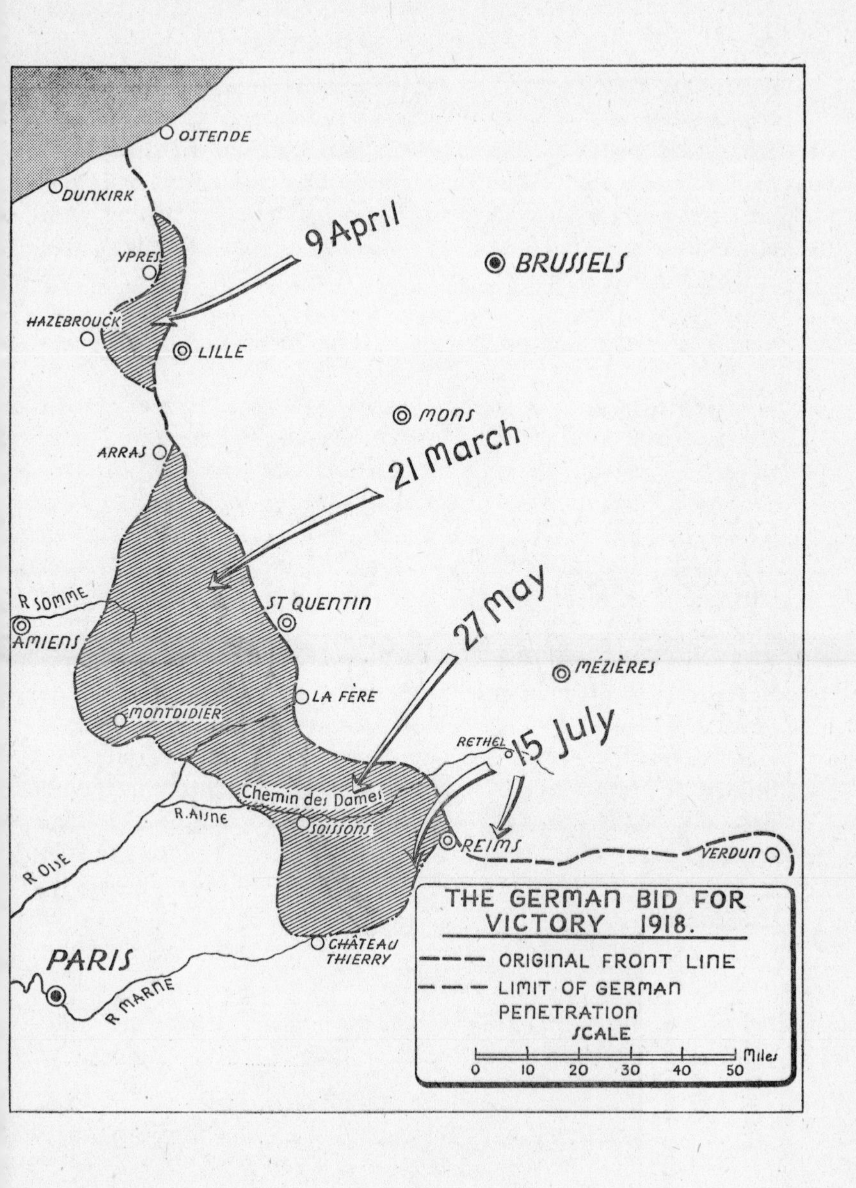
OSTENDE
DUNKIRK
9 April
YPRES
BRUSSELS
HAZEBROUCK
LILLE
MONS
ARRAS
21 March
R SOMME
ST QUENTIN
AMIENS
27 May
MÉZIÈRES
LA FÈRE
MONTDIDIER
RETHEL
15 July
Chemin des Dames
R.AISNE
SOISSONS
REIMS
VERDUN
R OISE
THE GERMAN BID FOR VICTORY 1918.
CHÂTEAU THIERRY
PARIS
ORIGINAL FRONT LINE
LIMIT OF GERMAN PENETRATION
R MARNE
SCALE
0 10 20 30 40 50 Miles

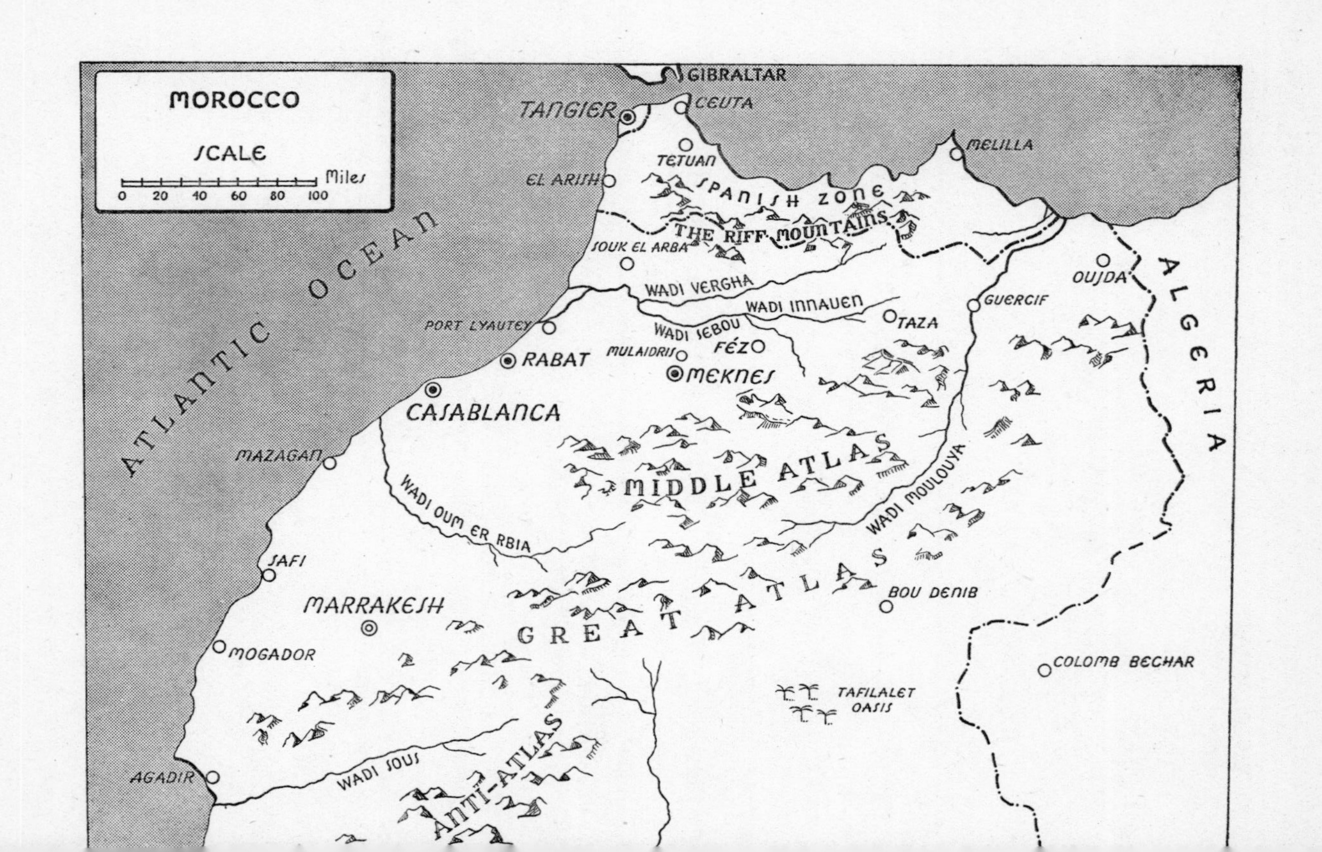
MOROCCO
SCALE
0 20 40 60 80 100 Miles
GIBRALTAR
TANGIER
CEUTA
TETUAN
MELILLA
EL ARISH
SPANISH ZONE
THE RIFF MOUNTAINS
SOUK EL ARBA
WADI VERGHA
WADI INNAUEN
WADI SEBOU
OUJDA
ALGERIA
GUERCIF
TAZA
PORT LYAUTEY
FÉZ
MULAIDRIS
RABAT
MEKNES
CASABLANCA
ATLANTIC OCEAN
MAZAGAN
MIDDLE ATLAS
WADI MOULOUYA
WADI OUM ER RBIA
SAFI
GREAT ATLAS
BOU DENIB
MARRAKESH
MOGADOR
COLOMB BECHAR
TAFILALET OASIS
WADI SOUS
AGADIR
ANTI-ATLAS

PART III

The Illusory Peace

1919–1939

7. MOROCCO

THE "War to end Wars" was over. There would be no more spring and autumn "pushes", as the offensives then were called. The casualty lists and the dreaded telegrams were things of the past. Although in France there were few families among whom death had not taken its toll, the relief that came with victory found expression in scenes of wild rejoicing. In Paris, the captured guns of the enemy were dragged from the Place de la Concorde, while men and women danced wildly round them. In the boulevards, soldiers—not always the most deserving—were kissed by sweet and grateful lips. London too went mad for a moment. But in both these cities, for all the rejoicing that marked that memorable day, there were thousands who mourned and wept once again.

De Lattre was now in his prime, and still under thirty. For those like himself, who had fought a good fight, life held many joys in those years that followed the Armistice. They were the objects of much adulation, and, for one so human as de Lattre, adulation was as champagne. In Mouilleron-en-Pareds he was a particular hero: the rosette on his Legion of Honour and the palms on his Croix de Guerre clearly told their story. But more eloquent still was the evidence of the men of La Vendée who had served with him.

It was in Mouilleron, soon after the Armistice, that de Lattre was to meet, for the first time, Georges Clemenceau. For years this anti-clerical and left-wing politician had been bitterly hated by the people of his village, but in the hour of victory much was forgotten. Even de Lattre's father agreed to open the doors of his *Mairie* to the veteran victor, now known as "the Tiger", and it was Jacques Daniau, the coachman, who one day followed him up the hill to the windmills, and surprised him by announcing that he would be welcome at the *Mairie*.

Later, Clemenceau was asked to distribute medals. Seeing young de Lattre standing near by, he turned to him and asked if he would pin on the medals himself, as he was the more worthy to do so. A great friendship between them dated from that occasion. In later years de Lattre would often recall conversations with "the Tiger", whom he used to visit in his small house on the coast, where in the evening of his life he wrote *Grandeurs et Misères d'une Victoire*. On one occasion he insisted on de Lattre sitting in his own chair. "One day you are going to be great," he said, "and I should like you to remember the day when you sat in my chair here." Shortly before his death, Clemenceau said that he wanted no soldiers at his funeral except Jean de Lattre de Tassigny. It seemed curiously incongruous, that friendship between him and Clemenceau, but, in his quest for intellectual companionship, differences neither of age nor of political outlook ever formed a barrier. De Lattre was never a great reader, and it was in conversation that his retentive mind derived its wide, if sometimes superficial, knowledge. At the dinner-table he could hold forth with convincing brilliance upon subjects of which he had only acquired knowledge in the course of conversation earlier in the day.

In February 1919 de Lattre joined the staff of the 18th Military Region at Bordeaux. Among his other duties, was the responsibility for organizing recreation and amusement for American troops before repatriation. It was not an occupation that would interest most soldiers, but for the imagination and talent of de Lattre as a showman it afforded great scope, and he set to work with his usual vigour and enthusiasm. The Bordeaux Theatre for a while became the theatre of de Lattre.

At the end of 1919 de Lattre joined the 49th Infantry Regiment at Bayonne. As usual, he made friends in many walks of life. In the social life of Biarritz and the country round, he could join as much or as little as he chose. When he went to a party, whether in uniform or plain clothes, he was always conspicuous by the immaculateness of his dress. Indeed, there were few days that passed when he did not visit his tailor, who became his friend, for he was a man after his own heart, who loved his work and was an artist. At these parties de Lattre was often reserved and distant in his manner, but, when he chose, he could exercise a charm that was invincible; women and men alike would fall under the spell.

At Bayonne, too, he was able to ride again, and he was asked to take on the mastership of the Biarritz foxhounds. Youth was still with him, and the thirst for speed and adventure as strong as ever. The inhabitants of the Basque country were as alarmed by his exploits as had been the villagers of Mouilleron when he was a boy. One day, while riding through Bayonne, he decided to jump the benches on the promenade and in the squares of the town.

For a time it was all great fun, but, as in England so in France, officers who had commanded battalions found themselves again commanding companies. There was much to discourage men like de Lattre, and, despite the gaiety and distractions which life then offered, in 1921 he applied to serve in Morocco, and his wish was granted.

At that time, Lyautey was completing in Morocco one of the most astounding achievements of the century. Among the great proconsuls who have served, not only their own country but also those whom they were called upon to protect, history can record no greater name than that of Marshal Lyautey. As recently as 1904, Morocco, although adjacent to Algeria and Gibraltar, had been a wild and almost impenetrable country. There had been little security and little happiness. There had been a Sultan resident successively in Marrakesh, Fez, and Meknes, who, in varying degrees, controlled a part only of his vast domains. More often than not he was playing off one tribe against another, exacting money from the vanquished and also from the victors as a reward for services rendered. There could be little progress under such a system of government, and the Moroccan people themselves would probably welcome a European master in preference to being exploited by the existing government. With her possessions in Algeria, and the danger of another European power seizing Morocco, it was inevitable that France should take a special interest in the fate of that country. But, to avoid complications with other European powers, she had hesitated to take aggressive action, and between 1904 and 1911 there were many conferences with the Sultan and with the other interested powers in Europe.

With Spain, France came to an agreement, and with the birth of the Entente Cordiale in 1904, Great Britain agreed in no way to interfere with the aspirations of France in Morocco. But by 1905 the German sabres had begun to rattle. In that year France asked the Sultan for a French protectorate. The reaction of Germany was dramatic. The Kaiser landed from his yacht at Tangiers and declared for the independence of Morocco. Upon the insistence of Germany, whose interests in Morocco were questionable, a conference was called at Algeciras in 1906. Great Britain stood firmly by France. Germany was forced to admit the special interests of France, and, among the other agreements reached at the Conference, France was allowed to patrol in the area near the Algerian frontier, and the country was to be policed both by France and Spain. But in 1908 relations between France and Germany were again strained, when a German Consul in Morocco gave refuge to deserters from the French Foreign Legion. In 1911, in the face of serious disturbances, the Sultan appealed to France for help. Again the German sabres rattled. The German warship "Panther" put in to Agadir, ostensibly for the protection of German interests. War seemed imminent. Great Britain again supported France, and in November of that year a treaty was signed, by which Germany finally accepted a French Protectorate in Morocco in return for the cession of a part of the French Congo. In 1912 Lyautey became the first Resident-General.

Lyautey was a man of outstanding independence of thought. Moreover, in Indo-China and Madagascar, he had acquired an unusual ability to get round regulations ("bousculer les réglements"), or at least to interpret them in the spirit rather than the letter. The office he hated, preferring to be on the move and to exercise direct command by the impact of his personality. A devout catholic himself, he respected the religions of those whom he came to protect. He respected also their traditions, their customs, and their laws. He came not to destroy, but to preserve. The chiefs of the country he would treat as the "grands seigneurs", which so many of them were, and, to win their respect, he himself would be more than the "grand seigneur". Whether at the Residency-General at Rabat, or in his tent in the middle of the desert, Lyautey reigned in splendour, and with the dignity that became the representative of France. If he went to see the Sultan, he would gallop, beautifully mounted, and clad in a flowing black "burnous" with gold fastenings. He realized that men liked to be governed, and that it was not unseemly that a Resident-General should look the part.

Under the imaginative drive of so remarkable a man, Morocco had achieved by 1921 a measure of prosperity that few would have thought possible. But, when war had broken out in 1914, he had been ordered to send every available soldier to France, to evacuate the interior of the country, and to hold only a fringe near the coast. The soldiers he sent, but he refused to evacuate one square yard of territory. With a mere skeleton force, and relying mainly on the influence of his own personality, he held the country throughout the war, and when it ended, the work of "pacification" continued. There were four main areas in which the French had to operate. To the north, near the Spanish Zone, there were the Djebala and Rif tribes. In the Middle Atlas were the Berber tribes. Round Marrakesh were the big Kaids, and, finally, there was the Southern front in the Tafilalet area.

Such was the Morocco to which de Lattre came in 1921, a country bubbling with activity. While month by month the Army pacified an ever wider area, hard in its wake came roads, railways, hospitals, and all that was best in the paraphernalia of European civilization. It was the policy of "la tache d'huile", as Lyautey called it. The contact which de Lattre had with Lyautey was only fleeting. Arriving at Casablanca, he saw him for a moment at the Residency-General at Rabat, but it would be surprising if the impressionable de Lattre had not been struck by the glamour that surrounded the person of the Resident-General. It would be unfair to say that he copied Lyautey. Already he had shown himself to be possessed of many of his qualities, which some might call eccentricities. But Lyautey was a man after his own heart, and there is little doubt that his contact with him, however brief, and his experience of the power that he generated, influenced his life as profoundly as the life of Gallieni had influenced that of Lyautey.

De Lattre was at once appointed to the Staff of General Poeymirau, then commanding the Meknes area. Poeymirau, or "the Poey", as he was called, was one of Lyautey's most faithful and successful disciples. Life at first was not easy for de Lattre. In France his exceptional war record had brought him admiration on all sides. In Morocco he was to find it otherwise; the old campaigners, or "blédards", as they were known, were an exclusive community who tended to look with suspicion upon the "roumis" (from the Arabic for foreigners), as were called the officers newly arrived from France and inexperienced in the way of life in Morocco. Their suspicion was the greater when this superbly dressed "roumi" arrived with the initials "J. L. T." emblazoned on all his belongings. He soon became known to all as "J. L. T."

De Lattre, with his abundant intelligence and power of assimilation, soon found his feet. "Pacification" operations in Morocco presented a problem that was very different from those to which he had been accustomed, but it was all common sense. Of the work of those admirable political officers, living lonely lives in the desert, of the organization of mobile groups and of the administrative problems involved, he soon acquired a working knowledge. Moreover, as always, to everything new he brought refreshing enthusiasm. Early in 1922, only a few months after his arrival, he was appointed head of the Third Bureau (Operations) of the Meknes area, and had to plan one of the operations that were to take place that summer in the area of the Upper Moulouya, a region that it was important to pacify, to ensure the security of communications with Algeria.

The character of most of these operations was similar. Two or more self-contained columns would converge on a given area. Generally the front, rear, and flanks were protected by a screen of cavalry. On an inner circle were the infantry, comprising anything from four to eight battalions, and in the centre were the artillery, the reserves, the headquarters, and the supply columns. Progress was often slow. Ten miles generally was the maximum that could be covered in a day, and columns had to halt at least two hours before dark so as to be leaguered up and secure by night. Within the column, manœuvre was limited by the need to protect the transport. For the staff, these columns provided an exhilarating contrast to the office. Staff officers were mounted, and from time to time they could gallop off to make contact with units of the column. For de Lattre in particular this form of warfare offered a pleasant change, after those grim battlefields of Verdun and the Chemin des Dames. Some of the foothills in which they operated were wild and forbidding, but the scenery had a grandeur of its own, with snow-capped mountains often towering in the distance. In such a setting war still retained a degree of pageantry. From column headquarters every unit was often in view, and through field-glasses could be seen those splendid squadrons of Spahis making good successive tactical features to the front or on the flanks, and holding on to those in rear till the column was clear.

The operations in the Upper Moulouya were completed without incident, but then impended the more difficult and important operation to clear up the area south of Taza that was known as the "Tache de Taza". Before the operations were launched, de Lattre had impressed superiors and subordinates alike by his energy. By day he was rarely in his office; rather was he constantly visiting units and discovering their wants. On one occasion he went to see a detachment of Goums.* Its commander who had long been serving in Morocco, was brutally frank and outspoken, and not over-fond of the staff. As the elegant de Lattre stepped out of his car, resplendent in bright yellow gloves, the old campaigner gave him a look as much as to say, "What the hell are you doing here?" De Lattre asked him if there was anything that his unit needed, whereupon, in a disgruntled voice, he poured forth a list of his complaints. A few days later everything for which he had asked arrived. The disgruntled commander was Captain Guillaume; he had discovered that the staff could be efficient and human. In later years Guillaume was to become one of the best divisional commanders in de Lattre's First French Army, and, later still, Resident-General in Morocco.

In 1923 the operations started, and for three months they continued. Again de Lattre gave proof of prodigious energy. By day he was generally to be seen riding with a unit that was engaged. Well might it be argued that his place was at headquarters, and that his gallops under fire were useless bravado; but morale was always the better for his presence.

For all his bravado, de Lattre could be prudent. Late one afternoon, one of Poeymirau's columns had reached its objective with relative ease. At headquarters there was a wave of optimism among the staff, who suggested that the column might well push on to the next hill. Poeymirau, often unorthodox, took

* The Goums were not a part of the regular French Army, but partisans recruited among the tribes for short periods and officered by the French.

the unusual course of putting the decision to the vote. To continue operations of that nature until dusk, was always a risk that played into the hands of the enemy, and de Lattre had been one of the few who disapproved of pushing on. But optimism prevailed. The hill was captured, but at dusk the enemy reacted with violence, and the French were dislodged with the loss of seventy killed. That evening de Lattre said to a friend, "Today I have learnt a lesson that I shall always remember: it is not sufficient to say 'I will'. The intention and the method of carrying it out must be expressed with conviction. You can't play tricks with chance." Indeed, at that period of his life, although he could never be accused of timidity, de Lattre never took foolhardy chances.

Hard though these months were, there were lighter moments. With their incomparable talent, the French had transplanted a little gaiety to the centre of Morocco. In Meknes and Fez there were hotels, night clubs, and parties, where charming voices could be heard again. For weary warriors the Hotel Transatlantique at Fez was a pleasant haven. Occasionally de Lattre and his friends would be seen to enter. He was always the centre of attraction. "There is J. L. T.," said people, just as at Mouilleron-en-Pareds they had said, "Voilà Monsieur Jean." No longer was he the mistrusted "roumi", but a legendary figure, who had fully earned the citation which he had received about that time:

> "A young officer with a remarkable gift of assimilation, enthusiasm, and energy. In battle his authority and courage are no less than his prodigious capacity for work. He is a brilliant officer in every respect; his intelligence is high, and he has an alert and ardent mind. In the interest of the Army, he should quickly reach the highest rank."

One day, just outside the Hotel Transatlantique, de Lattre was attacked by a fanatic and seriously wounded by a dagger in his right cheek. For three weeks he could neither speak, eat, nor drink, and the scar remained for the rest of his life. Meanwhile, in the north, stormclouds were gathering. In the Spanish Rif, Abdel Krim had raised the standard of revolt, and by the end of 1924 had achieved such substantial successes that he began to look southward towards the fertile plains of the Vergha, and the cities of Fez and Mulaidris. In the same year the "Poey" died, and a northern command was created at Fez under General de Chambrun, a descendant of Lafayette. To the new command de Lattre, although he had not been to the École de Guerre, was appointed Chief of Staff. He was happy with de Chambrun, who was a man of the world, and who had served with success as head of a mission to General Pershing, commander of the American troops, in the first World War. Serving under de Chambrun at the same time was Captain Juin. For more than a quarter of a century the careers of Juin and de Lattre were to run parallel.

The Wadi Vergha runs from east to west, just south of the Spanish-Moroccan border. This zone was not controlled by Abdel Krim, and was peopled by tribes to whom the French had given complete independence. The first concern of de Chambrun was to prevent their falling under the domination of Abdel Krim. In April 1925, the latter, who had continued to profess respect for the French zone of influence, came out into the open, and moved against them. He now had a formidable following. In addition to rifles and ammunition in plenty, he had about a hundred guns. De Lattre, although still only a captain, was Chief of Staff of the Taza area. His chief at the time was not a man who engendered confidence, and it fell to de Lattre to provide the impulsion that was lacking. Although his attitude to officers senior to himself was often overbearing, he galvanized the whole area into activity and determination. Giraud, who was to achieve renown in the Second World War, was then a lieutenant-colonel commanding a regiment in the area. In later years, he would often refer jokingly to this period when he was "under the command of Captain de Lattre". Such was the authority which J. L. T. already exercised; and it was the more to be commended, as he suffered much at the time from the heat, and from his many wounds. Indeed, there was much to excuse the outbursts of temper which began to increase. Already, too, he had declared war on mediocrity. Few things made him angrier than a badly written or badly expressed paper, to the preparation of which little care had been devoted. He argued, like Lyautey, that all work which was not a labour of love had little worth.

During the summer of 1925 the situation deteriorated rapidly. More and more tribes threw in their lot with Abdel Krim, and Taza itself was threatened. A change of government in France did not facilitate the making of quick decisions, nor was the task of the soldiers lightened by the stream of journalists and politicians who flocked to the scene. In the face of increasing pressure, French forts along the Wadi Vergha and the Wadi Innauen were only holding out with difficulty; but the worse the situation became, the more de Lattre seemed to dominate it. When morale became shaky, he steadied it not only by his own example but also by the use of his imagination. On his own initiative he organized an air-lift, carrying to beleaguered units not only ammunition and rations but also mail, decorations, and even slabs of ice from a requisitioned ice factory in Taza. This must have been one of the earliest air-lifts on such a scale to be recorded.

His chief was less cheerful, for the loss of Taza would mean the severing of communications with Algeria, the encirclement of Fez, and the spreading of the revolt to the Atlas. When his chief wanted to withdraw, de Lattre persuaded him of the advantages of going forward and occupying an important hill known as Msila. He was given a free hand to carry out the operation on his own. Among the subordinates to receive the clear-cut operation orders signed "J. de Lattre" were Giraud and de Monsabert, years later to command an army corps in de Lattre's First French Army. The operation was completely successful and de Lattre was recommended for promotion to the rank of major. Lyautey himself backed the recommendation with these words: "I support in the warmest manner this recommendation. Once again Captain de Lattre has given proof in difficult circumstances of his exceptional valour." He was only promoted a year later.

The action of de Lattre had momentarily averted a general withdrawal, but, as pressure of the enemy increased, Msila had to be evacuated, and even from Paris there came pressure for the abandonment of Taza. A staff officer was sent to visit de Lattre, to find out what he thought of the situation. He telephoned to Giraud and asked him the state of his regiment, particularly as regards morale. Giraud gave him an encouraging reply, as did, later, de Monsabert about his own group. That was enough to strengthen de Lattre's contention that Taza could be held. Although Lyautey himself had never listened to the pessimists, or been prepared to abandon Taza, he must have been greatly encouraged by the resolute views of the Chief of Staff at Taza. There was no further question of abandoning the place, and although several months were to elapse before Abdel Krim was brought to bay, the decision to hold Taza was one of the most momentous of the campaign.

One day, in the Autumn of 1925, de Lattre found a battalion having difficulties in reaching its objective. He himself virtually took over command, but while leading it forward with success he was seriously wounded in the knee. He was evacuated to hospital in Taza, where he found himself in a ward with Giraud. In September he received his final citation for the campaign. "An exceptional officer with a superb record in war. By his intelligence, determination, and profound knowledge of the country, and his prodigious work as Chief of Staff of the Taza area, he has contributed in a great measure to the success of the operations that resulted in the defeat of the Rif aggression."

Early in 1926 de Lattre returned to France. The years in Morocco had been rich in experience: his horizon had been immeasurably broadened. He had acquired an invaluable knowledge of a variety of units of all races and kinds: the Foreign Legion, North African "tirailleurs", Senegalese, and "Goums". Many such units he was to lead twenty years later from the Mediterranean to the Danube. But of all the impressions that he took with him from Morocco, the most vivid of all must have been that of Lyautey, that magnificent and inimitable ambassador of the grandeur of France. Only a few months before, Lyautey had resigned, and, as he passed Gibraltar on his return to France, two British destroyers put out to escort and pay tribute to this great Frenchman. In France, he was to experience the frigid welcome of an ungrateful government.

8. CAPRICIOUS FORTUNE

THE treatment which the French government had accorded Lyautey might well have convinced de Lattre of the futility of ambition, but when he returned to France, tired though he appears to have been, ambition burned within him. At the beginning of 1926 he was just thirty-seven, and upon few men of his age had fallen such heavy and varied responsibilities. Moreover, he had come to realize the full magnitude of his powers, and he had developed a degree of self-confidence that struck many as arrogance. "Am I arrogant?" he asked a member of his staff many years later. "Yes, General, you are a little," he replied. "All right," said de Lattre, "every night I will take up my rosary and pray that I may become less arrogant."

In the summer of 1926 de Lattre had leave; wounds and sickness made this imperative, and he spent several weeks with his parents at Mouilleron-en-Pareds. His mind was made up. He must go to the École de Guerre. But time was short, for he had almost reached the age limit, beyond which he would be ineligible to go there. Even during his leave, therefore, he set to work to prepare for the examination. As one of his subjects he decided to take English, and it so happened that at the college for priests of Saint-Laurence, on the outskirts of the village, there was a British novitiate named Jesse. Every afternoon de Lattre and Jesse went for a walk and talked in English, and between them there sprang up a great friendship. Jesse refused to accept any payment, but to the generous de Lattre such a situation was unthinkable. He therefore asked the Father Superior if there was any gift which the brothers would appreciate. He was told that any old clothes would be most acceptable. Up to a point it was an appropriate request, for no wardrobe was more plentifully stocked than that of de Lattre, although few of his clothes were old. As usual, he was most generous, but in order to hide from his mother the fact that he was giving away good clothes, he arranged for Jacques Daniau, the coachman, to stand under his window, while he threw out parcels of clothes.

Regaining his strength, he completed his preparations for the impending examination in Paris. It was at this time that he met Charles Bousquet, who was to become his lifelong friend. Few men came to know de Lattre better than Bousquet. He, too, was preparing for the École de Guerre, and they decided to work together. Already de Lattre had a profound dislike for working and reading alone. It was only in the company of other intellects that his mind acquired its greatest capacity for absorption. Bousquet seems to have proved an ideal companion for his purpose, and he helped to ensure that de Lattre did not stray too far from the path of orthodoxy that he had to tread if he wished to reach his goal. Often he would chide Bousquet for being too orthodox: "Mon petit Bousquet," he would say, "you don't understand anything. You fill me with pity, you, with your perpetual respect for the conventional. You are incapable of leaving the paths that are trodden by the whole world; you will never be anything but one among many, without any particular features, without character and without personality."

Bousquet has given an admirable account of their work together in those days. De Lattre was continually looking for new rooms of sufficient size to conform with his taste for grandeur and space. The Rue du Laos, the Avenue de Suffren, the Avenue Mozart, the Rue de Passy, the Jardins de la Muette, and the Champ de Mars, all these quarters were to be honoured in turn with a fleeting stay by the young commandant, who had been promoted in September 1926. The tempo of his life was already fast. He would be dashing in a taxi from one appointment to another; sometimes it was a social engagement, and sometimes to visit a professor who was coaching him in a particular subject. The activities which he crammed into a single day were astounding, and the money which he spent on taxis must have been out of all proportion to his means. Even in a taxi he would probably make a friend jump in with him to continue some unfinished discussion. One day he came to see Bousquet, carrying a bundle of books and papers: "Here are some books and documents on the battle of Wagram and the War of Secession. Read them quickly and come to my rooms tonight, after dinner, and give me a résumé of what you have read. See that it is short and clear. Here is a packet of those horrible cigarettes, with which you insist on smoking out my room. Smoke them until I come back. It will not be late." At two o'clock in the morning de Lattre returned, and until dawn the discussion continued. Then de Lattre put on one of his favourite gramophone records. Poor Bousquet just had time to catch the train from Pont Mirabeau Station to Versailles, where he was doing a course.

But love was to interrupt his work for the examination. That same summer, during an election campaign in La Vendée, he was invited to luncheon by a deputy for La Vendée. There he met Mademoiselle Simone Calary de Lamazière, the nineteen-year-old daughter of a Paris deputy. De Lattre fell in love. They met again at a party on the Île d'Yeu, off the coast of La Vendée. In the afternoon, de Lattre invited Mademoiselle de Lamazière to accompany him for a row. But the wind was blowing hard, and it was only with difficulty that he persuaded a boatman, who had served with him in the 93rd Infantry Regiment, to put to sea. His readiness to brave the perils of the deep cannot have failed to impress his charming companion, for soon afterwards their engagement followed. There was only one obstacle which had to be overcome. The parents of Mademoiselle de Lamazière were not happy about the disparity in their ages. Indeed, when de Lattre first broached the subject, he was told that a suitor much younger than himself had been turned down. It was unlikely that he would be deterred by that. Mustering all his charm, he triumphed, and on the 22nd March, 1927, Commandant Jean de Lattre de Tassigny and Mademoiselle Simone de Lamazière were married in the Church of Saint-Pierre de Chaillot in Paris. Jesse, who had now been ordained, celebrated Mass, and the Father Superior of Saint Laurence gave the address and blessing.

One of the first things which de Lattre did after his marriage was to take his young wife to meet Clemenceau, now nearly ninety. In the course of conversation, Clemenceau referred with sadness to the old windmills at Mouilleron, which he had loved for so long. "They are fast falling into decay," he said, "and soon they will disappear altogether. Why don't you buy one?" De Lattre, for whom these windmills had always retained their mystic appeal, was deeply touched; and, with his usual rapidity of decision, he went off to Mouilleron and bought one. His windmill at Mouilleron was his one solid link with the earth, and he never went to Mouilleron without walking up the hill to see it. It was rare for him to relax, but there, alone among the windmills, with that glorious view unfolding beneath him, he found peace and inspiration.

Only a few months were now left before the date of the examination. Few officers have passed it after so short a time of preparation. Into four months he condensed work that normally took two years, and his capacity to make the right contacts greatly helped him. His friend Captain Guillaume, whom he had helped in Morocco, was already at the École de Guerre, and it was Guillaume who coached him in tactics. "Like everything he undertook," said Guillaume, "it was a lightning preparation." One morning de Lattre telephoned to a Captain Ricard, who was coaching him for the artillery part of the examination. "At two o'clock this afternoon," said de Lattre, "I have got my oral examination in Anti-Aircraft Defence, and I know practically nothing." They lunched together, and he got through. Such were the methods that enabled him to follow up his matrimonial triumph with success in the examination.

Before starting the course, for a few months, de Lattre was given command of a battalion of the 4th Infantry Regiment, at Auxerre, on the road to Lyons and the South. Auxerre was sufficiently close to Paris to enable Bousquet to go there by train, and it was at the Hotel de l'Épée that their sessions continued.

At the École de Guerre, de Lattre was the senior officer of his year, and in that capacity he was responsible to the Commandant for the general conduct of all the students. No one could have been more fitted, for he always sought responsibility. It fell to him also to look after the foreign officers on the course, and as a man of the world, richer in experience and understanding than most, he was eminently suited for such a rôle. Moreover, the resultant contact with new and foreign minds served further to enrich his knowledge of men.

By the end of a year, although here and there he had begun to provoke envy and jealousy, de Lattre had already made his mark. He was reported on as an officer of "superior intelligence . . . with considerable pride and legitimate ambition, but with an excessive confidence in himself, which in his own interests he should check . . . an upright, forceful, and generous character." Of the two commandants under whom de Lattre served, one was General

Hering, who was so much impressed by the qualities of this student that ten years later, when he was Military Governor of Strasbourg, he asked for him to be his Chief of Staff.

On the 11th February, 1928, Madame de Lattre gave birth to their only child, a boy. He was christened Bernard. Although the care of the young Bernard occupied much of her time, Madame de Lattre still found moments in which to sort out her husband's papers, and to do a variety of things that a devoted wife can do to lighten the burden of a student at the École de Guerre. In their small flat in the Avenue de Versailles, she welcomed with a simple grace the numerous officers, including the foreigners, whom he delighted to invite. Soon she was to learn that dinners must be provided at short notice and for uncertain numbers, and that discussions would continue far into the night. She never complained, and, exacting though de Lattre could be, he worshipped her. Throughout his life, almost imperceptibly, she exercised a profound and steadying influence.

During the second year of the course it was customary, as at the Staff College in England, to hold a combined-operations exercise. In England the experience of the Dardanelles operations, in 1915, had led to unjustifiable pessimism as to the practicability of such an operation against a defended coast, but there were a few of the more thoughtful officers who rightly argued that, at the outset of a future war, England might well lose territory in distant oceans, which would have to be retaken. In France the interest in such exercises was even more limited than in England. In due course, it was the turn of de Lattre to participate in such an exercise, and upon him devolved the command of a force that was to take Cherbourg from the sea. For him it was a most congenial rôle, for his love of the sea was as great as ever, and under his imaginative and inspiring leadership the exercise became alive. He had a full grasp of the magnitude of the problem, and to its solution he brought refreshing originality. In the plan which he adopted, consideration was given to the employment of special landing-craft, and other devices as yet untried. When the admiral directing the exercise objected that the landing-craft did not exist, de Lattre replied, "It is unbelievable that your technicians should be unable to invent such craft through lack of imagination."

In March 1929, a few months before the course ended, Marshal

Foch died. He had raised the prestige of French arms to the highest pinnacle reached since Napoleon, and nowhere was his death more keenly felt than at the École de Guerre. Long after he had ceased to be its illustrious commandant, his spirit had continued to inspire the students of the future. As the senior student, it was de Lattre who was to have the honour of carrying the Marshal's baton at the funeral. But at the last moment sickness laid him low, and the honour fell to another. Years later, even his own Marshal's baton he was never destined to carry.

The report which de Lattre received at the end of the course was as satisfactory as that of his first year. It stressed his wide knowledge, and although it again referred to a self-confidence that sometimes made him hard to handle, it added that the uprightness of his character and his high conception of duty would always respond to understanding and firm handling.

De Lattre was now given command of a battalion of the 59th Infantry Regiment at Coulommiers, just east of Paris. He only commanded it for a year, but for months afterwards the people of Coulommiers spoke of the unusual happenings that marked his period of command. Paris was close at hand, and the minds of many officers and other ranks were more concerned with the joys of the capital than with the importance of their duties. All that was soon to change. Parades of unaccustomed length, night operations, alerts, and other surprises began to dissipate the torpor, and officers were made to devote themselves with greater zeal to the welfare of their men.

His period of command at Coulommiers was marred by one misfortune. For much of the time Madame de Lattre was ill, and unable to be with him. It was only two years since they had been married, and, with his consuming need for affection, her absence was deeply felt by de Lattre. His friend Bousquet had now become a civilian. At week-ends de Lattre in his loneliness, would telephone him. "Come," he would say. "Don't say you have not got the time. Faites-cela pour moi." Such pleading was difficult to resist.

It was not only to work that de Lattre applied reforms. His interest in the welfare of his men began to develop with increasing fervour. He wanted them to look back on their military service as a period, not of drudgery, but of memorable and spectacular occasions, in which their minds had been elevated above the mediocre and commonplace. The fêtes and galas at Coulommiers surpassed in magnificence anything that had before been seen, and no battalion funds would suffice to meet the cost. It seems more probable that de Lattre himself, although not a rich man, had come to the rescue with his own purse. But all that mattered was that ever afterwards the men should remember that they had served in the "Bataillon de Lattre", where routine never bored, and dormant minds were stirred.

If some were astonished at the quixotic actions of the officer commanding the battalion at Coulommiers, his superiors were not blind to his outstanding intelligence and gifts, and, in 1933, after a short period on the Staff in the 4th Bureau at the Ministry of War, he was appointed to the Staff of the Conseil Superieur de la Guerre, under General Weygand. In his rise to fame, this was a most important step.

When Weygand appointed de Lattre to his staff, he did not know him personally, although in 1914 Madame Weygand had visited him in hospital in Nancy and could recall his eagerness to return quickly to the front. He was soon to discover that the reports which he had received about him had not been exaggerated. Paying tribute to him later, Weygand referred to his unusually quick mind and to his love of taking risks, which somehow he contrived to combine with a measure of prudence. Weygand summed up de Lattre as "a thoroughbred who needed holding, rather than driving".

If the chief appreciated the qualities of his subordinate, it was no less true that de Lattre had an esteem for Weygand which he retained to the end of his life. His standard of conduct was of the highest, and, if not so forthcoming as his emotional subordinate, Weygand possessed a discreet and perfect courtesy that earned him the respect even of his enemies. Writing later of those years, de Lattre described them as the most fruitful that he passed between the two great wars.

Although fate was about to deal de Lattre an almost crushing blow, it was a happy partnership that he enjoyed with Weygand at "4 Bis", as his office in the Boulevard des Invalides had been familiarly known since the days of Foch. His new post acquainted de Lattre for the first time with the highest problems of strategy and world politics, and among the many tasks that confronted him was the daily presentation to his chief of a report summarizing the international situation. The compilation of such a report demanded much reading, and he was probably forced at that time to read more than at at any other period of his life, except when he was in prison at Riom. These reports did not provide the most pleasant reading. Neither abroad nor at home was there anything but news of a disquieting character. In Germany Hitler had come to power, and already the storm-clouds were gathering. In France, in a more vociferous form than usual, the Government had incurred the displeasure of a highly critical people. The threat from across the Rhine did little to unite the country, and, even in the matter of defence, there were profound differences of opinion. Lieutenant-Colonel Charles de Gaulle was writing a book advocating the creation of a professional army, and however sound his views they embarrassed the Chief of the General Staff.

De Lattre now had a poky little flat in the Rue Jasmin, on the fifth floor, with an ugly view over roof-tops, and again it was Bousquet who became his most frequent visitor. The old discussions continued. Others too would be asked to join, and, in the framing of his reports to his chief, de Lattre found these discussions an invaluable help. They brought him in contact with view-points to which, in the course of his normal duties, he would never have had access. In the face of the unhappy trend of events, it was understandable that this little band of patriots should feel the urge to give expression to their views, and ill-advisedly some of them combined to write an article which appeared under a pseudonym in the Paris Press.

On many issues the country was now divided. Since the signing of the Versailles Treaty, in order to avoid isolation in the event of another war with Germany, France had endeavoured to build up a series of military alliances. Czechoslovakia, Yugoslavia and Roumania had themselves banded together to form the "Little Entente", and of that alliance France commanded the loyalty. The Baltic States and Poland also became associated with the French system. But intelligent men, like de Lattre, realized that they were too weak to withstand an attack by Germany, and too distant to enable France to bring direct and timely aid. De Lattre was aware also, sooner than most, of the growing strength of the Soviet Army. Indeed, the only country which had the military strength to create that second front, which Germany so much dreaded, was Russia. The intelligent men prevailed. Military Attachés between France and Russia were exchanged, and negotiations were set in motion. These led in 1935 to the signing of the Franco-Soviet Pact. At a time when Communism was beginning seriously to shake the foundations of France, it is not surprising that the signing of this pact caused a wave of opposition throughout the country. However indirect was the part which de Lattre played in the events which preceded its signing, it was not forgotten by his enemies.

In January 1934, discontent with the alleged corruption of the Government reached its peak, as a result of the Stavisky scandal. Stavisky was a man of considerable charm, who was accused of swindling in connection with the municipal pawnshop at Bayonne. For months he had remained free and rumours gained ground that the Government was implicated and was protecting him. Anti-republicanism was in the air, and the situation became highly inflammable. It was essential for the Chief of the General Staff to be fully and accurately informed of the quickly moving events. Moreover, the problem of internal security demanded the closest liaison with the Ministry of the Interior. For all these tasks the services of de Lattre were fully used: not only did he constantly visit the Ministry, but, outside the Army, he redoubled his contacts with politicians and other leaders in various walks of life. At a time when intrigue was rife, he might have been wiser to be more discreet in these contacts, for they were to play into the hands of his malevolent and unscrupulous enemies.

At the beginning of February, Paris became the scene of serious trouble. Outside the Palais Bourbon, in the Place de l'Opéra, and on the boulevards demonstrations were organized. The Government resigned, and on the 6th February a new one took its place. While the Chamber debated, there were new demonstrations in the Champs Elysées, in the Palace de la Concorde, and at the Hôtel de Ville.

Accounts of these incidents have been most conflicting. The initial demonstrations were undoubtedly encouraged, if not organized, by right-wing elements, who were disgusted with the trend of events, but, however great the provocation, it is improbable that they intended violence. Bodies of ex-soldiers too had taken part; but these had paraded in an orderly manner with their banners, and were certainly not equipped for violent action. It seems that left-wing elements also took action on the same day, with a view to exploiting inflammable passions; they are said to have mixed with the demonstrators, deliberately inciting them to violence, and thereby exposing themselves to the accusation of having conspired to overthrow the government. Whatever the truth may have been, ugly scenes developed, troops were called out to assist the police, shots were fired, and people were killed. Passions now were roused, and on the next day demonstrations continued. Rather than be held responsible for the further shedding of blood, the President of the Council, Daladier, resigned.

Even today it is only in outline that the truth can be discerned. For de Lattre, these events were to cause some of the most unhappy days of his life. The ex-Minister of the Interior, Monsieur Frot, was accused among other things of having approached one of the proprietors of a right-wing newspaper through the intermediary of a staff officer. Later it was alleged that Lieutenant-Colonel de Lattre was the officer concerned. The outspoken manner in which he had criticized all that was wrong added fuel to the flames, and so grave were the accusations now made against him that a parliamentary commission of enquiry was set up to investigate them, and de Lattre appeared before it. In his evidence, given with incomparable lucidity, he maintained that he had always refused to dabble in politics. Admittedly, he had opportunities of meeting politicians and men of every shade of opinion, but his sole preoccupation was the service of his country. In any relations which he might have had with such people, his only object was to keep himself informed, and to ensure that they, in turn, should know the truth about certain matters which concerned the Army. He added that officers were often criticized for limiting the horizon of their knowledge to matters which concerned the Army only, and he regarded it as his duty not to expose himself to such criticism. For that very reason he always did his best to acquaint himself with all currents of opinion which might influence the destiny of the Army. There was other evidence that conflicted with that of de Lattre, and the enquiry did not end conclusively. Others have maintained that it was a right-wing newspaper that approached de Lattre with a view to subverting the Army. When de Lattre refused to have anything to do with such a project, the newspaper concerned encouraged that venomous campaign that was now launched against him.

Whatever the truth may be, it is only fair to de Lattre to stress that his wide and varied contacts were nothing new. Contacts he had always sought; for him they provided one of the necessities of life, and the misfortunes which they were to bring him in February 1934 in no wise deterred him from his lifelong pursuit.

Although officially the matter was dropped, the consequences for de Lattre continued to be unpleasant. When passions are roused, men tend to lend an all-too-ready ear to the most fantastic stories, for which there is no foundation in fact. The accusations made against Weygand's staff officer spread with rapidity, and, even in La Vendée, de Lattre was shunned by so-called friends. But throughout this time of trouble, apart from the immeasurable help and sympathy of his wife, there were staunch and faithful friends, who gave abundantly of their support. Bousquet was among them, and he spent hours with his friend helping to prepare the case that he was to present before the commission of enquiry. Referring to these events later, Bousquet recalled not so much the shooting on the 6th February, as the memory of his friend at grips with calumny, merely because he had sought political information that would enable him the better to fulfil the mission that had been given him. He had been the victim of underhand manœuvring, added Bousquet, and, as always, his sole desire had been to see his country united. Although friends might desert him, it is of interest to record that, despite differences of opinion, one of the few who wrote to him in that hour of trouble was de Gaulle.

From the highest quarters there now came pressure upon Weygand to remove his staff officer. But Weygand never wavered, and he gave him his full support. Indeed, there is little doubt that, although de Lattre may have been guilty of indiscretion, he was guiltless of political intrigue. He had no politics. In later years he was to badger politicians of all parties in his determination to get his way, but no soldier had a deeper respect for the established government. He had a profound belief also in the good sense and patriotism of all his compatriots, whatever their politics, and in the Second World War it was his proudest achievement to have blended in one army men of all political creeds.

The ordeal through which de Lattre passed could not fail to leave its imprint upon his character. It seems probable that the attitude of so many of his friends at this time developed in him a permanent mistrust of his contemporaries, and inclined him to seek the friendship of younger men. But whatever bitterness may have been engendered, there developed also an increasing determination to overcome adversity, and it was at this period of his life that he began to adopt as his motto: "Ne pas subir".

The heavy clouds which had so darkened his days at 4 Bis were soon to disperse and in the healthy air of new surroundings the sun broke through again. In 1935 de Lattre was given command of the 151st Infantry Regiment at Metz.

"LE REGIMENT DE LATTRE"

IT was in September 1935 that de Lattre took over command of the 151st Infantry Regiment at Metz. He was now forty-six. Just over twenty years had elapsed since, as a young cavalry subaltern, he had gazed upon the Cathedral of Metz from that hill at Pont-à-Mousson, and vowed with his troop that they would not rest content until Metz was French again. With his sense of the historical, de Lattre felt a special satisfaction at being given command of the regiment, and he set about proving to the inhabitants of Metz that France could produce as fine a regiment as any of those German regiments whom some of them could still remember.

Many of the men in the 151st Infantry Regiment came from the industrial suburbs of Paris, and the left-wing element within the regiment was considerable. The enmity, more often it was jealousy, which de Lattre had incurred as a result of the 1934 disturbances in Paris, still pursued him, and there were some who hoped that the command of this regiment might prove his undoing. If a new commanding officer has ideas that are at variance with those of his predecessor, there are two methods of taking over command. The one is gradual, and involves the introduction, step by step, of new ideas. The other is brutal, and involves a clean and immediate sweep. It was the latter method which de Lattre chose. From the outset, he determined to mark the regiment with the seal of his dynamic personality. It was a calculated process, therefore, that he now put into effect, and it involved a series of actions that would shake and astound. The first people to be shaken must be the officers. De Lattre decided that their marching was below standard. Every officer, therefore, including the battalion commanders, was made to parade on the barrack square, and to march past, while the men of the regiment looked out from their windows. Although similar scenes were familiar on the barrack squares in England, in France they were unusual. Many were shocked—"Who is this demagogue playing to the gallery at the expense of the officers?" they murmured. Many of the more senior officers did not approve, but the younger officers and the men were quick to respond to these novel methods.

The devices which he adopted to keep the regiment on its toes were innumerable. Sometimes without warning he would order an alert at night, and the hour chosen would often coincide with the arrival of the evening train from Paris. Some saw in this seeming coincidence an attempt to impress the returning passengers. On their way from the station to their homes, they would see units of the 151st Infantry Regiment on the move to some alarm post. In all his unconventional activities at Metz, there was one ally upon whom de Lattre felt that he could rely for support, and that was Giraud, the Military Governor, who had known him in Morocco.

In every field there were reforms. In his determination to enhance the prestige of the regiment, he set great store by the band. "The band of a regiment," he said, "is its visiting-card." In the building up of the regimental band he did not hesitate to place men of extreme political views in key positions. Some say he did it deliberately, but whatever the motives, the results were astounding.

In many units of the French Army at the time, the attention paid to turn-out and drill was negligible. The high place which de

Lattre gave to these matters would have gladdened the heart of a drill sergeant in the Brigade of Guards. His inspections became proverbial. To the perfect fitting of uniforms and equipment he devoted a revolutionary zeal. There was one standard only: everything must be "impeccable"—all else was "inadmissible".

Such reforms might have been considered superficial if they had not been accompanied by something more solid. But, from his earliest days, the welfare of his men, physical and moral, had been de Lattre's especial concern. The attention that was paid to physical training and games in the 151st Infantry Regiment must have been without parallel. But the development of the mind in a healthy setting was also the object of his unremitting care. Although canteens already existed, the amenities that were added under de Lattre were previously unheard of, and all was devised to uplift the mind. On the walls of the men's dining-halls were painted scenes depicting the grandest episodes in the history of the regiment.

The ingenuity of the engineers was taxed to the utmost by the need to keep pace with the demands of the officer commanding the 151st Infantry Regiment. Even more harassed was the staff of the Garrison Intendant. With de Lattre, considerations of finance and economy were never allowed unduly to interfere, but the grandiose schemes which he now developed could not be completed without funds, and these were rarely available. The Intendant must find a way round. De Lattre would invite him to his house, and by the exercise of charm, unbelievable miracles were wrought. If the funds were not available under one vote, they must be found under another. "Flexibility" was one of the guiding principles of his life, and his interpretation of financial regulations could be quite remarkable.

Among de Lattre's many gifts was the ability to remember names and faces. It was said at one moment that he knew by sight every man in his regiment. This was almost true, and he expected his officers to acquire the same ability. The increasing interest which officers began to take in the welfare of their men and their families was not the least of the factors that contributed to the efficiency and, above all, to the spirit of the regiment. It was a spirit that spread beyond those who were actually serving, for de Lattre was always inviting officers and non-commissioned officers on the reserve, who lived in the neighbourhood, to attend his exercises. In the same way he would invite those of an older generation who had served in the regiment in the First World War to come to reunions. The links of comradeship which were thus forged between the regiment and the outside world were almost unique.

Within a few months, the prestige of de Lattre had become legendary, and many will recall the inspiring sight of the "Regiment de Lattre", impeccably turned out, marching through Metz and the countryside, to the strains of its magnificent band, with its commander at its head, superbly mounted. For de Lattre there was a special thrill when the regiment marched through Pont-à-Mousson, where the exploits of the young subaltern of the 12th Dragoons of 1914 were still remembered. One day, as the regiment entered the town, and the inhabitants turned out to greet him, he noticed friends among them with one of their young children: he lifted the child into his saddle, and rode on thus. Such were the scenes by which he was remembered.

It was not only in his own regiment that the name of de Lattre became legendary. In Metz there was a joint mess for the officers of several units of the garrison, and, as they came in to luncheon, it was common to hear them asking if anything new or exciting had happened in the 151st Infantry Regiment. A young artillery officer who was stationed at Metz at the time, recalls meeting de Lattre one night at dinner: during dinner his host was discussing the horses in his regiment, and said that he would be pleased to let any officer outside the regiment come and exercise them. The young gunner, said he would like to avail himself of the Colonel's kind offer. It was therefore arranged that on the next morning he should report to de Lattre at his headquarters at eleven o'clock. When he arrived, he saw a queue of officers, including two of the Battalion Commanders of the regiment, waiting, outside de Lattre's office. In due course the door opened and out came a private soldier. The young officer was surprised to see that senior officers had been kept waiting while de Lattre interviewed a private soldier, but more surprises were to come. De Lattre asked him to come in, but he pointed out that there were two of his own commanding officers still waiting, "It is their duty to wait for me," said de Lattre, and proceeded to talk at length with his visitor. After some time, the latter was able to remind de Lattre of the purpose of his visit. "Of course," said de Lattre, as he pressed the bell and summoned the sergeant in charge of the stables. When the sergeant arrived, he was ordered to bring out some horses for the officer to try. The sergeant ventured to point out that it was now time for the men's dinners. With a cold and imperious glance, de Lattre said to the astonished sergeant: "The horses will be round at once. Is that understood?" Meanwhile the two commanding officers still were waiting.

De Lattre had barely two years in which to complete the infinity of reforms which he had in mind, and the enthusiasm with which he devoted himself to the service of his regiment left him little time for the other activities that characterize life in a large garrison town. Apart from his own exercises, there were the exercises that from time to time were set by his superior commander, and, as a normal prelude, voluminous papers would be sent to the participants on the eve of the exercise. The digestion of these papers and the marking of the map demanded considerable time which de Lattre was rarely prepared to give, and he relied generally on his capacity for quick assimilation. An officer serving in the regiment at the time recalls motoring out with him to one of these exercises. De Lattre had read none of the papers, and in the car he asked the officer to produce the map and run quickly through the exercise. On the ground, he contrived not to be among the first to be asked a question, and by the time others had spoken and his own turn came, his grasp of the situation was complete.

In September 1937 de Lattre was selected to undergo a course at the Centre of Higher Military Studies. Few commanders in so short a time can have left so indelible an imprint on a regiment as did de Lattre upon the 151st Infantry Regiment. Exaggerated stories gained ground as to the months required after his departure to settle the accounts, and of the despair of the Intendant at Metz. True, there had been great flexibility in the interpretation of financial regulations, and here and there some adjustments may have been necessary, but every sou was spent for the benefit of the regiment, and, more particularly, for the welfare of the men.

The regiment that he handed over to his successor had a spirit that was exceptional at a time when the morale of the whole Army was beginning to cause anxiety. The opinion then held of de Lattre by Giraud is reflected in his report on him at the time: "He is handing over to his successor a magnificent regiment, which is at the same time an excellent instrument of war. I strongly recommend his promotion at the earliest possible moment." The opinion formed by Giraud was reinforced by the Conseil Supérieur de la Guerre. General Billotte, an unfortunate leader, who was to perish in a car accident at the height of battle in May 1940, wrote as follows: "A young and brilliant commanding officer with intelligence, imagination, and a taste for reform. He has commanded his regiment by methods which lie off the beaten track.... The officers and non-commissioned officers of the 151st Regiment fully realize that the long and sustained effort which was demanded of them was in the general interest."

The officers selected to undergo the course at the Centre of Higher Military Studies were destined for the highest posts; indeed the Centre was sometimes known as the "School for Marshals". In this new and important phase of his life, there was full scope for the deployment of de Lattre's exceptional qualities. In the slippery climb to success, many officers have toyed with original thought, but few have had the courage of their convictions. Too many have been influenced by anxiety to produce the orthodox answer most likely to appeal to their superiors. To that mediocre company de Lattre did not belong. One of the exercises set at the Centre while he was there, dealt with the possibility of the Germans again disregarding the neutrality of Belgium and pouring through that country, while the French Army was concentrating on the frontiers of France. The particular problem to be studied was how best the French Army could intervene on the Albert Canal. The solution of the Directing Staff was to move forward in strength at once to the Canal. The majority of the students were content to move their cavalry forward. It was expected that de Lattre, with his cavalry spirit, would put forward an aggressive solution in the grand manner, but, to the surprise of all, he was one of the few to show prudence, for he considered that the armour and aircraft at his disposal did not justify an advance beyond the Escault. He could take risks, but he was not the irresponsible gambler that some have depicted.

It was during his course at the "School for Marshals" that de

Lattre lost his mother. At this period he was again seeing much of his old friend Bousquet, and the latter recalls the depth of the grief which de Lattre felt. To Bousquet he recounted all the memories which the death of his mother brought back.

In July 1938 de Lattre finished his course, and the report which he received on leaving left no doubt as to the high regard which his superiors had for him. It drew attention in particular to his outstanding personality, the breadth of his views, his enthusiasm in all that he did, and his capacity for concise exposition.

It was now that de Lattre was appointed Chief of Staff to General Hering, the Military Governor of Strasbourg, and Commander-Designate of the Fifth French Army. In March 1939, Hering reached the age of retirement and was succeeded by General Bourret. In that same month de Lattre was promoted to the rank of Brigadier-General. He was just fifty, and one of the youngest generals in the Army.

Ever since his early days in the 12th Dragoons, the mystique of Alsace and Lorraine had always appealed to him, and his love of that part of France was second only to his love of La Vendée. He was therefore happy at Strasbourg, and with his usual capacity for making new contacts, he soon had many new friends.

Meanwhile, momentous events were convulsing the world. While de Lattre had been commanding his regiment, Hitler had marched into the Rhineland. In March 1938 he had brought Austria under his yoke. The Munich crisis followed, and once again the lights of Europe were going out.

PART IV

Adversity

1940–1943

10. BLITZKRIEG

IN the autumn of 1938 it was a delirious and irresponsible crowd that welcomed the British Prime Minister, Mr. Neville Chamberlain, at Heston Airport on his return from Munich. In France, too, there was much rejoicing that war had been averted. But there were others, both in France and England, whose heads hung low in shame that honour had been sacrificed, and Czechoslovakia dismembered. So triumphed Hitler, not only against the Allies, but against the enemy within his own gates. "No more territorial ambitions in Europe", had been his cry at Munich, but within a year Czechoslovakia had been occupied and his raucous propaganda machine was fulminating against Poland. Feverishly the Allies strove to make good their deficiencies, and assiduously too they paid their artless court to Russia. But Hitler proved the more subtle suitor, and on the 23rd August was signed the Non-Aggression Pact between Germany and Russia. In a secret agreement a demarcation line was drawn for the partition of Poland.

At dawn on the 1st September Hitler marched into Poland, and Europe again was aflame. There had been years of warning, but when the moment came it was hard to believe that the war was real. Mechanically, almost listlessly, the armies of the Allies mobilized. In England, there was none of the enthusiasm of 1914, and yet there seemed to prevail a deeper sense of wrong. Whatever may be the verdict of history upon the leadership of Mr. Chamberlain, the fact that he had been so vilely tricked and cheated had stirred in the hearts of his countrymen an unwonted wave of anger. In France, however much men might also believe in the justice of the cause, the heavy sacrifices of the First World War had taken immeasurable toll of her strength, which had been still further sapped by insidious and intangible influences: in such a soil, enthusiasm and high morale could only thrive with difficulty, and it is against such a background that the rôle which de Lattre was about to play should be measured.

The front of the Fifth Army ran from the Swiss frontier along the Rhine, and therefore included that portion of the Maginot Line on which most work had been done. The rôle of Chief of Staff was not one which best befitted so dynamic a temperament as that of de Lattre, and the static nature of the campaign did not make the task more congenial; but his lively imagination and energy did not lie dormant. There was much that needed stirring. Army Headquarters were in the little town of Saverne, a conspicuous landmark, and therefore a vulnerable target for enemy aircraft. De Lattre persuaded his Chief to move to Wangerbourg, a small village on one of the heights of the Vosges, and he ordered the Officer Commanding Divisional Signals to see that communications were installed in the new headquarters within a week. "Technically that is impossible," said the officer. "Perhaps impossible for you," replied de Lattre, "because you are incompetent. The work will therefore be done by the Post Office technicians, and you shall watch and learn."

Although there was no indication or probability that the enemy contemplated an early assumption of the offensive in the west, and although many of those round him regarded the Rhine as a sure obstacle, de Lattre himself was never satisfied with the state of the French defences, and he strove to strengthen them. But the winter was exceptionally severe, and since few men in the Army had experienced heavy shelling, or indeed any of the unpleasantness of more active warfare, they did not readily see the necessity for such hard and monotonous work.

In other and less orthodox spheres, the imagination of the Chief of Staff was constantly at work. Much of the ground that lay between the French and German positions had to be evacuated; Strasbourg itself was a deserted city; factories ceased to function, and industry was at a standstill. De Lattre sensed, sooner than most, that gloom and lethargy were threatening to demoralize the Army, and he refused to accept a situation that to most seemed inevitable. He determined to react, and in a short time, with the help of the Army, many factories were reopened, and industry came to life again. In order still further to dissipate depression, de Lattre encouraged everywhere the cultivation of gardens, and in so far as was possible, the substitution of beauty for that ugly desolation that was the normal characteristic of the forward area. It seemed an unusual and fanciful outlook for a soldier, but once again the underlying theme was grandeur; even in war the mind could be elevated.

At this time de Lattre saw much of Colonel de Gaulle, who commanded the armour in the Fifth Army. Although their views had clashed and were to clash again, their respect for each other was considerable. How different they were! The one, austere, unapproachable, and seemingly self-sufficient; the other, intensely human, always approachable, and, indeed, in need of companionship. Different, too, were the rôles which they were about to play. France needed them both, and of both she was to be proud.

De Lattre remained with the Fifth Army until the end of 1939, but at the beginning of January 1940 he was given command of the 14th Infantry Division, an active division and therefore one of the best in the French Army. De Lattre's fortunes were still linked with those of Alsace, for the 14th Division included the 35th Infantry Regiment, which was the regiment of Belfort, and the 152nd Infantry Regiment, known as the Red Devils, which was the regiment of Colmar. The division also included a half-brigade of Chasseurs, comprising two battalions from Mulhouse, and the 25th Divisional Reconnaissance Group. The divisional artillery regiment was also from Colmar. When de Lattre took it over, the division was holding a sector between Sarreguemines and Forbach.

The ultimate test for a commander must always be battle, but despite the stagnation which then reigned, the powers of command of the new divisional commander were at once to be put to a test more subtle and difficult than battle itself. As soon as he had taken over, he realized that the division was already suffering from that lethargy which he had struggled so hard to combat in the Fifth Army. It had been aggravated by the severity of the winter, and all seemed numbed both in mind and body. Little or no work was being done to improve defences; digging and other work was regarded as impossible in such weather; men seemed to be sitting passive in their positions, waiting vaguely for something to happen. They seemed also to be imbued with an unwholesome fear of German patrols, who approached the French lines with impunity. In other spheres, too, all was not well. Arrangements for welfare were woefully inadequate; canteens were lacking; centres for receiving men returning from leave hardly existed; and such baths as there were, failed wholly to meet requirements. In fact the "Drôle de Guerre", as the French came to call it, was already playing havoc with morale.

It was only too evident that drastic action was required to pull the division together. Somehow it must regain the ascendancy over the enemy: despite the cold it must work, and above all it must struggle against boredom. When morale had sunk to so low an ebb, it presented a problem that needed careful handling: any false step might make matters worse. De Lattre decided that, although action must be drastic, it must be progressive. As a first step, he concentrated upon bringing the forward posts up to a pitch of alertness which they had not hitherto known. For two weeks, the division was to undertake no offensive patrolling: rather was it to devote its energies to improving fire discipline, and to acquiring confidence in its ability to keep the German patrols at a distance. The result of this action was that within a week, a German raid was repulsed with loss. From that moment the audacity of the enemy diminished. A great step forward had been taken.

A week later, the French in turn became aggressive. Their patrols pushed far into no-man's-land, and invaluable information began to reach divisional headquarters. De Lattre himself was never backward in setting the example, and on one occasion, with a suitable escort, he went forward to take Communion in an abandoned church in no-man's-land. News of this quickly spread throughout the division with heartening effect. As the weeks went by, the French patrols worked deeper into the enemy positions; prisoners began to come in, and information continued to increase. The artillery too kept pace with this new aggressiveness, and in two months all arms of the division had gained an ascendancy over the enemy.

In order still further to build up morale, the divisional commander launched a major offensive against the squalor and untidiness that had accumulated in the billeting areas occupied by the division. Again he encouraged the cultivation of gardens; canteens, baths, cinemas, and indeed all those comforts that had been lacking were quickly provided. On one occasion, he came across a man with long hair. To the familiar remonstrance that followed, the man replied that he knew of no barber's shop. De Lattre summoned his Chief Engineer Officer, and ordered the establishment of a barber's shop within twenty-four hours, complete with six assistants clothed in white overalls. Such was de Lattre. One who saw him at the time described him thus:

> "The impression that he gave was one of life and activity, and of a driving power that was extraordinary. For any form of laziness he had no use, and if anyone looked smugly content with his job, de Lattre would literally pulverize him. He liked to command, and yet he liked to charm. His mind, though tidy, was always on the move, devising projects for operations, projects for recreational facilities—indeed projects of every conceivable nature, which he would put into effect with a zeal that carried him along as it carried along those with him. He would brook no resistance."

To the writer who described him thus, de Lattre himself strove to explain what he was trying to achieve. No one must think of relaxing. In that monotonous and static struggle there was a danger of falling asleep. It was the bounden duty of everyone, every day, to shake himself and to renew his driving power. It was a matter of gaining the ascendency over oneself first, and then over the enemy.

In the middle of April the division was relieved and withdrawn to rest at Luneville. The rest was to be disturbed with brutal suddenness.

Of all the disadvantages from which the Allies suffered at the outset of the Second World War, none was greater than the handicap imposed upon sound military planning by the neutrality of Belgium. In the event of a German invasion of that country it could only be assumed that the Belgian Army would be able to hold its ground until the Franco-British forces could come to its aid. However gallant the Belgian Army might prove to be, in view of its size this was a dangerous assumption, and one to which the British General Staff had never subscribed; but French views prevailed. Although throughout the winter the Allies had worked feverishly on field defences that were to fill the gap between the northern extremity of the Maginot Line and the coast, it was decided that, in the event of a German invasion of Belgium, they should move forward from their defences to the help of the Belgian Army. Such, briefly, was "Plan D".

Meanwhile, the agreement between Germany and Russia had squeezed Poland out of existence. Although the prospect of an ultimate conflict with Russia was ever present in his mind, for the moment Hitler felt justified in denuding his eastern frontier, and once again, as in 1917, the whole of Germany's strength was transferred to the west. Hitler was now anxious, before Russia could intervene, to crush France; then, so he hoped, he could come to terms with Britain. By the beginning of May, all was ready for the launching of that momentous attack, which, by the rapidity of its success, was to astonish the attackers themselves no less than it staggered the unfortunate defenders.

The German Army was deployed in three Army Groups (see map on p. 69). On the right, was Army Group "B" under General von Bock; its task was firstly to overrun Holland and Belgium, and then to advance into France as the German right wing. In the centre, was Army Group "A" under General von Runstedt. To this army was entrusted the main thrust; it was to move through the Ardennes, cross the Meuse between Dinant and Sedan, pierce the French front, and then roll up the whole of the Allied left wing against the Channel. On the left, was Army Group "C" under General von Leeb, which was to pin the French Army along the Maginot Line.

Since it was the thrust through the Ardennes which was to interest de Lattre and his 14th Infantry Division, the operations of Army Group "A" under von Runstedt will be considered in some detail. Neither by the German nor the French General Staff had a thrust by armour through the Ardennes been considered practicable. But General Guderian, who in peacetime had made his mark as a tank commander of unusual enterprise, argued that the Ardennes did not constitute a barrier to armour; moreover resistance in the Ardennes was unlikely to be great, and the problem such as it was, was administrative rather than tactical. The main tactical problem was the protection of a myriad vehicles, moving through the steep and winding roads that led through that wooded country, against a major attack by the Allied Air Forces. Guderian convinced General von Manstein, von Runstedt's Chief of Staff, and the advance of the armour through the Ardennes was decided upon. It was to be followed by a rapid crossing of the Meuse. Once across the Meuse, the armour would be able to gallop to its heart's content over the rolling plains beyond.

To ensure the success of von Runstedt's thrust, six of the ten Panzer divisions which then existed were allotted to his Army Group. These were to comprise a Panzer Group under General Kleist. Guderian was appointed to command the spearhead of three Panzer Divisions. No one could have been better equipped for such a rôle, for in manœuvres he had fully tried out his ideas. Supported by an overwhelming force of dive-bombers, and exploiting success by night, he claimed not only that his columns would be able to penetrate deeply into the enemy positions, but also that, since the enemy would be taken by surprise, they need not worry unduly about the security of their flanks and rear. Such, briefly, was the conception of Guderian, but in the ensuing advance the pace was to be continually checked by his more timid superiors.

On the 10th May, at dawn, the might of Hitler's Germany moved forward against the West. In five days, more by the surprise effect of a small airborne force than by overwhelming superiority of numbers, Army Group "B" had forced Holland to her knees. The success of the German right wing had diverted the attention of the Allies from the real danger point in the Ardennes. Plan "D" was at once set in motion. The Ninth, First, and Seventh French Armies, with the British Expeditionary Force interposed between the latter two, raced forward with redoubled speed to the aid of their new Allies; but the very speed of their advance led them deeper into the trap.

On the front of Army Group "A", moving forward in three vast blocks, was the Panzer Group of Kleist. In the leading two blocks were the armoured divisions, and in the third were the motorized infantry divisions. Behind the Panzer Group came the Twelfth Army. Although nine days had been allowed for the advance to the Meuse, the opposition was even lighter than expected, and the sixty miles that separated the Meuse from their jumping-off place had been covered by the armour in three days.

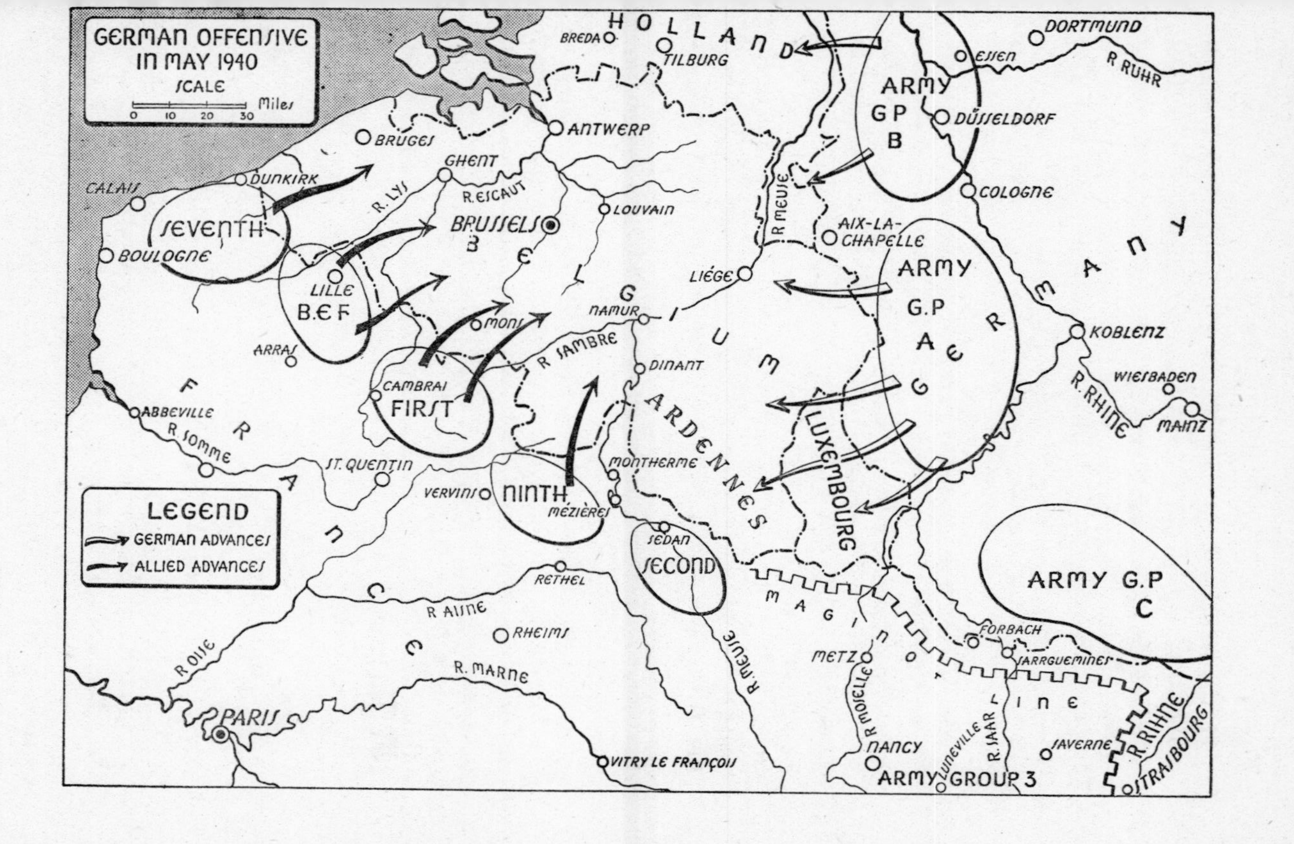
GERMAN OFFENSIVE IN MAY 1940
SCALE
0 10 20 30 Miles
LEGEND
GERMAN ADVANCES
ALLIED ADVANCES
HOLLAND
BELGIUM
GERMANY
FRANCE
LUXEMBOURG
ARDENNES
MAGINOT LINE
ARMY GP B
ARMY G.P A
ARMY G.P C
ARMY GROUP 3
SEVENTH
B.E.F
FIRST
NINTH
SECOND
BREDA
TILBURG
ESSEN
DORTMUND
R RUHR
DÜSSELDORF
COLOGNE
ANTWERP
BRUGES
GHENT
DUNKIRK
CALAIS
BOULOGNE
R. LYS
R. ESCAUT
BRUSSELS
LOUVAIN
R MEUSE
AIX-LA-CHAPELLE
LIÉGE
LILLE
NAMUR
MONS
ARRAS
R SAMBRE
DINANT
KOBLENZ
WIESBADEN
R. RHINE
MAINZ
CAMBRAI
ABBEVILLE
R. SOMME
ST. QUENTIN
MONTHERME
VERVINS
MÉZIÈRES
SEDAN
RETHEL
R AISNE
RHEIMS
R. OISE
R. MARNE
PARIS
VITRY LE FRANÇOIS
R. MEUSE
METZ
FORBACH
SARRGUEMINES
R MOSELLE
NANCY
LUNEVILLE
R. SAAR
SAVERNE
R. RHINE
STRASBOURG

On the morning of the 13th, therefore, from the wooded heights to the north, Guderian's armour overlooked the Meuse. Many of his superiors with more orthodox views hesitated to attempt a crossing before the infantry had been brought up, but Kleist decided to cross at four o'clock that same afternoon. A mass of dive-bombers—"almost the whole of the German Air Force" to quote Guderian's operation order—was to support the attempt. By the effective and protracted efforts of these aircraft, the French defences were virtually neutralized, and crossings were made both east and west of Sedan.

Shortly before midnight on the 13th, Guderian issued his orders for the immediate exploitation of the bridgehead, and in view of the subsequent part that was to be played by de Lattre's 14th Infantry Division, the general scope of those orders is of particular interest. The 2nd Panzer Division on the right was to advance through Boutancourt on Poix-Terron (see map facing p. 96); the 1st Panzer Division, with its left on the Aisne, was to advance through Vendresse and le Chesne on Rethel; the 10th Panzer Division was to protect the left flank of the advance. The armour of Guderian and the infantry of de Lattre were soon to meet.

Such, briefly, was the opening of the Blitzkrieg. The armies of the Allies were quickly placed at a cruel disadvantage. To those, therefore, who stood their ground, the greater credit is due. If, in the French Army at the time, there were divisions whose morale had been impaired by the insidious poison then at work, there were others who fought as valiantly as ever Frenchmen have fought. Not least among them was the 14th Infantry Division.

11. THE GIANT OF RETHEL

ON the 10th May, when the blow fell, the 14th Infantry Division was still at rest near Luneville. Many were on leave. A training programme based on the lessons of the Polish campaign was due to start on the 15th May. By the 11th, everyone had been recalled from leave.

By the morning of the 12th the German punch had already more than dented the fragile surface that it struck, and on that same morning Fourth Army warned the division by telephone to be prepared to move any time after dawn on the 13th. This warning order was confirmed later in the day, and between seven o'clock on the morning of the 13th and the morning of the 15th, a series of trains conveyed the division to the area near Rheims. The motor transport of the division was to proceed by road. Particular attention was paid to camouflage, and, despite the enemy air force, the entrainment of the division at the seven stations allotted proceeded without incident.

It was at four o'clock on the morning of the 14th May that de Lattre received the first indication of what was happening. An officer on the divisional staff telephoned from Rheims station to say that the situation round Sedan was extremely confused, and that the first elements of the division to detrain had at once been put into lorries and sent north of the Aisne towards Sedan. Guderian had in fact crossed the Meuse at Sedan on the previous day, and was already exploiting the bridgehead westward (see map facing p. 96).

The most imaginative exercise could never have devised a more harassing situation than that which confronted the commander of the 14th Infantry Division on the 14th May and the days that followed. Such information as he received regarding the enemy was conflicting. Communications both with superior headquarters and with his neighbours were precarious, and they were no better within the division, which was spread out over a large area between Luneville and Rheims, partly in trains and partly on the roads. Units could only be engaged piecemeal as they arrived. The collecting of information and the issue of orders were often only possible by the use of the divisional staff, and invaluable energy was often dissipated in this way. Moreover, the rapid tempo which Guderian's armour had brought to the battlefield caused orders and information often to be out of date by the time they were received. The resulting orders and counter-orders left both flanks of the division continually in the air. But these disabilities were as nothing to that unnerving atmosphere that overshadows a retreating army. The sky was overcast with enemy aircraft, and not only did the more familiar noises of the battlefield haunt the ears, but also the incessant whine of the dive-bombers. Moreover the roads were encumbered by transport and weary men, soldiers and civilians. Under no conditions could the personality of a commander exercise so profound an influence, not only upon his own exhausted staff and those whom he commanded, but also upon his superiors and upon his neighbours.

By the 14th, in a confused situation, it was at least clear that the Germans had crossed the Meuse and driven a wedge between the Second and the Ninth French Armies; they had in fact lost touch with each other, and it was to close the gap between them that General Corap, commanding the Ninth Army, was forming an Army Detachment under General Touchon. But as yet the detachment, of which the 14th Infantry Division was to form part, was hardly in being, and in the emergency early that morning Colonel Manhes d'Angeny, de Lattre's Chief of Staff, was himself summoned to Ninth Army Headquarters at Vervins to receive orders direct. The division, while covering its own detrainment, was also to cover the right of the Ninth Army near Omont. On the right it was to establish contact with the left of the Second Army round La Cassine, and on the left with the Ninth Army's right flank near Villers-le-Tilleul. Manhes rejoined de Lattre later in the morning, and the latter at once ordered the leading company of the 152nd Infantry Regiment, which had just arrived, to hold the northern outskirts of Rethel, while the remainder of the leading battalion was sent in lorries to Omont.

De Lattre himself reached Rethel later in the day, and established his headquarters in an abandoned house in the middle of the town. It might have been wiser to have selected a site outside Rethel, and remote from the attention of the Luftwaffe and the distracting confusion caused by retreating soldiers, civilians, and vehicles in the middle of the town. But in view of the precarious state of arrangements for intercommunication, the site selected was probably easier for liaison officers, despatch riders, and others to find.

Although on the 14th he was not yet heavily engaged, for the leading elements of Guderian's Panzers were only just beginning to move forward from the Meuse, the situation of de Lattre's own division, arriving company by company in the battle zone, was sufficient to cause him the greatest anxiety. But through all the fog and fluctuations of the situation, he retained his grip, and though gloom and depression surrounded him, he towered like some giant beacon, radiating encouragement and hope to the weary and faint-hearted. Colonel de Camas, head of his operations staff at the time, has given the following picture of his commander on that day:

> "In the room which he had chosen for his office, the General was in conference with his staff, while the clerks were collecting tables and chairs, and laying out maps. Through the open windows came the roar and rumble of that unending stream of vehicles and men in flight to the south. Suddenly there was the whine of the Stukas diving to drop their bombs. The noise was infernal. Quite quietly, just as if it was merely a hailstorm, little Dequenne, the clerk who never left the General, shut the windows. Immediately there was another explosion, and the windows flew in all directions, covering the General's table with bits of glass. Dequenne was hurled to the ground, and the General, with a touch of humour in his voice, said, 'Quick! clear all that away for me.' And as the clerk left the room with the bits of broken glass, he added, as though speaking his thoughts aloud, 'What a good little chap he is! If everybody on the Meuse had shown equal sense and coolness in shutting their windows because of the noise of the Stukas we shouldn't be where we are today.'"

De Lattre's affection for little Dequenne was typical. The qualities of this excellent man had first come to his notice when he was Chief of Staff to the Governor of Strasbourg, and Dequenne had been added to that little band of followers, in whom de Lattre inspired a loyalty akin to veneration. A few weeks later, Dequenne was killed during the fighting on the Loire. De Lattre never forgot him. Three years later, after his escape from prison, it was the name of Dequenne that he chose for his forged identity card.

De Camas recalls further impressions on that same day:

> "The General had gathered his staff round him. In that hour when such vital and irrevocable decisions had to be made, he gave an impression of complete self-possession. His calm and serenity increased as the noise of the bombs grew louder, and reports of the great rout grew worse. His lucidity was something quite supernatural; he seemed to grasp the situation better by intuition than if he had been in possession of a hundred

situation reports. On the map he described the enemy's intentions, where he would stop him and where he himself would link up with his neighbours. It was because he visualized that situation so intensely that he dominated it. He gave at that moment the impression af a magician soaring high up in the sky, and bending both men and events to his will. 'And now,' said de Lattre, 'let's get on with it. You, Pommier [head of his 4th Bureau], off you go at once in a car, reconnoitre the whole railway down to Rheims, and as units detrain, direct them to Rethel, and send their commanding officers to me. You, Manhes [Chief of Staff], and you, Lamont [an officer in the 3rd Bureau], I want you to reconnoitre in the direction of Sedan, and see if there is anyone holding out in front of us. And you, Camas, move off towards le Chesne on the right, and see if you can find any units of the 5th Light Cavalry Division, who should be in action in that area. Tell them that we are on our way up, and ask them to hold on to the line of the Aisne, joining up with us at Attigny.' And as they moved off he called them back. 'For the love of Heaven,' he added, 'don't get killed or taken prisoner. You are far too useful at this moment. Besides—I'm very fond of you all.'"

The spirit of de Lattre permeated the whole division, and spread to the disintegrating units of others. Indeed, the 14th Infantry Division became a rallying point for all. The artillery regiments of at least two other divisions threw in their lot with de Lattre. It was reported that north of Rethel there were several French "B" tanks immobilized through lack of fuel. De Lattre was quick to appreciate the rôle they could play. They must be salved. Seizing hold of a member of his staff he said, "Get a car at once and go off to Mourmelon, Rheims, or even Paris if necessary, and get hold of some petrol and oil. I give you six hours." At a time when he was trying to deploy his division and there was hard work ahead, this may seem an unnecessary additional burden to have imposed upon his staff, but, as a result, many tanks were salved, which in the coming battle were to play an invaluable part.

Thus was the fight conducted. There were few written orders. Most were given verbally by de Lattre direct to regimental, battalion, or even company commanders, and the tone and manner of their issue were adapted to the personality of the subordinate concerned. For some, a few words only would suffice;

for others, more were needed; and for others again, a little anger was more effective. From each man his maximum capacity was obtained.

On the evening of the 14th, de Lattre himself went to Army Headquarters, and discovered that the rapidity of the German advance would necessitate a modification of the orders already issued, and upon which action had already been taken. The line he was now to hold was Poix-Terron–Signy-l'Abbaye. Poix-Terron was the objective which had been given to one of Guderian's Panzer divisions. In fact, while de Lattre, with fragments of his division, was trying to take up a position facing north, Guderian's Panzers were rapidly approaching from the east, and at any moment might strike his fragile flank.

De Lattre now ordered the Divisional Reconnaissance Group, which was on the road near Vitry-le-François, to move at once to Rethel, which incidentally was the objective which had been given to the 1st Panzer Division. Meanwhile, a few more elements of the 152nd Regiment had detrained and moved forward in the direction of Omont. They were to establish contact on the right with the 5th Light Cavalry Division. They were now near Bouvellemont.

Throughout the 15th May, events again moved swiftly. Information was still uncertain and conflicting, and as more units of the division reached the battlefield in driblets they were bustled forward. Of all the burdens that men bore on that day, none was heavier than that which fell upon the shoulders of the liaison officers. In a large and unfamiliar area, in which Guderian's tanks already roamed, they were constantly ferreting out the scattered units of the division to give them their orders. Returning exhausted to divisional headquarters, they would find that the remorseless and ever-changing situation had brought about the need for new orders, and off they would set again.

At Rethel, in the very early hours of the 15th, de Lattre had met General Touchon, who was just beginning to assemble his heterogeneous detachment which, in addition to the 14th Infantry Division, was to include the 2nd Reserve Armoured Division and all units and establishments of the Ninth Army in the area. De Lattre was never an easy subordinate, and at their first meeting there was disagreement. In view of the continual danger of the enemy, with his greater mobility, turning the flanks, Touchon, with considerable justification, was anxious to withdraw at once south of the Aisne, in order to make the best use of that anti-tank obstacle. But, although information was still very scanty, de Lattre appreciated that the enemy was directing his main thrust westward, and that he would want to reach the Aisne in order to use it as protection for his southern flank; he also appreciated that he would want to use the east and west road running through Rethel: therefore, argued de Lattre, they should cling to the ground north of the Aisne, and deny the enemy the use of the road through Rethel. Furthermore, by holding a bridgehead north of the Aisne they would better be able to cover the withdrawal and reorganization of the vast number of disintegrating units withdrawing southward. Finally, claimed de Lattre, the maintenance of such a bridgehead would provide an indispensable jumping-off area for a French counter-attack. His plan, therefore, was to build up a defensive position based on the positions ahead held by the 5th Light Cavalry Brigade near Omont, and his own 152nd Infantry Regiment now near Bouvellemont.

The appreciation which de Lattre thus made in regard to German intentions could not have been more accurate. Indeed, the Germans had from the outset feared a French counter-attack from the south, and it was a part of the German plan, in the wake of Guderian's armour, to deploy a strong force of infantry along the Aisne to meet such a threat. The plan also envisaged the use of the road through Rethel. But de Lattre's own plan was perhaps a little audacious, based optimistically on the positions which the 5th Light Cavalry Brigade and the 152nd Infantry Regiment were supposed to be holding. And at that stage de Lattre certainly did not know the strength of the enemy armour that threatened to charge through.

A compromise was reached with Touchon, who agreed to the holding of a small bridgehead north of Rethel. He left to de Lattre the initiative to withdraw south of the Aisne, if, in his view, the situation should warrant it.

Meanwhile, however, confirmatory orders had arrived from Army Headquarters for the holding of the line Poix-Terron–Signy-l'Abbaye, and on these orders de Lattre had to act. He decided to leave the elements which had already reached Bouvellemont where they were. The front allotted was about thirteen miles, and he decided to hold it with all three regiments forward. At that moment, however, only about one battalion in each regiment had reached the area, so that three battalions had to hold the whole front. Special arrangements were made for covering the left flank, where the situation was obscure, and no touch had been established with friendly troops. The half-brigade of Chasseurs, which had just arrived, was ordered to Launois. The divisional reconnaissance group was ordered at once to organize a bridgehead at Rethel itself, and to defend the northern exits of the town. The establishment of this backstop proved to have been a wise precaution.

During the afternoon, elements of the 152nd Infantry Regiment became heavily engaged with enemy armour round Chagny, Bouvellemont, and La Bascule. Although they disabled a number of enemy tanks, they lost most of their own anti-tank guns and suffered heavy casualties; only through the skill of junior commanders were they extricated and saved from encirclement. During the night they withdrew to the general line Jonval–Wignicourt. It was Guderian's 1st Panzer Division that they had met.

While these events were taking place, de Lattre attended a conference at Chateau Porcien, together with General Touchon and General Germain, commanding XXIII Corps, under whose command the 14th Infantry Division now came. Information continued to be contradictory, but there was a fleeting moment of optimism when it was reported that the 53rd Infantry Division was holding firmly the line Poix-Terron–Launois, on the left of the 14th Infantry Division. Based on this information there was even talk of counter-attacking. Orders were therefore given for the 14th Infantry Division to move forward, and secure the line Omont–Poix-Terrom.

The return of de Lattre to his headquarters at Rethel coincided with that of a liaison officer bringing news not only of the heavy fighting in which the 152nd Infantry Regiment had been engaged but also of the virtual disappearance of the 53rd Infantry Division. The orders which had just been issued were thus already in part impracticable. But with modifications they were still to stand. Two battalions of Tirailleurs had now come under de Lattre's orders, and they were ordered to thicken the front between the 152nd Infantry Regiment on the right, and the half-brigade of Chasseurs on the left. These orders in turn could not be executed. At seven o'clock in the evening, the leading Chasseurs units, who were moving through the northern outskirts of Faissault on their way up to Launois, were heavily attacked by enemy armour, which was probably the left flank of Guderian's 2nd Panzer Division. A fierce engagement ensued, in which six enemy tanks were destroyed.

For the moment all thought of holding out north of the Aisne had to be abandoned, and during the night orders were issued for withdrawal to that river. For the 14th Division it had been the first day of battle, and for those units which had detrained and been pitched straight into battle the test had been severe and the casualties heavy. One battalion of the 152nd Regiment lost four officers and 245 other ranks. But at least thirty enemy tanks had been destroyed, and on the whole divisional front the enemy had been checked, however slightly. In no case had there been withdrawal without orders.

During the night of the 15th, the bridgehead at Rethel organized by the divisional reconnaissance group, formed a welcome shield to cover the withdrawal of those weary units of the division who, after long marching and hard fighting, made their way back in good order throughout the night. Other units crossed at Attigny and Givry.

The events of the 14th and 15th do not seem to have made a serious inroad into the energy of de Lattre, and on the 16th he applied himself as vigorously as ever to organizing his thirteen-mile sector along the Aisne from Attigny, where he was now in touch with the 36th Infantry Regiment, to just west of Rethel. He was still without the 35th Infantry Regiment, and only two batteries of his own divisional artillery had reached the area; but his artillery commander had roped in odd units from all over the place to provide the infantry with the most effective artillery support that the circumstances allowed. In all spheres everyone was improvising, and the liaison officers were busy impressing upon all commanders that their positions must be held at all costs, and "sans esprit de recul".

For the most part, the forward line ran along the Aisne, to the south of which was the Aisne Canal running parallel with the river and forming a second anti-tank obstacle. At Rethel only was a small bridgehead retained. Odd German detachments approached this on the 16th, and were severely dealt with. Upon one German officer, who was killed, were found the orders for the advance of the German armour, and it was clear that it had been their intention to use the roads passing through Rethel. The stand, therefore, of the division north of Rethel had at least inconvenienced the westward thrust of the enemy.

During the 17th, continual enemy movement was observed from east to west, and de Lattre struggled to impress upon the Corps Commander the vulnerability of the enemy, and the desirability of a strong northward counter-attack. He was informed, however, that the absence of reserves made his proposal impracticable.

It would seem appropriate at this point to leave the 14th Infantry Division reorganizing on the Aisne and to consider for a moment the intentions of the enemy, and in particular the operations of Guderian's Panzer Corps since its crossing of the Meuse on the 13th.

On the 14th, the situation of Guderian on the left bank of the Meuse was not entirely happy. One division only was across, and the one bridge was subjected to heavy attacks by the allied air force. However, the strength of the German anti-aircraft defences at that vital spot was highly effective, and Guderian was determined to push on; on the previous evening he had already issued orders for his corps to exploit due westward on Poix-Terron and Rethel, while the 10th Panzer Division was to stave off any French attempt to break into the bridgehead between Stonne and Sedan.

It was not until the 15th that Guderian was really under way again, and in the afternoon the 2nd Panzer Division came up against opposition north of Faissault, while the 1st Panzer Division also ran into trouble round Bouvellemont. It was de Lattre's Chasseurs whom the Germans met at Faissault, and the 152nd Infantry Regiment at Bouvellemont. In both cases, the Germans, after losing a number of tanks, circumvented the opposition, moving round to the north, and by the evening both Panzer divisions were established in the area round Poix-Terron, whence the 1st Panzer Division swung south. On that same day, while he was exploiting his success, a timid and restraining hand was placed on Guderian by his superiors: their minds were still greatly exercised by the fear of a major French counter-offensive being launched from the south. It is true that on the 14th sporadic attacks were delivered near Stonne, but they had been driven back. Nevertheless, Guderian was ordered to confine himself to the bridgehead. It was only with difficulty that the infuriated Panzer leader obtained permission from Kleist to continue his advance for another twenty-four hours, in order to allow the Infantry Corps to follow up.

In view of the resistance of the 152nd French Infantry Regiment at Bouvellemont on the 15th, it is of interest to note that Guderian himself passed through that place on the 16th. He found the troops very tired, having had no real rest since the 9th May. Ammunition was running low, and the men in the front line were falling asleep. The local regimental commander described the fighting on the previous day. His own officers, he said, had complained against the continuation of the attack, and it was only when the commander himself said he would lead it that the attack was continued, and the village captured. Referring later to this battle, Guderian stated that the French had fought very bravely. This was a fitting tribute from the enemy to the 152nd French Infantry Regiment.

By the evening of the 16th, Guderian's Panzers were well on their way westward, but, on the 17th, there was again an attempt to check his dash to the coast. In his anger at this second attempt to thwart his plan, Guderian asked if he could hand over his command. But General List, commanding the Twelfth Army, supported him, and he was authorized to carry on "strong reconnaissance". These instructions he interpreted in his own manner.

Away, therefore, went Guderian for the coast. For the moment he was to be parted from the 14th French Infantry Division, but a few weeks later they were to meet again. The German Twelfth Army was to have followed Guderian, but it was now ordered to swing south and take over from Guderian's corps along the Aisne. A new army, the Second, replaced the Twelfth in the wake of Guderian. It may well be that this decision to divert the Twelfth Army from its original rôle was prompted by an increasing fear of a French counter-offensive from the south. To that extent the decision was a tribute to the gallant fight of the 14th French Infantry Division, and other French formations in the area. But it seems unlikely that the diversion of the Twelfth Army brought more than twenty-four hours' delay to the general advance. It was the XIV Corps of that army which was now to face de Lattre along the Aisne.

12. THE PAUSE ON THE AISNE

THE XIV Corps of the Twelfth German Army was now probing forward with a view to making good the line of the Aisne and securing the southern flank of von Runstedt's westward thrust. De Lattre was still clinging to his small bridgehead at Rethel, which, in addition to the divisional reconnaissance group, was now being held by the remaining battalion of the 152nd Infantry Regiment, which had only just reached the battlefield, and had therefore missed the hard fighting in which the remainder of the regiment had been engaged on the eastern flank of the division.

In the afternoon and evening of the 17th, under cover of a heavy artillery and mortar bombardment, the Germans attacked Rethel from the direction of Château Porcien; but they suffered heavy casualties and eventually withdrew, leaving behind much equipment. In the repelling of this attack, one of the salvaged French "B" tanks, which had been incorporated in the defences of Rethel, played a most effective part. No further attacks developed until the 19th, and in view of his warm reception two days before, the enemy attacked in strength and with overwhelming artillery support. Once again the hard-pressed defenders put up a great fight, but by evening the bridgehead at last had to be abandoned. In their withdrawal the infantry again received valuable support from the "B" tank.

The Germans seemed determined to clear up the Rethel situation once and for all, and throughout the night they continued to try to exploit their success, and both east and west of Rethel they got small parties across the Aisne, although not south of the canal. In both areas, where the enemy had secured a crossing, the French counter-attacked, driving them back over the

Aisne and capturing much equipment. The French were everywhere back on the Aisne, except at Rethel itself, where they held the canal. But the enemy persisted, and at dawn on the following morning he obtained a footing over the canal south-east of Rethel. An immediate counter-attack by the 152nd Infantry Regiment drove him back to the canal. Prisoners taken in this counter-attack reported that an enemy battalion was assembling on the slopes north of Rethel, with a view to exploiting the success of the morning. Most of de Lattre's divisional artillery had now reached the area, and a heavy concentration was put down north of Rethel. From prisoners taken later it was discovered that this concentration fell right into the middle of the German battalion and virtually cut it to pieces in its assembly area.

Meanwhile, von Runstedt's spearhead under Guderian had reached the coast. The northern wing of the Allies, comprising about a third of their total forces and the most modernly equipped formations, had been severed from the rest of their forces. It only remained for the Army Groups of von Bock and von Runstedt to complete the discomfiture of the severed wing. For the moment, therefore, the Aisne front became static.

For more than a week the scattered units of the 14th Infantry Division had been marching and fighting. If little rest was yet possible, at least his division was now concentrated, and de Lattre could begin to organize his defences on a more solid basis. The division now came under XXIII Corps, which at this stage was under the newly-forming Sixth Army. Later it was to come under the Fourth Army.

De Lattre set about his new task with vigour undiminished. In the later stages of the war, fifty was regarded as old for a divisional commander. De Lattre was now fifty-one, and, despite the disability of his early wounds, he seems to have withstood the strain of the last ten days better than many who were younger. Age is not always the criterion.

The main pre-occupation of the divisional commander was the security of his flanks. His division was now the extreme right of the Sixth Army, and although on his right he was in touch with the left of the Second Army near Attigny, it was unsatisfactory that the boundary between the two armies should be the important road Attigny–Suippes–Châlons. It was more than likely that the enemy would use that road when he tried to resume his advance. Moreover, he feared that the attention of the Second Army was riveted eastward. De Lattre therefore devoted particular attention to the arrangements for liaison with the 36th Infantry Division, which was the left division of the Second Army. His attention was particularly focused upon the important road junction of Mazagran, where he organized a defensive area to be held jointly by units of the 36th Infantry Division and of his own. On the left flank, the 2nd Infantry Division was due to take over the Rethel sector, and this would make possible a welcome reduction of his front.

The disturbing depths to which the enemy had penetrated through his new tactics had made de Lattre very much alive to the danger of continuing to think in terms of linear defence, involving a line of infantry, a line of guns, and then a line of administrative services and units. He now completely reorganized his division into what he called a Mobile Group, capable of all-round defence. Leaving only four battalions to hold the line of the Aisne, he established three defensive zones: one round Vaux-Champagne–Mazagran, to protect his right; one on the River Retourne, to protect his rear; and a third round Annelles, to protect his left. The divisional reconnaissance group was to be located centrally with a view to intervention in any direction. The artillery was disposed with a view to its ability to put down concentrations along the whole front, and more particularly round Rethel and Attigny. It was also to be able to give support to either flank, and to establish anti-tank barrages. Essential services were located centrally; the remainder were sent well back. Hard work was accomplished by all to implement this plan, and most villages were turned into strong points, with all-round anti-tank defence. No commander had ever driven his engineers as hard as did de Lattre. Apart from the organization of these defence works, there were demolitions to be prepared on all bridges along the front.

During this period the Germans displayed no exceptional activity on the front of de Lattre's division, except to bring into action loudspeakers which blazed forth "Great Germany bears no ill-will towards France" and similar messages. With this propaganda de Lattre dealt in summary fashion. "To put an end to these manifestations, the artillery will reply in a brutal and no uncertain manner."

Very different was the activity displayed by the infantry of the 14th Division in the forward area. North of the Aisne, their patrols were continually aggressive. Every unit took its turn. Although it would be invidious to single out the operations of any particular patrol, the action of a platoon of the 35th Infantry Regiment is worthy of mention. It had received orders to lie up during the night in a farm on the far side of the Aisne. Its presence was detected by the Germans, who at dawn sent at least a company against it. In the face of heavy casualties, including the loss of their commander, the Germans withdrew, only to be replaced by a second company which was launched to the attack. Céhin, the French platoon commander, had been able to get one section back to warn his company commander as arranged. Uncertain as to whether it had got back, he sent back a Corporal Leger, who had volunteered for the job, to report the situation to the company commander. Although twice wounded in the course of his duty, Leger succeeded in crossing the river and reporting to the battalion. With the support of artillery, another platoon succeeded in extricating Céhin. Five of his twenty-five men were killed and five wounded, but more than seventy German dead were counted round the farm.

It was the exploits of Lieutenant Céhin, Corporal Leger, and others like them, which combined to establish the reputation of the division, and few compliments have been better deserved than the one it received about this time in a general order published by the Sixth Army Commander: "He would always remember with emotion the arrival on the battlefield of the 14th Infantry Division, calm and determined in the middle of general confusion; nor would he forget the courage and tenacity of its leaders and of their men, in re-establishing the situation on the Aisne."

Although the fate of France was hanging in the balance, de Lattre still found time to write not only to his wife, but also to Bernard, who was now twelve years old. To Bernard, he had always continued to write very full letters, containing advice about his work and guidance for the future. Even on the 2nd June he wrote: "Continue to write me these good letters, as you are doing, mon petit Bernard. They give me such pleasure.

1. De Lattre at Auberge Saint-Pierre, 14 September, 1914. Painting by Müller

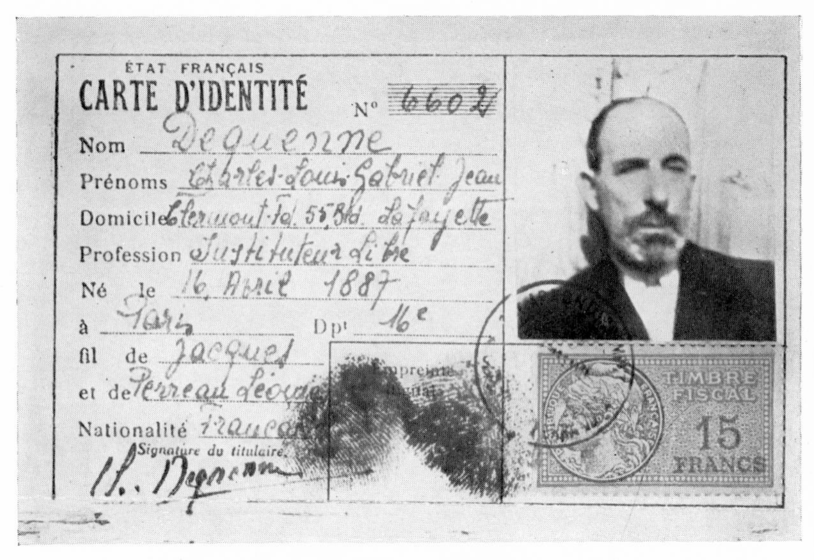

ÉTAT FRANÇAIS

CARTE D'IDENTITÉ N° 6602

Nom Deguenne

Prénoms Charles-Louis-Gabriel Jean

Domicile Clermont-Fd. 55 Bd. Lafayette

Profession Instituteur libre

Né le 16 Avril 1887

à Paris Dpt 16e

fil de Jacques

et de Perreau Léo

Nationalité franca

Signature du titulaire.

Ch. Deguenne

Empreinte

TIMBRE FISCAL

15 FRANCS

2. De Lattre's forged identity card

3. Window of the prison cell at Riom

But do also make an effort to write well. If you will do that, then I shall have proof that you are applying yourself, and that you really are trying to please me." This insistence on perfection was always recurring. A few months before he had written in the same strain: "Get it well into your head, that you must never send off a letter that is slapdash, for the disappointment I feel on seeing that you lack care, takes away all the pleasure which I would otherwise have had in receiving a letter from you."

Meanwhile, the first phase of this titanic battle drew swiftly to its close. The northern wing of the Allies was almost encircled. Then, on the 24th May came the strange pause before Dunkirk that was to allow the British Army and many valiant Frenchmen to escape and fight again. The responsibility for the pause is uncertain: the main reason which seems to have prompted it was impatience to redeploy for the second phase of the battle, which involved the destruction of the remainder of the French Army. There seems also to have been an exaggerated confidence in the ability of the Luftwaffe to complete the seaward encirclement of the Allies, and to prevent their escape from Dunkirk.

However much the Germans may be criticized for their blunder at Dunkirk, the rapidity of their deployment for the second phase of the battle commands unstinted praise. In the first week of June, despite the losses in tanks, and the wear and tear on those that remained, von Bock, on the right, and von Runstedt, on the left, were ready to strike again, across the Somme and the Aisne, along which line the sorely tried French were trying to reorganize. By the 1st June Guderian himself, now in command of a Panzer group, comprising two corps, each of two Panzer divisions, and one motorized infantry division, was back in the same area, where only a fortnight before he had first been engaged with the 14th French Infantry Division. Only a few days before he had been operating on the coast, and, in view of the many bridges which had been demolished, some of his units had been compelled to move two hundred miles to their new assembly area. In the impending battle it was de Lattre again, who was to be his most effective opponent.

13. THE LAST PHASE

THE dates of the resumed offensive were staggered. Von Bock had rolled forward on the 5th June, and, on the 9th, von Runstedt was due to follow. On the Aisne it was still the Twelfth German Army that lay opposite de Lattre, and it was the infantry of that army which on the 9th was ordered to establish eight bridgeheads over the river and the canal to the south, between Château Porcien and Attigny. When these bridgeheads had been established and the bridges thrown across, Guderian, now under Twelfth Army, was to attack through the infantry. Depending on how the situation developed, he was then to move on Paris, Langres, or Verdun. Buoyant with confidence, as a result of his recent successes, Guderian felt that his own group was fully capable itself of establishing a bridgehead. Moreover, he disliked the idea of attacking through infantry, whose unwieldy transport columns might well block the advance of his tanks. He therefore asked if the task of capturing some of the bridgeheads might be allotted to his own divisions. His request was refused, and once again his impatience had to be curbed. But he was not going to waste a moment more than was necessary. At five o'clock on the morning of the 9th, he went forward to an observation-post north-east of Rethel to watch the progress of the infantry. He would thus be the better able to launch his armour the moment the bridgehead was established.

While the eager Guderian was moving into his observation-post on the opposite side of the river, de Lattre and his division were enduring the final hour of the bombardment that preceded the enemy's attack. The weary 152nd Infantry Regiment was resting, and the front was now held by the 35th Infantry Regiment, on the right, and the half-brigade of Chasseurs, on the left. At six o'clock in the morning the bombardment lifted, and the enemy infantry came forward to the attack, directing their main efforts on Givry and Thugny-Trugny. Although the Germans gained ground everywhere, local counter-attacks successfully flung them back to the Aisne or to the canal, and by one o'clock in the afternoon, the situation seemed in hand. Only on the left was there some anxiety in regard to a battalion of Chasseurs. Although encircled in Thugny-Trugny, it was resisting heroically and still in touch with division by wireless. In the afternoon a counter-attack by a mixed force, including tanks, drove the enemy back to the canal, and the battalion was extricated.

A notable feature of these counter-attacks was the confidence and self-sufficiency of local commanders. So often, under similar circumstances, a divisional commander would be pestered with demands for help from every corner of the battlefield. This was spared de Lattre. Indeed, the spirit of confidence he had already infused into his subordinates greatly reduced the weight of the burden he was now called upon to bear. During the morning, the officer commanding the 35th Infantry Regiment sent reassuring messages to division that he was capable with his own resources of dealing with the situation. Similar messages came in from at least one other commander during the day.

But with his neighbours on the flanks, events were far less reassuring. On the right, the enemy had crossed the Aisne south-east of Attigny, and, under orders from the neighbouring corps commander, the centre of resistance at the Mazagran road junction, so carefully organized by de Lattre, was evacuated by its garrison, which was needed for a counter-attack. De Lattre at once reinforced it, and succeeded in obtaining the corps reconnaissance group from his own corps commander to assist in the protection of the right flank.

On the left, the situation was much worse. The 2nd Infantry Division also had been heavily attacked. The enemy was across the Aisne south of Château Porcien, and counter-attacks had failed to throw him back. The divisional commander then informed de Lattre of his intention to withdraw two miles south of the Aisne. De Lattre received this information personally on the telephone, and accounts vary as to the torrent of abuse with which he greeted it; but those who knew de Lattre will probably agree that the accounts were not exaggerated. Although de Lattre pointed out that the withdrawal of the 2nd Infantry Division would wholly uncover his own left flank, the commander of that division would make no radical change in his decision. He did, however, agree to leave his right regiment still on the Aisne, under de Lattre's command.

Throughout the afternoon the attacks continued along the whole front with increasing violence, but they were all repulsed. From subsequent reports of prisoners, of whom several hundred were taken in the course of the various counter-attacks, it became clear that the half-brigade of Chasseurs alone had been attacked by at least a division, and, from one French observation-post, about thirty enemy batteries could be counted in action in the open. While the French losses had been relatively small in view of the hard digging and other work that had been done, the German losses, apart from prisoners taken, were extremely heavy.

On the following day, after a lull in the morning, the attacks continued and were again repulsed. It is now known that on the 9th and 10th June the best part of three German Infantry Divisions, the 73rd, 86th, and 17th, had attacked de Lattre.

Although the situation on the divisional front was in hand, that on either flank continued to deteriorate. On the right, the 36th Infantry Division still held Attigny, but the enemy was dangerously threatening its right flank. On the left, the situation which de Lattre had so clearly foreseen when the 2nd Infantry Division withdrew south of Château Porcien materialized only too quickly, and on that morning, enemy armour was reported as far south as Bergnicourt, almost behind his left rear. Indeed, Guderian had not let slip the fleeting moment. In the morning it had been a disappointing spectacle that he beheld from his observation-post north-east of Rethel. Instead of bridges swiftly spanning the river, he had only seen the hard-hit infantry of the XIV Corps staggering back northward to the river bank. But he would not be absorbed or discouraged by the local scene. About midday he received reports that a single bridgehead had been established south of Château Porcien. He at once went off to that area and arranged for his right corps, the XXXIX, comprising the 1st and 2nd Panzer Divisions, to push elements into the bridgehead during the night with a view to exploitation at dawn. At six-thirty on the morning of the 10th he had launched them to the attack. Only too true, therefore, had been the reports which reached de Lattre on that morning of the enemy armour at Bergnicourt.

The disturbing nature of the tidings that now reached the

commander of the 14th Infantry Division was the harder to bear in view of the fact that his own troops had so successfully repulsed the onslaught of the enemy infantry, and were still firmly holding their ground. But the situation on the flanks made withdrawal now inevitable. When the order was given, it was met with consternation and bitter disappointment by the whole division.

To recount in detail the confused operations, which now led inexorably to so tragic a climax, would be tedious. The left flank of the 14th Infantry Division was now virtually in the air; and while Guderian's Panzers began continually to move round him, de Lattre strove to cling successively to the water-courses and other anti-tank obstacles that were available between the Aisne and the Marne. It was only by keeping his division, to the best of his ability, in box formation, that he was able to maintain any form of cohesion and to extricate himself. Indeed, there were times when elements of Guderian's armour were cutting diagonally from north-west to south-east, through his retreating columns. Just south of the Aisne, there were instances of the most stalwart conduct on the part of many units. A battalion of the 35th Infantry Regiment, encircled in Machault, held on until its ammunition was spent. The German commander, who had attacked it, stated later that the resistance of that battalion had delayed his advance by twelve hours. Guderian himself reported that the German infantry had to fight hard for the barricaded streets and houses of the villages.

In the extrication of his division from the Aisne (see map on p. 93), de Lattre owed much not only to his own divisional reconnaissance group but also to other mobile groups that were placed under his command. Deprived of sleep for four days, they made continual sacrifices to enable their comrades in the infantry to get clear. On the 12th June they played a conspicuously valiant rôle at the camp of Mourmelon, where a part of the division made a final stand in an effort to ensure the withdrawal to the Marne. Indeed, by that day it had become only too clear that no further stand north of the Marne would be possible. In the event, it became doubtful whether the division would be able to reach the Marne at all, for the objectives which Guderian had given that day to his XXXIX Corps were Châlons-sur-Marne and Vitry-le-François.

By a miracle de Lattre himself succeeded in crossing the Marne at Châlons, where he had been ordered to organize a position along the river, east and west of the town. But before the bulk of his division reached him, the northern part of Châlons was in the hands of the enemy. Fortunately for de Lattre, the foremost German reconnaissance troops failed to prevent the demolition of the bridge. In his account of the operations on this day, Guderian refers with some bitterness to the fact that these troops had captured the bridge intact, but that, despite explicit orders, they had failed to examine it at once for demolition charges.

De Lattre now found himself on the southern bank of the Marne, while Guderian on the northern bank was between him and his division. The probability of the divisional commander ever being rejoined by his division now seemed remote. But such was its spirit of cohesion, that while Guderian moved south-east along the northern bank of the Marne, virtually in its midst, the greater part of the Division succeeded in crossing the Marne at Vitry-le-François to the south-east.

Meanwhile, south of Châlons, de Lattre had been endeavouring to build up a defensive position along the river with the remnants of another infantry division which he found in the area. But he was precariously thin on the ground, and for the protection of his own headquarters he could rely on only a few clerks and other headquarters' personnel. It was on the 13th that the weary remnants of his division began to cross the Marne at Vitry-le-François. To see his division as it then was, having lost nearly two-thirds of its effectives, must have nearly broken the heart of its commander, for with all his courage, physical and moral, he was the most sensitive of men. But there was to be no respite. VIII Corps under whose orders he now had come, called upon him for another effort to hold south of the Marne. His appeal to his troops was phrased in characteristic language: "Once more this order must be carried out in the tradition of the 14th Infantry Division" (" . . . dans la manière de la 14e. Division d'Infanterie").

De Lattre's superiors were well aware of the tribulations through which he was passing, and a personal letter which he received from the Army Commander, dated the 12th June, ran as follows:

My Dear Friend,

The 14th Infantry Division, together with yourself, its commander, is worthy of a citation in Army Orders, for its discipline, its courage, and its spirit of sacrifice.

Have confidence. I know you will not be beaten, whatever may be the realities of the situation, and of these I am fully aware. I am continually thinking of you and your troops, for whom I have so great an affection.

Already I have informed General Georges of their magnificent conduct, and of your own.

A vous de tout cœur,
Requin

De Lattre was not insensitive to such encouragement, and it materially helped him in making yet another appeal to his men.

The next phase would carry the division from the Marne to the Loire. Guderian and de Lattre now parted, for the former's line of advance now took him south-eastward, while de Lattre was withdrawing southward. Events followed the same pattern as with the withdrawal from the Aisne to the Marne, but the tempo became faster and the scene more chaotic. Air bombing too gathered grim momentum, destroying in rear of the division the bridges by which it was to cross. The scene at those bridges which remained intact may well be imagined. The congestion on the roads anyhow had assumed immeasurable proportions, and de Lattre himself with a few staff officers would often be seen endeavouring to clear a way for the men and transport of his division. Although additional lorries had now been allotted to the division for troop transport, attempts to stand, first on the line of the Aube and then on the Loire at Nevers, were in turn frustrated by the relentless pressure of the enemy on the left.

The situation now deteriorated rapidly, and by the 16th June, VIII Corps was out of touch with the Army. De Lattre himself went to General Headquarters at Vichy, where he saw General Georges, who acquainted him with the situation. There is little more to be told. When hostilities ceased, the 14th Infantry Division was south of Clermont-Ferrand. Many formations by that time had disintegrated, but the conduct of de Lattre during those last few tragic days was typical. From an artillery depôt south of Clermont-Ferrand he carried along with him 500 young soldiers of the 1939–40 class; they had volunteered to form provisional anti-tank units. Few men could have exercised so robust an influence under such conditions of gloom. In Clermont-Ferrand itself there were large stocks of equipment of every sort, including new clothing. Lorries from the 14th Infantry Division were soon on the spot, and de Lattre virtually re-equipped and re-clothed the remnants of his division. The following is an extract from an order he issued on the 23rd June, the day before hostilities ceased: "In the present circumstances, the 14th Infantry Division owes it to its reputation to set an example by impeccable turnout and the strictest discipline. Opportunity will be taken while in billets to give this matter the fullest attention." De Lattre had wanted to be a sailor. When his ship sank, he was on the bridge, with colours flying.

It is probable that in the whole of his spectacular and eventful career, de Lattre was never greater than he was during those weeks that preceded the momentary downfall of his country. The conditions in which his division was engaged at the outset, the uncertainty of the information and orders upon which he had to act, the demoralizing effect of a superior enemy air force, and of frightened civilians streaming down the roads have already been described; but tactically, also, he had laboured under constant disadvantages. He had first engaged his division in positions that were not prepared, and on ground that had not been reconnoitred. These were not the best conditions for infantry to withstand armour. Moreover his division was not motorized, and, when his flanks were turned, he had not the mobility to facilitate disengagement from his more swiftly moving opponents. In so unequal a struggle, when feebler wills collapsed and crumbled, the story of the 14th Infantry Division, and its leader, is as an oasis of refreshing glory in a desert of despondency and gloom. The action of the division may have done little to influence the course of the campaign, but in the hearts of those who served in its ranks it kept alive the will to win.

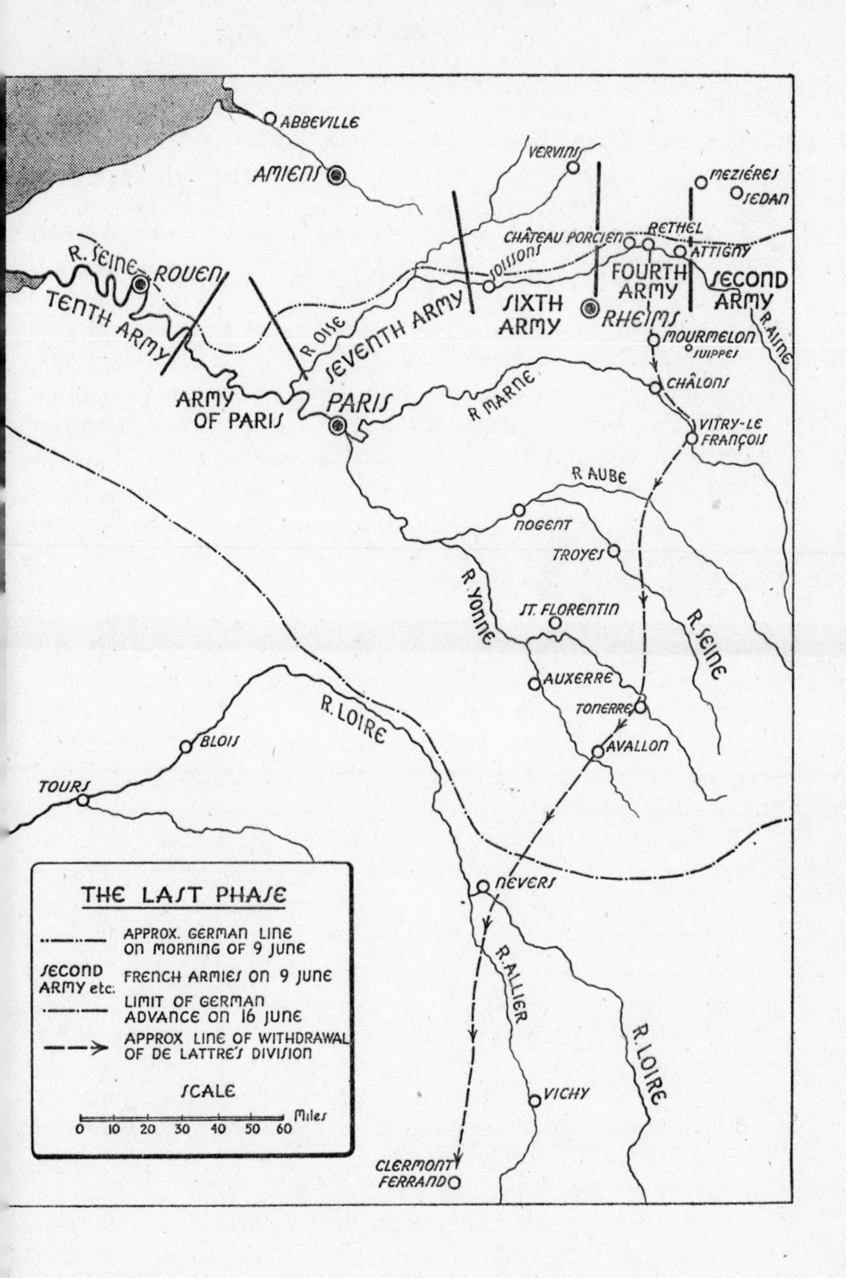
ABBEVILLE
AMIENS
VERVINS
MEZIÉRES
SEDAN
CHÂTEAU PORCIEN
RETHEL
ATTIGNY
R. SEINE
ROUEN
TENTH ARMY
SOISSONS
FOURTH ARMY
SECOND ARMY
SEVENTH ARMY
SIXTH ARMY
RHEIMS
R. OISE
R. AISNE
MOURMELON
SUIPPES
ARMY OF PARIS
PARIS
R MARNE
CHÂLONS
VITRY-LE FRANÇOIS
R AUBE
NOGENT
TROYES
R. YONNE
ST. FLORENTIN
R. SEINE
AUXERRE
TONERRE
AVALLON
R. LOIRE
BLOIS
TOURS
NEVERS
R. ALLIER
R. LOIRE
VICHY
CLERMONT FERRAND
THE LAST PHASE
APPROX. GERMAN LINE ON MORNING OF 9 JUNE
SECOND ARMY etc:
FRENCH ARMIES ON 9 JUNE
LIMIT OF GERMAN ADVANCE ON 16 JUNE
APPROX LINE OF WITHDRAWAL OF DE LATTRE'S DIVISION
SCALE
0 10 20 30 40 50 60 Miles

14. THE CALL OF VICHY

THE full magnitude of the calamity that befell the French nation is not easy to comprehend. Memories of defeat in the Franco-Prussian War had been obliterated by the Allied victory in the First World War, and the prestige of bygone days had been restored by Marshal Foch. Again the French Army was supreme. That it should have been overrun and crushed in so short a time had left France stunned. For those whose countries have not been subjected to the humiliation of an enemy occupation, it would be presumptuous to pass judgment on the reactions of Frenchmen in that sombre hour of tragedy. Only those close to them at the time, who saw the dilemma with which they were faced, can even begin to understand the conflicting calls of conscience that led men to tread such divergent paths. There were those who argued that, while the French Empire overseas was still intact, it would be shameful to ask for an armistice; while there was yet time, the Government should fly to North Africa. In the view of others, such a course would involve the overrunning of France, and the exploitation of success through Spain to North Africa.

Weygand, who had been commanding the French Army in Syria, was already seventy-three when he was recalled to France to retrieve a situation already heavily compromised. The ugliness of the scene which met him upon his return might well have dismayed a younger man. Flying north to acquire a first-hand picture of events, his aircraft was subjected to continual attacks, and, although those with him have commented on his remarkable coolness, the experience can have done little to cheer his outlook. However much he may be criticized on account of the Armistice, and however sinister were some of the characters with whom he now had to work, he himself was a devout and honest man, and for his Allied sympathies he was eventually to be deported to Germany. But it was a disappointment to his friends in England, of whom there were many, that he should have had so little faith in the capacity of the British to continue the struggle.

When the Armistice had been signed, the minds of Frenchmen, in France, and overseas, were to be exercised for months to come, in their efforts to discern the path of duty. There were those, like Leclerc, who felt irresistibly impelled to escape from France and to continue the struggle beyond the seas. There were others, particularly those of an older generation, who could not bring themselves to rebel against so illustrious a figure as Pétain. For them the path of duty was to stay in France, and to preserve the cohesion of such units as would be allowed to France under the terms of the Armistice. Whatever the decision of individuals, it would not have been possible for everyone to escape from France.

There were a few, fewer than is often imagined, who decided to cut their losses and wholeheartedly to collaborate with the Germans. It is easy to speak lightly of collaboration, of which there were varying shades. At the time, to the outside world, anyone associated with the Vichy Government was regarded as a collaborator. But, if the truth had been known, there were many in those days outwardly subservient to that Government, but inwardly determined to continue the struggle at the earliest opportunity. A humorous observer of the early scene at Vichy said that, apart from the more contemptuous elements, there were two categories—those who said, "pourvu que les anglais gagnent", and those with cooler feelings towards their late allies, who said, "pourvu que ces cochons d'anglais gagnent". But whatever their intentions or feelings, prematurely to have avowed them might have been fatal.

The choice before Frenchmen overseas was even more difficult. In general, in those parts of the world which were remote from France, and from the influence of Pétain, the will to continue the struggle was greatest. Catroux, in the Far East, and Legentilhomme in Jibuti, threw in their lot with de Gaulle. At the outset, too, Mittelhauser in Syria decided to continue the struggle. But, in North Africa, Nogues followed Pétain, and it was his decision, combined with the spell which Pétain cast upon men of an older generation, which caused Mittelhauser to reverse his decision. Moreover, as one Frenchman said at the time, "after the age of seventy, one does not become a rebel". And so the nation divided.

Leclerc and others like him, devoted husbands and fathers of large families, risked all to continue the fight overseas. Above all, they risked separation from their families for a period that might well drag on for years. For at the time they made their decision, the hopes of an Allied victory seemed remote. For such men it was difficult to be indulgent towards those who had not chosen a similar path. Some of those, on the other hand, who remained in France, and experienced, in all its cruelty, the moral degradation of an enemy occupation, could not always feel sympathy for those who were continuing the fight overseas, and who, in their view, had escaped from the miseries which they themselves were suffering.

If Frenchmen became divided among themselves, they tended also to blame the British for their misfortunes. However indulgent one may be towards Pétain, it is not easy to forgive him for the part he played in bringing this about. In a broadcast to the French nation at the time of the Armistice, he referred to the failure of the British to contribute a larger force. But the French knew what the strength of that force would be, and that much of the available British man-power would be absorbed by the demands of the Royal Navy, the Merchant Service, and the indispensable requirements of industry. German propaganda was quick to exploit the Marshal's broadcast and to fan the flames of hatred against the British. But there were Frenchmen who risked condemnation to death and reprisals against their families for the steadfastness of their loyalty towards their former allies. The courage of these men, and of their families also, will not soon be forgotten by their friends across the Channel.

Despite all the bitter passions which were then engendered, there were in all camps great French patriots who, with equal courage, genuinely followed the dictates of their conscience. For a moment they were divided, but in the fullness of time their paths would converge on the highway to victory.

Accurately to portray the workings of de Lattre's mind when he, like others, was faced with the great dilemma, and had to choose his path, must be in the nature of conjecture. But some at least of the considerations that influenced his decision are not difficult to recapture. A few days before the Armistice, when the defeatists were already beginning to make their voices heard, he had proposed to General Georges that he should take his division to North Africa or England to continue the struggle. But his proposal had been rejected. Whether it would ever have been practicable is doubtful. After the Armistice, de Lattre, with his division near Clermont-Ferrand, was at the very doorstep of the Government which had asked for the Armistice, and in the closest touch with the workings of its mind. Moreover, Weygand, his former chief, to whom he owed so much, was now Minister of Defence. Doubtless the proximity of the Government, and particularly that of Weygand whom he greatly respected, contributed to the making of his decision. But, whatever may have been his motives, it would be less than fair to the commander of the 14th Infantry Division, who had battled so staunchly to the end, to accuse him of having thrown in his lot with collaborators.

One night in July, he asked to dine with him an officer who was due for demobilization on the following day. After dinner, de Lattre said to him and to others who were dining, "We have been beaten, but, when the battle starts again, we shall hurl them out of the country. On that day, all of you who have served under me will get a command." In the atmosphere of suspicion and intrigue which then prevailed, these words were hardly discreet. They were certainly not the words of a defeatist, and those to whom they were addressed were to form the nucleus of a commando, which four years later was to participate in the liberation of France. "Ne pas subir" was the motto which de Lattre had fervently adopted when fortune had frowned on him in 1934. With such a motto, he could never accept the situation in which the Armistice had placed his country; but he would react in his own way and in his own time.

On the following day, de Lattre asked the same officer to accompany him for the last time to see the changing of the guard. Many who watched were shocked to see the men in white gloves. Was it right that in the hour of defeat the vanquished should go about like victors? It was against that very tendency to appear ashamed and penitent that de Lattre reacted with all the vigour at his command. Dark though the hour was, belief in the grandeur of France must still be kept alive. Pride must conquer, and *panache* again was to come to his aid.

By a General Order dated the 12th July, de Lattre was made a Grand Officer of the Legion of Honour for his services "as a young divisional commander of the first order, who, as much by his courage as the skill of his dispositions, proved one of the main elements in re-establishing the defences of the whole Army on the Aisne". Weygand himself decorated him, and to the men of the division who were on parade he said, "You at least have the right to hold your heads high."

Later in the year, de Lattre was promoted from Brigadier to Major-General, and given command of the Puy-de-Dôme, or Massif Central region. A command in France at that moment, under the cloud of defeat, must have seemed very unreal. With the control of the German Armistice Commission growing tighter each day, there seemed little that he could do. How could the morale of a defeated army be sustained or keenness infused? But it was the very difficulty of the situation which stimulated him. Lack of weapons did not matter; he would train leaders, for sooner or later France would need them. And so was conceived the project of forming a training centre for officers and non-commissioned officers. To the creation of that centre de Lattre applied his full energy and imagination. As ever, uppermost in his mind was the cult of grandeur. The camp must be in a grandiose setting. The site chosen was Opme, on the plateau of Gergovie, where, centuries before, the Gauls under Vercingetorix had beaten back the legions of Caesar. Upon such a site, and with such associations, the spirit could not fail to be elevated, and it was there that he set out to restore pride and confidence in a defeated army.

In the task that lay before him, he derived much comfort from the fact that his wife and Bernard had now joined him. Bernard was twelve, and he and his mother had spent the early months of the war in Touraine, at the home of Madame de Lattre's family. Before the Armistice, Bernard had written continuously to his father for whom he had a profound admiration. In one letter he wrote: "I have read with great pleasure the article in 'Paris-Soir' about yourself and your division. How proud it made me feel of you and your courage! I hope that when I grow up I shall be as frank, loyal, and brave as you." His letters were full of a fervent love of France. In one he described a history lesson dealing with the Middle Ages: "I have drawn a splendid map," he writes, "all in colours, and with arrows showing where the Barbarians passed. . . . I hope that in the year 3000, students studying the campaign of 1939 will not be drawing maps with arrows going from east to west, but in the other direction—and very far." How disillusioned he was to be! Bernard had all the sensitiveness of his father, and the tragedy of 1940 was a cruel blow to this ardent young patriot.

De Lattre's letters to Bernard reflected his own ideals and aims. In later life he was constantly urging men to be "generous", that is to say, never to spare themselves, but always to give everything they had to the task of the moment. He urged Bernard too to be generous, and in one letter he wrote: "May St. Bernard protect you, and ensure that all your life you have an upright mind and a noble and generous heart." The same exhortation is repeated in other letters.

Bernard soon recovered his youthful fervour. In order the better to supervise the work at Opme, de Lattre installed himself in a tower of the old château, so that his family also was caught up in the atmosphere of faith and hope that he radiated. Bernard himself took part in the physical and other appropriate training at this Spartan camp. His father's memory for names and faces, which had been so remarkable a feature of his command of the 151st Regiment at Metz before the war, again came to the fore. He watched the progress of every individual who passed through the camp, and his ability to pick out future leaders was uncanny.

The Opme Training Centre absorbed all his energies. It was as though he had one mission in life at that time—to infuse into those who passed through it his own dynamic faith in the future of France; and all had to be done without exciting the curiosity of the German Armistice Commission. Every device for the betterment of morale was employed. Physical training played the largest part. A series of lectures was instituted, which he called "Les Fiertés Françaises", in which all the great figures of French history—Saint Louis, Turenne, Lyautey, Foch, and others—had their place. He also attached the greatest importance to community singing, and nightly from the camp could be heard the strains of "Vous n'aurez pas l'Alsace et Lorraine". Few passed through the Opme training centre whose minds and bodies were not the better for the experience. At least they were sheltered from the more demoralizing influences of the Vichy Government.

Engrossed though he was with this work, he also began to

formulate other plans. Already he was in touch with General Cochet, whom he had known when the latter was commanding the Air Forces supporting the Fifth Army. Cochet became later one of the best known of the Resistance leaders in France, and at that time was forming the nucleus of resistance groups in the Massif Central.

In September 1941 Weygand was appointed Delegate-General of the Vichy Government in North Africa. Although he had remained loyal to Pétain himself, he had found it distasteful to work with the more worthless intriguers in his entourage. To some extent, therefore, it was a relief to leave France and to breathe fresh air; but he felt that intrigue had been responsible for his removal from France. He was still convinced that the Armistice policy was in the best interests of France. He felt, therefore, that his task was to knit together the divergent elements in North Africa, and to prevent the disunity caused by the influence of de Gaulle. To use his own words, Weygand considered that "a Sovereign State, unless drifting to destruction, should under no circumstances, even under the impulsion of sentiments of chivalry, allow its component parts to secede. Still more was this true in a moment of adversity when it was the duty of the Government to preserve intact the unity of its forces, which alone would enable it to exploit its national resources when the opportunity arose."

If such were the underlying principles which guided the conduct of Weygand in North Africa, he was none the less determined to resist any pressure from the Germans or Italians. If his utterances in public, were guarded, in private he constantly expressed his hopes of a British victory, and proclaimed that it was his object to enable the Army once more, when the moment came, to take up arms against the enemy. Whether Vichy or de Gaulle were to command the allegiance of the Army in North Africa, there was much to be done. In one of his first reports, Weygand said: "My impression is detestable: training and turn-out are mediocre, and commanding officers are inactive." Any reorganization had of course to be approved by the Armistice Commission in Turin. Every argument, therefore, which French ingenuity could devise was brought into action to persuade both the Italians and the Germans that large French forces were required

4. Regimental Commander, 1935

5. *En route* for France with Bernard, 1944

6 De Lattre and Montgomery

7 De Lattre in Indo-China

in North Africa to ensure its security against violation by the Allies. It was eventually agreed that an army of 120,000 should be allowed, together with a theoretical police force of 20,000 Goums. Whatever judgment may be passed upon the Armistice policy, these measures at least resulted in North Africa becoming virtually an Allied bridgehead, and its garrison was later to contribute a welcome reinforcement to their armies.

In July 1941, Weygand asked for de Lattre to come to North Africa to take over command of the French Forces in Tunis; and so once again de Lattre was to serve immediately under his former chief. No one was more delighted with the prospect of a move than young Bernard de Lattre, who was now thirteen. There would be a better chance of being able to "passer de l'autre côté", as the expression then was for going over to the Allies. The thought of going overseas filled him with hope.

On his arrival in Tunis, de Lattre's first thought was to build up morale as he had done in France, and so there rose at Salambo, by the waters near Carthage, another Opme. De Lattre could not often be persuaded to codify his intentions, but he did set out in general orders what he meant to achieve at this camp. Leaders were to be found possessed of strong character, a passion to serve and command, and a determination to work. They were to be imbued to the full with the welfare side of their duties: they must get to know and to understand their men intimately; and lastly they must strive with fervour, not only to improve their physique but also their moral, intellectual, and professional standards. Such aims were typical of the ideals for which de Lattre was always striving. Instructors of exceptional enthusiasm were needed to transmit the driving power that came from above.

Meanwhile, in the Eastern Mediterranean, the ebb and flow of Allied fortunes, and, in particular the British advance in the spring of 1941 against superior Italian forces, and the possibility of the latter being driven westward to the Tunisian frontier raised awkward problems for Weygand. He made it clear that if the Italians were to cross into Tunis, they would be disarmed and interned. But that was not the only problem. The strategic importance of Bizerta, as an alternative base for feeding their forces in Africa, made the Axis powers bring heavy pressure upon the French for its use. Weygand resisted.

The appointment of Weygand to North Africa had never pleased the Germans. As early as December 1940, Hitler had written to Mussolini that he was dissatisfied with the appointment, and, at his trial in 1946, Abetz, who had been Hitler's representative in Paris, stated that the Germans had always suspected that Weygand would form in North Africa a bastion against the Reich. The firm resistance with which Weygand now opposed German pressure and other "Bocheries", as he called it, made his presence in North Africa more distasteful than ever. In September 1941, Abetz sent a note that was a virtual ultimatum to the Vichy Government, stating that the continued presence of Weygand in North Africa would prove an insurmountable obstacle to the establishment of constructive collaboration between Germany and France. His manner of speaking of Germany, said the note, in the presence of Frenchmen and foreigners, made it obvious that he would never overcome his unfriendly prejudices.

In these events, the fortunes of de Lattre were inevitably linked with those of Weygand. In compliance with the latter's orders, the defences on the Eastern Tunisian frontier, including the Mareth line, had been strengthened to resist a possible incursion of Axis troops. In the event, it was Montgomery's Eighth Army, and not the troops of the Axis, who had to assail that line. Such is the unpredictable course of history. De Lattre made little attempt to conceal his intended course of action, in the event of Axis troops threatening to cross the frontier. Moreover, he made it equally clear that he would prevent any attempt on the part of the Axis to supply their forces through Tunis. The limit of German patience had been passed: in October 1941 Weygand was recalled to France; and in bringing this about, Darlan had not been inactive. Four months later, de Lattre in turn was recalled.

The work of Weygand for his country was ended. The flames of passion which then devoured and divided unhappy France have not all died down. Not until the last flickering embers are dead, will dispassionate judgment be possible on the conduct of one who at the age of seventy-three had been called upon to bear so heavy a burden. This at least can be said: the North African bridgehead remained secure, and those who held it played no inglorious part in the final march to victory. But without de Gaulle this happy outcome might well have been in doubt. Though envious men might seek to dim its light, in the hour of darkness, it was the torch that he lit which sustained the hopes of all his countrymen, whichever the path they had chosen to tread.

15. THE DRAMA OF MONTPELLIER

THE paths of Weygand and de Lattre now began to part. While the former retired to live under suspicion in the South of France, de Lattre was allowed another chance, and given command of the XVI "Military Division" at Montpellier. Although called a division, it was in fact an area. Under German pressure, the Vichy Government might well have reserved for him a less pleasant fate, but de Lattre at that time seems for a moment to have lost his customary buoyancy.

It was not surprising that momentarily his capacity for robust reaction should have been impaired. Under clear Tunisian skies he had been able to breathe a purer air, and refreshing breezes had swept from the Libyan desert, bringing puffs of hope from men still free to fight for freedom. It must, therefore, have been with heavy heart that he returned to France, where the stranglehold of Hitler was growing ever tighter. Moreover, the fear must now have haunted him that by returning to France he might well be jeopardizing his future. Would he not have been better advised to try to escape from the clutches of Vichy while yet there was time, and to throw in his lot with de Gaulle? There is little doubt that a mind so active must often have considered the alternatives that lay before him. But now, in France, he was suspect, and his movements were closely watched. There was good reason for momentary dejection.

Bernard too was unhappy. No one had been more pleased than he to leave France, with the prospect of being able to "pass over to the other side". To all those dreams an end had come, and for Bernard the return to France and to school in Montpellier was like a return to prison.

De Lattre was soon to overcome that wave of depression that so ill befitted him, and after a few weeks his will-power returned, and he began to apply his familiar technique. The indispensable Training Centre was soon established at Larzac, in the middle of a wild and thinly populated area; but its very wildness gave it that touch of grandeur that he always sought, and there, once again, he began to infuse his reborn hopes into the hearts of the young.

Things were going better for the Allies. In October, Montgomery had won his resounding victory at El Alamein, and the war had reached its turning-point. De Lattre now began to consider the possibility of an Allied landing in the South of France. Inevitably this invasion would be followed by a German invasion of the unoccupied zone, and in such an eventuality he would have to decide upon his own course of action. Counting only on his own troops, he decided to form a bridgehead, the right of which would rest on the coast, in the wild and rocky country-south-east of Carcassonne, known as Les Corbières. He quickly set in motion the necessary reconnaissances.

Before a month was out, against that complex Vichy background, there was to take place the greatest drama of his life. There were many who believed that if the Germans marched into unoccupied France Pétain himself would resist, and in his entourage, apart from the more despicable individuals, there were many who played the double game, and while outwardly subservient to Vichy were secretly working for the Allies. But, in such an atmosphere, suspicion was rife everywhere, and few could trust their so-called friends. Darlan was Commander-in-Chief of the Armed Forces, Bridoux was Secretary of State for War, and his "chef du cabinet" was General Delmotte. Whatever lay at the back of the inscrutable Darlan's mind, it was fair to assume that Bridoux and Delmotte thought with him. But the Chief of the General Staff, General Verneau, who was later to die in a German concentration camp, was head of the Secret Army, planning to resist the Germans.

De Lattre had already been reported as undertaking Gaullist activities, and one of those deputed to watch his movements recommended that he should be moved to a post where he could do no harm; otherwise it would be necessary to watch him still more closely, and if necessary eventually to "neutralize" him. But there was two-way spying. De Lattre was in close touch with Verneau, the Chief of the General Staff, and kept himself fully informed of the manœuvres and machinations of Vichy.

Meanwhile there had occurred a curious action on the part of Darlan. In the event of an Allied landing in the South of France, the whole of the Mediterranean coast, including Corsica, was to come under one command, to be known as the "Théâtre d'Opérations de Provence" (T.O.P.). The commander whose name Darlan put forward for the T.O.P. was de Lattre, but he was only to assume command when the emergency arose; then he was to establish his headquarters at Avignon, replacing his superior there, who commanded the Group of Military Divisions of which de Lattre's division was one. The motives behind Darlan's wish to appoint de Lattre to the T.O.P. will ever remain as obscure as much else that the Admiral did. But although he despised the intellect of soldiers, or "Terriens" (landlubbers) as he called them, he seems to have acquired a degree of respect for de Lattre; and yet it had been Darlan as much as anyone who had been responsible for recalling him from Tunis.

Once again the dilemma that confronted so many Frenchmen at that time was to baffle de Lattre. While he himself, in conjunction secretly with Verneau and the 3rd Bureau of the Army, was planning to form a bridgehead facing north against the Germans, he received orders from his superiors to face south and be prepared to oppose an Allied landing. On the latter orders he took little or no action, nor did he make any attempt to improve the coastal defences in his area. However, under pretence of complying, he was able to stock stores and ammunition in the area of his intended bridgehead. Meanwhile, he had contrived, in so far as it was possible, to surround himself with officers upon whom he could rely. Most of his staff and subordinate commanders were by now acquainted with his plans. In early November he himself went to visit the area, staying in La Preste.

It was at La Preste in the early hours of the 7th November that Colonel Albord, his Chief of Staff, arrived with a momentous message from the Admiralty, stating that several hundred ships had passed through the Straits of Gibraltar, and were heading eastward. De Lattre at once returned to his headquarters at Montpellier, thinking that at any moment a message might arrive from Darlan, ordering him to assume command of the Théâtre d'Opérations de Provence at Avignon. By an extraordinary coincidence, which was profoundly to influence the course of events in North Africa, the Admiral had left on the 5th for Algiers, where his son was seriously ill. No order, therefore, came from Darlan for de Lattre, and there was no need for him to proceed to Avignon.

In the absence of Darlan from Vichy, uncertainty prevailed for forty-eight hours. For de Lattre it was an anxious period, for there could be little doubt that soon he would have to make momentous decisions. Those near him at the time have remarked on the exceptional coolness which he always displayed at such moments. About one o'clock in the morning of the 10th November, the following instructions were received from the General Staff of the Army:

T.O. 128/3 E.M.A.

1. With a view to avoiding contact between the Armistice Army and foreign troops, General Officers commanding Military Divisions will be prepared, in the event of a German advance over the line of demarcation, to move their troops and staffs away from their garrisons and the main routes of penetration. All ammunition will be taken with them.

2. The above measures will be carried out on the initiative of Military Divisional Commanders, and only upon receipt of definite information that the line of demarcation has been crossed.

These orders made no mention of resistance to the Germans. But they gave de Lattre almost complete freedom of action. Moreover, the initiative given to Military Divisional Commanders would preclude the risk of these orders, given by superiors during their last hours of liberty, being supplanted by later orders given under captivity. De Lattre therefore went ahead with his arrangements. Warning orders were issued to all units for the move to their concentration area in the Les Corbières bridgehead. He also made efforts to ensure the co-operation of the Military Divisional Commander at Toulouse on his left. But he was not reassured. Indeed it began to appear more and more likely that, in the dangerous enterprise that he was contemplating, he might have to act virtually alone, with a remote possibility that the Allies might come to his support. It was to be a great gamble, the greatest of his life; but he considered that the honour of French arms left no alternative.

Among his contacts at Vichy at this time, upon whom he felt he could rely, was General Revers, Chief of Staff to Pétain. On the morning of the 10th, de Lattre tried to get in touch with him by telephone. It so happened that Revers was in the office of General Delmotte, "chef du cabinet" of the Secretary of State for War, and it was Delmotte who answered the telephone. "My attention has been drawn to considerable activity in the area of the XVI Military Division," said Delmotte, "and the Minister would like an explanation." "But I am merely putting into effect the instructions contained in General Staff telegram No. 128," replied de Lattre. "But this is all imagination," said Delmotte, "the Germans will never cross into the unoccupied zone." That same evening an officer arrived at Montpellier and confirmed verbally the instructions contained in telegram 128. A little later, while they were dining, de Lattre was handed a message, which he took with him to his office, returning a few moments later to tell those present of its contents: "Admiral Darlan has just ordered the Cease Fire throughout North Africa. The end of hostilities in North Africa is the end of the Armistice. The Germans know it, and their Panzers are probably already descending the Rhône Valley."

During the day, de Lattre's superior commander at Avignon had telephoned continually to de Lattre's headquarters to find out his intentions. The latter gave him no satisfaction, basing his attitude on the independence that had been given him in telegram 128. It seemed clear that his superior could not be counted on; moreover, there was one senior officer in de Lattre's own entourage whose loyalty gave cause for concern. It was the general who commanded his infantry. Attempts to get in touch with him during the same day had failed.

The next morning, the 11th November, the Germans crossed the line of demarcation. The hour for action had struck. De Lattre had slept little, and he himself woke up his Chief of Staff and gave orders for the prescribed plan to be put immediately into effect. His own headquarters was to move in two echelons.

One, comprising a few officers and non-commissioned officers from a local training centre, four platoons of lorried infantry, and two anti-tank guns, was under Captain Quinche, an officer who had served him well at Rethel. The other, comprising the clerks and wireless section, was under de Camas, head of his operations staff, and an officer who had also served him well on the Staff of the 14th Infantry Division at Rethel.

At eight-thirty, as he was leaving his hotel for his office, he was called to the telephone. It was Bridoux, the Secretary of State for War. "Hullo, is that you, de Lattre? No troops must move." "Is it true," replied de Lattre, "that the Germans have crossed the line?" "Yes," said Bridoux. "Thank you!" concluded de Lattre, and he put down the receiver. He proposed to ignore the cancellation by telephone of a written order. But at about eleven o'clock, by which time he was in his office, the following message was received from his superior at Avignon:

By order of the Secretary of State for War:

1. No movement until further orders.
2. Troops and Staffs will remain in normal barracks.
3. Any movements started will be cancelled.
4. Ensure maintenance of order through prefects, and avoid all contact.
5. Troops confined to barracks.

Military Divisional Commanders will explain to their subordinates the necessity for maintaining the French Army.

Tearing up the order, and throwing the pieces into his wastepaper basket, de Lattre said to his staff that the die had been cast, and that he had no intention of obeying the order. Movements as already ordered by himself were to start at midday.

De Lattre had no illusions as to the danger of the game that he was playing. He went off to say good-bye to his wife. He explained to her fully that the action he was taking might well have fatal consequences for himself, and he asked her whether she approved of his intentions. With her usual courage and sense of duty, Madame de Lattre at once gave her husband the encouragement he wanted. In many moments of crisis throughout his life de Lattre went to confession. He now told his wife that he would like to confess, and while he made final preparations for leaving, he asked her to telephone to Father Bureau, who was the Superior of the Jesuit College at Montpellier, where Bernard was then a pupil, and to ask him to come. He sent his own car to fetch him, and within a quarter of an hour Father Bureau was there to hear de Lattre's confession. Shortly before midday, with Tabouis, his A.D.C., Constans, his "chef du cabinet", and a few other officers, he moved off through Saint-Pons to the heights of Les Corbières, where he hoped to arrive before dark, make further reconnaissances, and send back officers to meet and guide the troops.

But while de Lattre and his faithful band of followers set forth to champion the honour of French arms, behind the scenes a sordid and sorry tale was unfolding. At ten-thirty the same morning, the senior officer in de Lattre's entourage, whose loyalty was in doubt, telephoned behind his chief's back to de Lattre's superior at Avignon to say that he had the impression that de Lattre was intending to disobey the orders not to move. De Lattre's superior at Avignon referred to the Secretary of State for War, who ordered him to proceed at once to Montpellier to clear up the situation. He also telephoned to the Prefect of the Montpellier region, ordering the arrest of de Lattre. The Prefect said afterwards that the whole of that day they talked to him a lot about arresting de Lattre, but never about stopping the Germans. In the confusion that followed, these two senior officers, who had decided to thwart de Lattre were able to stop the movement of any units. Thus de Lattre, with his headquarters and small escort, was left stranded in the wilderness, betrayed.

Only Frenchmen are entitled to pass judgment on the conduct of the two officers who betrayed de Lattre on that fateful November morning. With some justification they might argue that the oath they had taken of allegiance to the Marshal was still binding and that orders from Vichy overrode all others. But it is interesting to read the text of the oath: "I swear fidelity to the person of the Head of the State, promising to obey him in everything that he shall command me to do for the good of the service, and the success of French Arms." No more need be said.

In vain de Lattre waited. He sent out his officers to scour the roads, but they did not return. No one came. It was only as evening began to fall that his A.D.C., Tabouis, found his way back to the General. He had with difficulty got past a barrier set up by the Gendarmerie. All was now clear. His plans had failed.

There was still one course open to him that might lead to freedom. He had a forged passport, and might well have tried to make good his escape over the Pyrenees. But he regarded such a course as selfish and cowardly, for he would be leaving behind the others, whom he had implicated, to face the consequences of his act. Besides, he felt that he had a duty to his men. As these had not been able to get to him, he would get to them. On the following morning, therefore, before six o'clock, he drove up in his car, still proudly flying the tricolour, to the Gendarmerie at Saint-Pons. From there he telephoned to the Regional Prefect, who begged him to return to Montpellier, assuring him that his command would be restored to him. He refused, and an hour later he wrote to his wife as follows: "I refused. They can do what they like with me. Nothing matters except what I have tried to do—to save the honour of our poor Army. Beside that, my liberty and life are as nothing to me." Having refused to comply with the request of the Regional Prefect, he was arrested. In a brief, ironical communiqué, the Vichy Government summed up the story: "After wandering about the countryside, General de Lattre de Tassigny gave himself up to the first gendarme he met. His career as a rebel was short. Now he is in the hands of Justice."

That evening de Lattre with his A.D.C. and some of his other followers were removed to the military prison at Toulouse. When the identity of the distinguished new arrival and the reason for his detention became known to the other prisoners, the walls of the old prison vibrated with a resounding Marseillaise. Rarely had de Lattre been so moved, and, at such a moment, no tonic could have been more effective.

For three weeks the prisoner was interrogated at Toulouse, and on the 10th December he was removed to Montluc at Lyons, where he was to be tried. The accusation of treason deprived him of the right to choose his own lawyer to defend him. A certain Puntous was appointed, but François Valentin, who had served the General with distinction on the Staff of the 14th Infantry Division, was allowed to assist him. During the weeks that remained before the trial was due, François Valentin was to see him frequently. His memory of the General at that time was of a supremely calm man, who did not seem unduly anxious about his immediate fate, of which he spoke little. Convinced that he had done his duty as a soldier, de Lattre had no personal regrets; he did not keep referring to the past, nor did he harbour excessive bitterness against those who had betrayed him; indeed, he was remarkably indulgent. The thought of languishing for years in prison had naturally exercised his mind, and already at Toulouse he had planned, if no worse fate awaited him, to plunge deeply into intellectual study. He had discussed such plans fully with the prison chaplain, and later he was to apply himself with his usual passionate concentration to the study of the Scriptures.

The trial, which took place in a very small and very cold room in the Court of Appeal at Lyons, started at nine o'clock in the morning on the 9th January, 1943. A special "State Tribunal" had been set up for the purpose. Such tribunals had been created at the beginning of the war for the trial of traitors and black marketeers. A magistrate presided, and the court included an admiral and a general. The prisoner was arraigned on the charges of abandoning his post, and treason against the State. It was not possible to make a charge of abandoning his post "in the face of the enemy", for the Vichy Government did not recognize Germany as an enemy.

The size of the room precluded the attendance of many people, but Madame de Lattre was present with a few close friends to support her. Never was the courage of his devoted wife greater than on that lamentable occasion. De Lattre appeared in uniform. He had brought with him some notes to facilitate his replies. In the margin he had written, in his clear handwriting, "Sobriété–Force". Recalling the scene later, François Valentin stated that those two words summed up his own impression of the General's attitude throughout the trial. To every question de Lattre replied with precision and clarity, and with a skill that was remarkable. In that little room he retold, with his grand command of language, the tragic tale of the Army of the Armistice. He seemed to forget that he was on trial. It was as though he were delivering a most inspiring talk on the duties of a commander. He spoke of the Army as the only force remaining in the country which could preserve the traditions of France and be the symbol of her patriotism. That Army must resist aggression. Such was his conception, and such too was the conception which had inspired telegram 128, upon which he had acted. By leaving their garrisons, the troops would have been free. They would have been as a card that could still have been effectively played; but shut up in their barracks, they were as a card that had been played and lost. Moreover, they brought dishonour upon their country. Was it reasonable that, beyond the oceans, skeleton French units should resist their British Allies in Madagascar, while, on the soil of France, to resist the enemy was a crime?

To those who sat in judgment, the weight of these words, and the bearing of him who spoke them, brought a measure of discomfiture and perhaps, to some, a little shame. Later, the subordinate who betrayed him was called upon as a witness. At first it was said that he was too sick to attend, but later he appeared. When asked if he had any questions to ask this witness, de Lattre replied drily, "None".

At four o'clock the court retired. The charge of treason had been dropped. After three-quarters of an hour the court reassembled. The prisoner was found guilty of abandoning his post, and sentenced to ten years' imprisonment. The prosecution had asked that he be degraded in rank, but he was spared the ignominy of this. Madame de Lattre was soon beside him; mustering all her courage, she said to him calmly, "Don't worry, you will never have to serve this sentence".

During the day, the Germans had taken possession of Fort Montluc, where he had been imprisoned; now, therefore, he was to be removed to the prison of Saint-Joseph, returning to Montluc only to collect his belongings. Madame de Lattre, however, feared that if he should set foot again inside that prison, he might well fall into the hands of the Germans, and she was able to prevent his returning, by going there herself to pack up his clothes and bring them away. Later he was transferred to Riom.

De Lattre was not the only ship to founder in the waves of this new invasion. The plight of Weygand was still more pitiable. At the moment of crisis, Pétain had summoned him to Vichy to ask his advice. At the meeting which followed, there was a conflict of opinion as to the path that should be followed. Weygand spoke in heated and uncompromising terms of the Germans. He then left by car for home, accompanied by his son and daughter-in-law. On a lonely part of the road, a fast car overtook them, and pulled up in front. Out stepped his German kidnappers. He was deported to Germany, and it was two and a half years before he and de Lattre were to meet again. How different were to be their destinies!

PART V

Triumph

1943–1945

16. FLIGHT TO FREEDOM

THE cell at Riom was of a reasonable size, and a limited amount of furniture was allowed. Among the few things which he had with him was a picture of Notre-Dame de France, by his old friend Ambroselli, and also a small statue of the Virgin, by Roger de Villiers. But whatever they might do for his comfort, his gaolers were determined to make escape impossible. Originally the number of men detailed to guard him was twenty, but these were soon increased to forty. Outside there was a permanent sentry under his window, which was thirty feet above the ground. Other sentries patrolled the perimeter, and outside his door there was also a double sentry.

Already de Lattre had spent two months in prison before his trial. Eight more months of captivity were to be his lot, and during that period the Allies were to be deprived of his services by the very men whom they were marching to liberate. Such was the miserable handiwork of Vichy. But the prisoner did not give way to such melancholy reflections. Indeed, it seems that at this moment he was possessed of great tranquillity of mind. He applied himself in earnest to the intellectual studies which he had planned at Toulouse. For the second time only in his life, he became a great reader. Among other books that he read, apart from his study of the Scriptures, were *Letters to a young man*, by Father Lacordaire. These letters must have served to inspire many of the letters which he wrote to Bernard, who during the early months of his father's imprisonment was in Touraine, continuing his studies under a village priest. The education and future of Bernard were a constant preoccupation that served greatly to distract de Lattre's mind. On the 11th February, 1943, Bernard's fifteenth birthday, his father wrote as follows:

" . . . and now you must do what you have promised me—work, and work not with your head in the clouds, but in all seriousness, making a real effort. If there are days when you feel disinclined to work, think of your father in prison, who sometimes gets very bored, and is often unhappy, and who hopes that one day he may be proud of you. So take yourself in hand, and catch up on lost time. Think of the future and work loyally. Everything that you do, do it well. [Fais bien ce que tu fais.] Strive for more orderliness in your work—I want you to be neat and tidy."

Few things were more obnoxious to de Lattre than untidy work and ill-prepared papers. Everything had to be impeccable. But work was not the only subject which father and son were considering. Bleak as were the walls of his cell, in one of them, high up and near the ceiling, there was a small semicircular window, with forbidding bars that began to intrigue him. Gradually his plans for escape took root. Already there had been chances, but, until he was certain that none of those whom he had involved at Montpellier would be compromised, he had resisted the temptation. At this time Bernard had only one object in life—to see his father free.

After a few weeks, Madame de Lattre succeeded in finding accommodation for herself in a house in Riom, at the back of which was a garden adjoining the walls of the prison. Bernard rejoined his mother there in the spring, and she and Bernard were allowed to visit the prisoner twice a week. They were not allowed beyond a waiting-room, and there was always a witness present. Moreover, the little parcels containing eatables and other articles, which they brought to cheer his existence, were always searched.

It was clear that escape would not be easy, and de Lattre was intelligent enough to make no move that might prove premature. Firstly, he must charm his gaolers, and for this he was amply equipped. But there were other brains at work to oppose his designs. *Agents provocateurs* deployed all their cunning to extract from him a disclosure of his plans. Only with difficulty did he escape the trap; but if his intentions were divulged, the details remained secret.

As the weeks passed, more and more privileges were extended. His wife and Bernard were allowed to visit him in his cell. Bernard would bring a brief-case full of books, and work that he had done for his father to correct. Madame de Lattre would occasionally bring flowers. The visitors continued for a while to be searched, but in the course of time the searching ceased, and he was allowed to receive his wife and Bernard without the presence of a witness. Plans now began to ripen quickly, and by the end of the summer they were almost mature.

All escapes involve two distinct phases—the actual escape from the prison itself, and then the get-away to a safe distance. For the second phase, often the most difficult, de Lattre would have many accomplices. Apart from his valiant wife and Bernard, Louis Roetsch, his loyal and devoted Alsatian driver, was to play a key-part. He was to collect round him other helpers, mostly men who had served some time under de Lattre, and were then serving at the headquarters of the Clermont-Ferrand region. On the appointed day they were to produce two cars at Riom. But the first problem was how to get out of the window of his cell. The bottom of the window was at least twelve feet from the floor, and about thirty feet from the ground outside. To get through the window itself would involve first of all breaking through the glass, and then the vertical iron bars. If de Lattre could solve that problem, he would then have to surmount the exterior wall of the prison.

In the hatching of these plans Madame de Lattre and Bernard played their full part. Among the tools which they smuggled in either among the flowers, or the washing, or the books and work that Bernard used to bring in for his father's correction were a hammer, a screw-driver, a gimlet, paint, a paint-brush, and putty. Roetsch also managed to loot a length of rope from the Germans, and this was smuggled in with Bernard's books. Outside the prison de Lattre had found two accomplices—a Corporal Leblanc, who had served in the 14th Infantry Division, and a gendarme named Courset, but better known by his nickname "Bouboule". It was arranged that the attempt must be made on a night when Bouboule was to be on guard outside the prison wall. He would cause a diversion by feigning drunkenness. To enable de Lattre to surmount the exterior wall of the prison, Bernard was to throw a rope ladder over the wall from the outside. Roetsch was to be a mainstay in the execution of this part of the plan, and indeed of all the arrangements not only for getting de Lattre himself away, but also for getting away Madame de Lattre and Bernard, who would both immediately become targets for reprisals.

During these days de Lattre thought much of Bernard. He was only fifteen and a half, and upon the manner in which he carried out his part in the impending adventure, the whole future of his father was in large measure dependent. Few more moving or uplifting letters can ever have been written by a father to his son than those which de Lattre wrote to Bernard from the prison at Riom. In the middle of August he wrote to him thus:

> "The need that I feel to lean upon you with complete confidence grows ever stronger. Please let me feel that I can do this, without illusion to-day, or deception to-morrow. Keeping close together let us put all our hopes and all our faith in God. But let us do it wholeheartedly, with complete submission to His will and a conception of daily life which is one of confidence in Him. I want you again to be the Bernard of Father Marie [a Benedictine monk]—with a heart that is pure and noble, and with impulses that are earnest and deep, dominating these earthly miseries, of which perhaps already, for your age, you have seen too many examples. Yes! you must dominate them . . . go forward nobly, be my son, my friend and my comrade, worthy of the task which lies ahead for both of us. . . ."

By the 1st September all was ready, and after eight months' imprisonment it was probable that a measure of laxity should have crept into the routine of the prison guards. From personal observation, de Lattre discovered that, at night, the sentry underneath his window, instead of being relieved at his post, used to go himself to wake up his relief. For a period of five or ten minutes, therefore, there would be no sentry under the window, and that was the factor which was to facilitate his escape and decide the hour of the attempt. What an eruption there would have been if de Lattre had discovered such laxity in any unit under his own command!

All the phases of the operation would demand a considerable physical effort. De Lattre was already fifty-four and prison life did not tend to perfect his physical fitness, but he had always made the most of the limited time given to him for exercise in the courtyard. In that courtyard, normally reserved for those condemned to death, he would dig as well as walk. He discovered, also, that if he could cut away one of the vertical bars outside the window, he would just with difficulty be able to squeeze through. It so happened that the space between the two rails of the towel-horse, which he was allowed in his cell, was just about the same as that between the bars through which he planned to squeeze, and daily in his cell he would practise squeezing through the rails of his towel-horse.

About six o'clock in the evening of the 3rd September Madame de Lattre and Bernard were just leaving the prison when Corporal Leblanc informed Bernard that Bouboule would be on guard outside the prison that night. So the great moment had come. That very night the attempt must be made. The hour fixed was between one-fifteen and one-thirty. There was, therefore, little time to lose, and much to be done. Bernard took the last train into Clermont-Ferrand and warned Roetsch, who in turn collected other helpers. The plan was for Madame de Lattre to leave that night by train for Paris. Twenty minutes only before the train was due to leave, Roetsch and his men arrived. Some of these were to be led by Bernard, through a gate at the end of the garden, to the spot beneath the prison wall from which the rope ladder was to be thrown.

Already the General had perforated the wooden window frame in several places with a gimlet, and had removed all traces of his work by means of the putty and paint that had been smuggled in. He was able to reach the window by placing his dressing-table on the top of his writing-table. The window-frame came away easily as a result of the preparatory work done, and in less than three-quarters of an hour he was able to saw through the bottom part of the iron bar, to pull out the upper portion and to attach the rope. Then came the anxious moments while he waited for the sentry to go off and wake up his relief. When the moment came, the operation of squeezing through the bars, which he had thoroughly rehearsed, was accomplished in a few seconds, and down the rope he slid. He had an unpleasant landing, for the rope was several feet too short, but he was undamaged, and rushed to the outer wall. These were the worst moments of all, for there was no sign of the rope ladder. Bernard had in fact at the last moment mislaid the key of the garden gate, and only just found it in time. The minutes passed and seemed like hours. Then at last over the wall came the ladder, and up he climbed. The emotions that must have stirred father and son as they were united on the other side of the wall may well be imagined. But emotion had to give place to action. There was not a moment to lose. Meanwhile, Bouboule had done his drunken act, diverted attention, and escaped, leaving his rifle behind him.

It was not easy to bring up a car in the middle of the night to the vicinity of a prison without arousing suspicion. The two cars which Roetsch had arranged to be brought up to a point a few hundred yards away, had already attracted the attention of a few gendarmes, who were asking questions. But the ingenuity of Roetsch had left nothing to chance. The papers were in order, satisfactory explanations were given, in jumped de Lattre with Bernard, and away they went into the night. Roetsch was at the wheel, the faithful Roetsch who had driven de Lattre throughout those memorable and tempestuous days in May and June 1940.

The devotion of subordinates of all ranks played a great part in the life of de Lattre, and now that he had to flee from justice and assume a false identity, it was the name of Charles Dequenne that he chose to assume—Charles Dequenne, the gallant little clerk whose conduct had so impressed him at Rethel, and who later had given his life for his country at Nevers, on the Loire.

The new Dequenne described himself on his identity card as a private tutor, and Bernard was to be his delicate pupil. Roetsch took them first to a lonely farm near Compains in the Puy-de-Dôme, and there de Lattre lay low for a time, and grew a beard. It is amusing to think of de Lattre with a beard, for beards were anathema to him, and many will remember the occasions when some unfortunate man was given five minutes in which to shave one off!

These were busy days for Roetsch; not only was he busy organizing hide-outs for de Lattre and Bernard, but also he was concerned with the safety of Madame de Lattre, and keeping her in touch with the General's movements. Madame de Lattre, who had assumed the name of Mademoiselle Suzanne Lalande, reached Paris and later went into hiding in a Benedictine convent, where the Mother Superior was a Protestant convert named Waddington, descendant of an English family which had settled in Normandy.

New plans were now on foot for de Lattre's future. It would hardly have been in the best interests of France that this proven commander in the field should limit his activities to service with the Maquis. Communication was therefore established with London. The position of de Lattre *vis-à-vis* de Gaulle was not easy. They knew each other, and they had respect for each other, but their swords had already crossed even in peacetime, and now their paths had widely diverged. De Gaulle could not feel the same towards de Lattre as towards those who had rallied to him in the earlier days. Both men were proud, proud to a degree that was at times intolerable. Would de Gaulle accept the services of de Lattre, or de Lattre agree to serve his junior? It is to the credit of both, that, in the interests of their country, they were able to sink their buoyant pride, and arrangements were completed for flying de Lattre out of France and bringing him to London.

Meanwhile de Lattre had been forced to leave his hide-out in the Puy-de-Dôme. It had become unsafe. On the 1st October several of those who had helped him to escape were arrested, and it would have been imprudent to remain where he was. He made his way eventually to Clermont-Ferrand, where he took the train to Lyons. From Lyons he travelled to Macon, and thence to Pont-de-Vaux on the Sâone. There, on the night of 15th October, in the company of Claudius Petit, a future member of the French Government, and others who had come by devious ways to the rendezvous, de Lattre proceeded to a lonely clearing that had been improvised as an air-strip. Armed villagers escorted them. There was only a little moon. Just before midnight a van drove up, and out jumped some men who started signalling with lamps. A little later the distant hum of an aeroplane reached their eager ears, and then from Macon, a few miles away, came the disturbing moan of the sirens. Would they ever get get off? Surely every German for miles had been alerted! But there was worse to come. Without any warning a thick damp mist enveloped them: the aircraft could not land, and the dejected little cavalcade tramped back to the village, hoping for better luck on the next night. With nerves so tensely strung it was difficult to sleep, and de Lattre and Petit talked until the early hours. The experiences of the past year, and particularly of the last few weeks had told on the General. Petit, writing later of these events, said that de

Lattre seemed very weak and cold, and so he made him stay in bed and drink "tisane".

On the following night, the cavalcade set forth again. Suspense and doubt were soon to end. Down from the skies swept Livry-Level, piloting a British aircraft. De Lattre was wafted to London, and to fame. Poor Bernard, who had played so great a part in his father's escape, had banked on being able to accompany him, but it was not found practicable. Through the help of an officer who had served in the 14th Infantry Division, he was able to reach Paris and subsequently to see his mother. Both were now wanted by the police, and he too had to assume a false name, so he became Robert Laurent. They could now only hope to receive spasmodic news of the General by code messages broadcast by the B.B.C. On the 17th October the following message was received: "The Screech-owl has arrived safely, and embraces the Sparrow and the Chaffinch."

17. NORTH AFRICAN SPRINGBOARD

ONE dark night in October 1943, in the London blackout, a well-known English peer was asked to dine with Monsieur Viénot—de Gaulle's representative in London. He took a taxi to the street where Monsieur Viénot lived, just off Eaton Square. The night was too dark for the taxi to be able to pull up at the right house; so Monsieur Viénot's guest got out and with the aid of a torch began to search for the house. On the pavement there flashed the torch of another distinguished Englishman, also looking for the same house. Inside the house, in addition to Monsieur Viénot, were two well-dressed strangers. A few hours before they had been bearded peasants, plodding the roads of France; for the strangers were de Lattre and Claudius Petit. They had landed in the early hours of the morning at Tangmere near Chichester. De Lattre, always meticulously careful about his clothes and appearance, had wasted no time after his arrival in

London. The beard had soon been removed, and he had set about finding respectable clothing; his proudest purchase of that day was a new hat that he had bought at a well-known hatter in St. James's Street. "No mediocrity" was one of his many mottoes. Clothes, like everything else, must be impeccable.

Neither during nor after dinner did de Lattre seem very communicative. Even he must have been bewildered by the sudden contrast and the strange new world into which he had dropped from the skies. After nearly a year in prison, followed by weeks as a fugitive from justice in his own country, he was now free—free to play a part at last in the liberation of his country. His one object was to take up arms again at the earliest moment. He was determined also to see that France should live down the defeat of 1940, and again take her rightful place in the Councils of Europe. But what role was he to play? And how would de Gaulle welcome him? He was out of touch with the differences which had existed between de Gaulle and Giraud. This inevitable aftermath of an enemy occupation was sufficient to confuse the mind of de Lattre who had suddenly been plunged into the middle of it. The added and constant anxiety as to the fate of his courageous and devoted wife and Bernard, and the fatigue brought on by his recent exertions, helped also to account for his unusual silence at dinner that night.

De Lattre telegraphed to de Gaulle, who was now in Algiers, asking if he might serve under General Giraud. His contemporary, General Juin, had just been given command of the French Corps in Italy. No immediate departure could be arranged, and the delay must have sorely tried him, but he did not waste his time. He enjoyed a little well-earned comfort at the Ritz Hotel, where the visits of his tailor restored a few of the long-lost pleasures of life. He had many contacts, not only with the British but also with the American authorities in London, and any prejudices which may have existed against one who had been associated with the Vichy Government he quickly broke down by his gift of eloquent persuasion. If he did not attempt to defend the Vichy Government, at least he was able to throw light on the situation in France, and to give his views on the various resistance groups, about whose activities there was much ignorance. With especial fervour did he stress the need for a French Army to form the spearhead to any projected Allied landing in France. Among the many distinguished men with whom de Lattre made contact in London was General Jacob Devers, commanding the United States troops in Great Britain. A year later, he was to find himself commanding an army in Devers' Army Group.

After a few weeks in London, the strain of months in prison began to tell. He became seriously ill, and had to spend some time in the Middlesex Hospital. He always spoke of his time there in terms of the warmest praise. He in turn was a model patient, and exercised all his charm upon those who attended him. On the 11th December, therefore, when he left the hospital, the sisters gave him an unusually touching farewell. On the 19th December he left Prestwick Airport for North Africa.

Arriving in Algiers on the 20th December, he at once asked to be received by de Gaulle. The meeting would not be easy. Apart from the divergent paths which they had chosen, evil tongues had spread stories to the effect that de Lattre was to have been one of the judges deputed by the Vichy Government to try de Gaulle. Actually de Lattre had said he would resign rather than sit on such a court. But the interests of France were supreme, and on this occasion de Gaulle would stoop to no pettiness. "You haven't aged," said de Gaulle, towering above de Lattre. "But you have grown," rejoined de Lattre with a smile.

From de Gaulle, de Lattre went to see Giraud. They were not strangers to each other: twenty years earlier they had served together in Morocco, de Lattre as a captain, and Giraud as a colonel and they had occupied the same ward in hospital after being wounded. Later, when de Lattre commanded the 151st Infantry Regiment at Metz, Giraud had been Military Governor of the city. De Lattre was at once given command of the army subsequently to be known as "Army B".

The new Army Commander set about forming a headquarter staff in characteristic if unorthodox fashion. A colonel on Giraud's staff received the visit one afternoon of one of de Lattre's A.D.C's. "General de Lattre invites you to dine with him tonight," said the A.D.C. "I am very sorry," said the colonel, "but I have already accepted an invitation to dine with General X." The A.D.C. seemed surprised that anyone, whatever the pretext, should decline to accept an invitation from his chief, whose invitations were expected to be regarded as royal commands. Indeed, in due course, de Lattre came to earn the nickname of "le Roi Jean". The A.D.C. returned later in the afternoon to the colonel. "It is all right," he said, "it has all been fixed. You are dining with de Lattre." Le Roi Jean had fixed it. Two or three other officers had also been invited to dine. As they sat down to dinner, de Lattre said to the colonel, "You are to be the head of my 3rd Bureau," and to another he said, "You are to be the head of my 2nd Bureau," until each in turn had been told what he was to be—and that was that. It would have been as useless for them to decline as for their superiors to protest.

On Christmas Day, de Lattre visited an armoured regiment and attended mass. The fact that the majority of the officers were on leave struck him as a sign of extreme slackness and apathy, which he took the appropriate measures to remedy.

At first sight it might have seemed an easier task to build up the morale of an army in 1943, when the Allies were rapidly gaining the ascendancy, than it had been to sustain the morale of the 14th Infantry Division in 1940, in the hour of defeat. But the new problem was far more subtle. The elements of which his army was composed had reached North Africa by those divergent paths which had divided Frenchmen since 1940, and the bitterness which had been engendered was not to disappear in a moment. There were the veterans of the Free French, for whom there had been no respite since 1940. There was the army in North Africa, which until November 1942 had been under the control of the Vichy Government. There were Europeans and natives; some were volunteers, and others were called up when maximum mobilization was introduced after Vichy lost control. Frenchmen living in North Africa, and in Corsica, contributed their share, and the ranks were reinforced also by a continuous stream of men escaping from France. Twenty thousand Frenchmen, leaving their families at the mercy of the enemy and the collaborators, escaped over the Pyrenees to join their compatriots in North Africa. Of such was composed the army which de Lattre was now to command. All would be fired by the common ambition—to liberate France. But that was not enough. De Lattre was determined that this army should be symbolical of a new and united France. Of course it must be organized, trained, and equipped. But, first of all, it must be moulded into one entity. There must be one outlook for all, and no bitterness. All must be made to understand and make allowances for much that had happened in France, and which hitherto had passed the comprehension of some. They must be prepared to understand and co-operate with the various resistance bodies with whom they would come in contact after landing. To the moral preparation of his army, de Lattre now devoted all his energy and all his genius.

Familiar methods were set in motion. Within a few hundred yards of his own residence at Douera he formed his Training Centre. It was Opme and Salambo all over again, and from his headquarters at the Château he could bring to bear the full weight of his personality upon all who passed through, moulding and fashioning them to his liking. He was never satisfied, and often he was criticized for demanding the impossible. "But by always demanding the impossible", he would say "I have often obtained it".

It seemed difficult on occasions to know what he really did want. One day an officer on his staff ventured to suggest that a written directive might better ensure that his wishes were carried out. "They will never know what I want," replied de Lattre in anger. Commenting on the incident later, the officer concerned said that this was typical of his methods; if he committed such details to paper, they would know what he wanted, and it would be too easy. It seems to have been a part of his technique to keep people guessing and on their toes. It was not a method that was any easier to defend than much else that he did, but the results were outstanding. In a matter of weeks, a divided mass of men had become a dynamic and united army.

The establishment of the Douera Training Centre recalls another episode that typifies the unusual methods that de Lattre employed. One day the General went to inspect an artillery unit near the coast. The commanding officer was fully aware of de Lattre's tendency to be unpunctual; he was even prepared for him to arrive after dark, and had therefore installed searchlights, so that, if necessary, the inspection could still take place in darkness. In the event, the General turned up just before dusk, and the services of the searchlights were duly required. De Lattre was so delighted that he asked the commanding officer, after the inspection, to call up all his non-commissioned officers. He then selected personally all those whom he considered to be the best, and said that he wanted them as instructors at Douera. The commanding officer was thus deprived without warning of all his best N.C.O.s. Could it not be put to them, he protested, whether they wished to be appointed to Douera or remain with the regiment? "Je ne fais pas de plebiscites," replied de Lattre, in a paroxysm of wrath. That there should be any question as to whether they would prefer to serve under himself or their commanding officer was intolerable to him. So the commanding officer had to build up his regiment anew. Effective as were such methods in the hands of de Lattre, they were not to be commended to others, nor did de Lattre himself commend them. To a subordinate commander, who once kept his unit waiting, de Lattre remarked, "Il faut suivre mes grandeurs et non mes servitudes."

While de Lattre had become fully absorbed by his new activities, his wife and Bernard were still in France, and wanted by the police. Madame de Lattre, now Mademoiselle Lalande, was in the convent at Vanves, and Bernard, now Robert Laurent, was at the Jesuit College at Rheims. From time to time only were mother and son able to meet. One day Bernard picked up a newspaper, and saw in it a photograph of his father in London. His excitement was so intense, that for the first time he became indiscreet. "That is my father," he said, showing it to a friend. His indiscretion cost him much remorse, but he confided to the Father Superior what had happened, and there was no unfortunate sequel.

In March, the following message was broadcast by the B.B.C.: "Request immediate evacuation Sparrow and Chaffinch via Spain. Study best means carrying out operation with François and Christian." François was François Valentin, and Christian was a certain Gilbert Getten, a well-known figure in the Resistance Movement. So at last they were to rejoin the General. On the evening of the 31st March, they left the Gare d'Austerlitz in Paris for Toulouse. It was not until the 7th May that they reached Algiers, by air from Gibraltar. It had been an adventurous journey, for not only had they to avoid the Gestapo, but there were the Pyrenees to be crossed, and the health of Madame de Lattre often gave cause for anxiety. For greater safety, mother and son crossed the Pyrenees separately. Bernard crossed at a higher point. His party had to spend two bitterly cold nights in a mountain hut, prevented by bad weather from completing the crossing at once. They had to continue, in snow which was sometimes knee-deep. Some members of the party suffered from giddiness, and others from exhaustion, and it was not without a series of adventures that they got across. The guide who led them recalls the courage which Bernard had shown, and his gratitude on reaching the far side of the mountains. "He threw himself into my arms, in gratitude at getting across, and being able to proceed on his way to his father and to liberty." In Barcelona, he was rejoined by his mother, and on the 6th May they reached Gibraltar, where they were warmly welcomed by the Governor and Lady Eastwood. On the following day they left by air for Algiers, where, at the Maison Blanche Airport, the family was reunited. "All that we had suffered for eighteen months," wrote Bernard later, "was forgotten. We could only revel wildly in the joy of finding that we were all three united again on a soil that was French and free." He was soon taking full part in the activities of the Douera Training Centre, as he had done in 1940 at Opme.

When de Lattre first took over command, no definite task had been assigned to his army, but on the 18th April he was informed that ultimately he was to assume command of the French forces destined to participate in Operation X, the projected landing in the South of France. He was therefore to get in touch with the Allied High Command, and to make initial preparations.

Meanwhile, de Lattre's first contacts with the Americans had not been entirely happy. In January 1943, Giraud had signed an agreement with the Americans which envisaged the creation of a French force of eleven infantry and three armoured divisions. With great difficulty, for their own needs were considerable, the Americans had more or less armed and equipped three infantry and three armoured divisions. But de Lattre was not satisfied. He rarely was. He visualized that once his Army had landed in France, its ranks would be swelled by thousands of Frenchmen who would need to be armed and equipped. But the Americans would not consider basing any calculations upon such uncertainties. They had to be realists, and it was not always easy for them to understand and sympathize with the viewpoint of a nation whose country had been overrun, and was at that moment occupied by the enemy. De Lattre and his men were fired with the spirit and fervour of crusaders, setting forth to liberate their own land. Moreover, it was on French territory that the liberation was being planned, and on that account, too, French *amour-propre* was more than usually sensitive. De Lattre may have been difficult, and not always appreciative of the magnitude of the American effort, but co-operation would have been easier if greater allowance had been made for the state of the French mind at the time. In the planning of complex operations there may be little room for sentiment, but when morale is affected it cannot be ignored. Eventually it was agreed that the maximum French force that could be equipped was eight infantry and three armoured divisions. Of the latter, one was Leclerc's division, which was to train in England and take part in the landings in Normandy.

These were not the only difficulties that rendered so difficult the smooth running of relations between the French in North Africa and Allied Force Headquarters, first under Eisenhower, and later under Maitland Wilson. The question of command created many difficulties. It was natural that the French should have striven for an independent French Army to land on the Mediterranean coast of France, but in their eagerness to achieve this, they failed at times to appreciate the difficulties that made it impracticable. All the administrative machinery and the vast resources that would be required for the operations envisaged were to be controlled by the Americans. There could only be one solution. In the long arguments that continued, de Lattre was not always popular with Allied Headquarters, but at least he had shown that he was a force to be reckoned with.

18. "DRAGOON"

ALLIED strategy for the year 1944 had been the subject of much discussion between the Americans and the British. To many in America the defeat of Japan was probably of greater immediate interest than the defeat of Germany, and for a time this factor exercised considerable influence upon the projects of the Allies. When it was eventually agreed that the defeat of Hitler in Europe should have priority, the Americans were anxious that all available resources should be used for the operations in Normandy, and they were at first opposed to what they considered to be a dissipation of these resources on operations in the Mediterranean. Moreover, they tended to suspect British Mediterranean projects as being based on political rather than military expediency. The British, on the other hand, argued that it would be uneconomical to tie up large forces in North Africa in a purely defensive rôle. Indeed, it might well result in large German forces being set free, and becoming available, firstly to overwhelm Russia, and subsequently to switch westward and oppose the Allied landing in Northern France. The British view, in short, was that the forces in North Africa should be used to strike against what Mr. Churchill called the "under-belly of the Axis", on the northern shores of the Mediterranean.

After the invasion of Italy, there was a strong current of opinion among the British against the decision to land in the south of France. The mere threat of a landing in that area, so they argued, would ensure the desired dispersal of German forces. Mr. Churchill had always been drawn away from the southern coast of France, and had favoured operations through the Balkans which, in his view, would constitute the more potent threat. His romantic and lively imagination had dreamed of a rendezvous with Stalin on the banks of the Danube in Vienna. In this course he was supported by Maitland Wilson, who had succeeded Eisenhower as Supreme Commander at Allied Force Headquarters in Algiers. Indeed, it seemed questionable whether sufficient troops or resources were available to conduct an operation in southern France, simultaneously with those in Italy and Normandy. Maitland Wilson was of the opinion that all his available resources should be used to support Alexander in Italy, and he further proposed an amphibious operation against the Istrian Peninsula, to be exploited through the Ljubljana Gap, into the plains of Hungary.

Whatever the ultimate decision was to be, it would profoundly affect the French forces in North Africa. For them, the only course was to land in southern France, and liberate their country; the dispassionate consideration of any other alternative was impossible. If such a course had been abandoned in favour of an advance through the Balkans, the course of European history might well have been happier; but it would have been a bitter disappointment for de Lattre and his crusaders, who were counting the days until they could land on the shores of the motherland.

Until the last moment, the decision was in doubt, but meanwhile there was to be a subsidiary operation that would give experience, both to de Lattre and to his troops, of amphibious operations. Maitland Wilson, planned to capture the island of Elba (see map on p. 133), and he was anxious that the operation should be carried out by French troops.

Allied Force Headquarters were still preoccupied with the difficulties which the French raised over questions of command and matters had not been made easy by the differences among the French themselves. Although Giraud could be difficult, Allied Force Headquarters had found him easier to work with than de Gaulle, and when Giraud and de Gaulle fell out and Giraud retired from the scene, it was with regret that they saw him go. De Gaulle seemed obsessed by the fear of being accused by his compatriots of being the tool of the British and Americans, and in his efforts to obviate such an accusation he became at times intolerably difficult. It had been decided that the operation for the capture of Elba should be carried out by the French 9th Colonial Infantry Division, under the direction of General Henri Martin, their Corps Commander in Corsica. At the last minute de Gaulle insisted on the insertion of a French Army Commander between Maitland Wilson and Henri Martin. The task of planning and conducting the operation was much complicated by this last minute intervention, but General Devers, then Deputy Supreme Commander under Maitland Wilson, smoothed over the difficulties, and de Lattre was the Army Commander chosen.

This was the first experience which the Allies were to have of co-operating with de Lattre in battle, and they were not to find him easy. The first difficulty to arise was the question of the date. By the end of May Rear-Admiral Tom Troubridge and Colonel D'Arcy, U.S.A.A.F., commanding respectively the Naval and Air Task Forces, had everything ready when de Lattre asked for a postponement. How far this request was justified is difficult to say. Both Magnan, commanding the 9th Colonial Division, and Henri Martin were of the opinion that the recent strengthening of the German defences on Elba necessitated a more thorough preparation, and de Lattre supported them. But the delay entailed the locking up of limited and valuable resources for a long period, when they might well have been needed elsewhere.

Yet a further complication was to strain inter-allied harmony. De Lattre asked for the use of a French parachute battalion to support his attack. Maitland Wilson had agreed to this request, providing the aircraft could be made available. In the event, four days before the operation, de Lattre was informed that he could not have the aircraft, as they were needed on the mainland. De Lattre threatened to call off the operation. It is difficult to blame de Lattre for trying to obtain all he could to ensure the success of this his first operation since his escape from captivity. Indeed, it is a commander's duty to ensure, within reason, that his troops have the maximum support possible. De Lattre was never backward in pressing his claims, and at times he placed a severe strain on the patience and tempers of his superiors. But just as he knew how far he could go in driving his subordinates, so generally he knew where to stop in persecuting his superiors. When Maitland Wilson made it quite plain that there were prior claims on the aircraft, de Lattre agreed to carry out the operation without them.

It was thought that the strength of the enemy in Elba was in the neighbourhood of 2,000. It was known, however, that during recent months much work had been done on the defence of this rocky island, which is about twenty miles in length, and it was known also that over and above anti-aircraft and anti-tank guns, there were at least sixty pieces of artillery, including coast defence and other heavy batteries. Most of the bays were therefore fully covered, both by light artillery and small-arms fire, and the heavier batteries inland could bring fire to bear on almost any part of the coast that might be threatened. Moreover, the island was surrounded by underwater mines, and the only course considered practicable was to use the narrow channel in the main bay to the south, through which the Germans used to supply the island.

The force allotted for the capture of the island comprised the 9th Colonial Division under Magnan, and a detachment of

Moroccan Goums of about brigade strength, together with some commandos and a so-called "Choc" Battalion, which was more lightly equipped than the commandos. The main condition for the success of the operation was to destroy, or at least to neutralize, firstly the shore defences, and secondly the coastal and other heavy batteries, which could bring converging fire to bear on the bays. The heavier batteries presented a difficult problem, since neither the Navy nor the Air Force could guarantee their destruction. The "Choc" Battalion was to provide the answer. It was a magnificent unit, composed entirely of volunteers, many of whom had only recently escaped from France, and it had a first-class commanding officer in Lieutenant-Colonel Gambiez. This unit was to land three hours before the main assault, and seize the batteries by surprise.

By the time all was set for the operation, de Lattre had recovered from his anger at failing to obtain the use of the parachute battalion. He was in a happier frame of mind, and this may in large measure have been due to that love of the sea and ships which had never left him. When at three o'clock in the afternoon of the 16th June, from his headquarters at Bastia, in Corsica, he looked out upon the array of ships weighing anchor, and setting sail for the south, with a view to deceiving the enemy, he was greatly stirred. His happier frame of mind may also have been due to the fact that Tom Troubridge, the British Admiral in command of the Naval Task Force, was not only a first-class sailor, but also a man of the world, who fully understood the French. Tom Troubridge, with his outstandingly buoyant, cheerful, and very human personality, was a man after de Lattre's own heart, and between this sailor and soldier there developed a mutual and exemplary understanding. In later days, it was always in terms of deepest affection that de Lattre referred to Tom Troubridge.

At eleven o'clock on the night of the 16th June, the "Choc" and Commando detachments slipped silently ashore. Their operations in the main were crowned with success. Apart from destroying the most dangerous batteries, they penetrated to the interior of the island, causing all the havoc they could. At four a.m. on the 17th, the first two waves of the assault force went ashore under cover of every available supporting weapon. At four-thirty, the third and fourth waves went in, but two of the

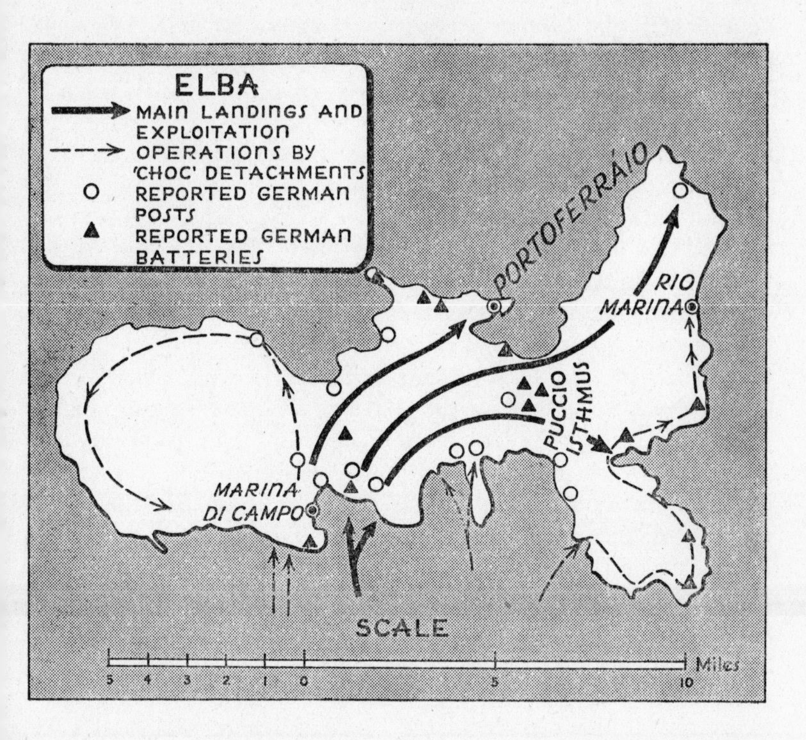

five landing-craft were at once hit. The leading waves had been unable to mop up along the shore, and some of the enemy, who had been overrun, re-emerged at this critical stage. Fortunately, an alternative plan had been envisaged in the event of the main beach proving difficult. This was now put into effect by agreement between the head of de Lattre's 3rd Bureau and Troubridge, who were in the same ship. It involved a landing in a small creek to the east of the main bay, and was completely successful. By five-thirty the main force was ashore; but it was not until the afternoon that the bridgehead was secure.

Although the Germans fought with determination, the issue was now no longer in doubt. Gall, the enemy commander, had hesitated to commit his reserves at that fleeting moment when the French landed, and were most vulnerable, and by the evening of the 17th the western half of Elba was in French hands. Although on the 18th the Germans clung desperately to the bottleneck formed by the Puccio isthmus, by nightfall the capture of the island was complete. It was the anniversary of de Gaulle's stirring appeal to Frenchmen in 1940; and it was also, as Troubridge laughingly remarked to de Lattre, the anniversary of Waterloo.

The operations of French units during these two days' fighting had not only served to give confidence to the French themselves, but had also dispelled any doubts that may have existed at Allied Force Headquarters as to their capacity to contribute in full measure to the operations that impended. Moreover, it was proved that, however difficult de Lattre might be, co-operation with him was possible, if reasonable tact and firmness were used.

The decision to land in the south of France was continually deferred. Among the many factors affecting the decision was the date upon which the required amount of landing-craft would become available, after the landing in Normandy. But the main reason for the delay was the conflict of views between the Americans and the British. General Eisenhower recalled that this subject introduced one of the longest sustained arguments that he had with Mr. Churchill in the course of the whole war.

Eisenhower maintained that he could not rely on sufficient ports in Brittany becoming available to allow American divisions to land in France at the rate required. In fact General Marshall told Maitland Wilson, whom he visited at this time, that unless further ports became available, about forty American divisions might well be held up in the United States. Eisenhower therefore strongly advocated the landing in the south of France, with a view to making available the port of Marseilles, which would facilitate the disembarkation of troops coming both from the States and from North Africa. Finally, he argued that if an army landed in the south of France and advanced northward, it would effectively protect the right flank of his own armies advancing eastward from Normandy. Without such protection he would have to dissipate much of his strength by deploying divisions from the base of the Brittany peninsula to the most forward point reached by his attacking spearheads.

Mr. Churchill argued that the Brittany ports would become available for use by troops coming both from the States and from North Africa. Moreover, he pointed out the risk of forces landing in southern France being held up, and unable to advance northward in time to act effectively on Eisenhower's southern flank. Maitland Wilson strongly supported Mr. Churchill. He argued that the diversion of the required air power from Italy to support a landing in Southern France would seriously compromise the successful conclusion of the Italian campaign. Again the Adriatic project was strongly put forward.

But the Combined Chiefs of Staff supported Eisenhower, and it was decided at last that operation "Dragoon", previously known as "Anvil", should be carried out. De Gaulle, too, had been active in pressing such a course, and at last the dreams of de Lattre were to be realized. The code-word "Dragoon" was a felicitous choice for an operation that was to take place just thirty years after de Lattre, as a young officer in the 12th Dragoons, had first achieved fame on the battlefield.

Allied Headquarters were to be responsible for the planning of the operation, and a composite Franco-American Army, to be known as the Seventh Army, under General Alexander Patch, was to carry it through. Patch was an excellent choice, for he had gained considerable experience of combined operations as a successful corps commander at Guadalcanal in the Pacific. For the actual landing, de Lattre would have a mixed headquarters comprising partly an Army Headquarters Staff and partly the Corps Headquarters Staff of the first French corps to land. Patch would therefore exercise command of the French corps through de Lattre. As soon as two French corps should be in the field, de Lattre would assume complete tactical control of his own army.

On the 14th July, de Lattre had moved his headquarters from Algiers to Naples. He now had to take over command of those divisions of his army who had hitherto been serving with distinction under General Juin in Italy. For de Lattre this was a peculiarly delicate task, for there was that almost feminine side to his character which made it essential for him to be able to count on the affection of those whom he commanded. But in the divisions concerned, Juin had, by his masterly leadership, inspired the deepest devotion. Would they be able at short notice to transfer their affections? It might not be easy. There was now only a month left before the operation was due to take place, and those who visited de Lattre's headquarters at Naples will remember the busy scene. He wanted to know personally all those who would be working with him or under him, and every day his mess was full of visitors.

He also contrived to leave Naples and to visit most of the units in his army. He paid increasing attention to dress, for he attached supreme importance to the first impression that his army would make upon landing. It must compare favourably with the best units of the occupying army, to whom his unfortunate compatriots had grown accustomed. To achieve his purpose, he rarely visited a unit without finding some pretext, however trivial, for the discharge of one of those resounding broadsides that were the familiar expression of his wrath. On one hot sunny day, he came across a sentry wearing dark spectacles. "Inadmissible," he roared, and everyone within reach was sent for at the double, and regaled with an impassioned dissertation on the iniquity of soldiers wearing dark glasses.

His visits to units had another object. Only a small proportion of his army had been in France under the occupation, and there was a tendency to minimize the achievements of the Resistance Movement. He was determined to suppress any such antipathy, and with every unit he pleaded for an understanding of the difficulties which had confronted their compatriots in France. "You have been lucky," he said, "to fight a victorious war. But remember those who have lived hours that were humiliating and painful. Many have been fighting in a murderous underground war. All have suffered—suffered greatly. Try to understand them and forget your own glory, so that they shall not feel too keenly their own misery."

The decision to carry out operation "Dragoon" involved a great sacrifice on the part of Alexander, who was commanding in Italy. With his usual selflessness, he made no complaint. He was to lose no less than seven divisions, three American and four French, which were to be transferred to Patch's Seventh Army. Although shipping facilities and other considerations would preclude the immediate employment of the whole of Patch's Army, its eventual composition would be the VI U.S. Corps of three infantry divisions, and two French corps totalling two armoured and five infantry divisions. There was also available an Anglo-American Airborne division.

Information as to the opposition which Patch might expect to encounter was fairly complete. South of the line Lyons–Bordeaux the Germans had two armies, the First Army (Headquarters Bordeaux) which was responsible for the defence of the Atlantic Coast south of the Loire, and the Nineteenth Army (Headquarters Avignon) which was responsible for the defence of the French Mediterranean Coast. The Nineteenth Army was commanded by General Wiese, and it was that army with which the Allies would be mainly concerned. It is interesting to reflect that the task of the Nineteenth German Army was the very same which Admiral Darlan had allotted to de Lattre nearly two years earlier. He therefore had an unusual knowledge of the problems which confronted the enemy Commander.

The Nineteenth German Army was disposed with three corps covering the Mediterranean Coast respectively in the Montpellier area, the mouth of the Rhône, and the Riviera coast round Cannes and Nice. These corps totalled eight infantry and one armoured division, but they might well be reinforced by an infantry division from the First Army. It was appreciated therefore that the eleven Franco-American divisions might be opposed by ten divisions of the enemy; but this comparison takes no account of a variety of other units at the disposal of the enemy, including twenty battalions of the Eastern Legion,* three Luftwaffe regiments, two marine brigades, and several territorial units. Moreover, there were the formidable fixed defences of Toulon and Marseilles, with their coastal and anti-aircraft armament.

At first sight, therefore, the Allies do not seem to have had that preponderating superiority that would ensure success. But their complete mastery of the sea and air were the factors that mainly told in their favour. Moreover the support upon which they could count from Resistance Groups in South-east France under General Zeller, known as "Joseph", was by no means negligible. The general scope of the projected operation was to:

(1) Establish a bridgehead East of Toulon (see map on p. 153).
(2) Capture Toulon and Marseilles.
(3) Exploit northward to Lyons.
(4) Join up with the right of Eisenhower's forces advancing from Normandy and Brittany.

* The Eastern Legion (*Ost Legion*) consisted of Russians, mostly recruited from the Ukraine and Georgia.

The beaches selected for the assault were those between Agay and Cavalaire. The VI U.S. Corps, with 1st Combat Command* of the 1st French Armoured Division was to carry out the assault, which was to be preceded by the landing of the airborne division on the heights to the north and east of Le Muy and north of Grimaud. The French were to land on D + 1 and move westward to capture Toulon and Marseilles. In the time-table worked out for the successive phases of the operation a large safety margin was allowed. Maitland Wilson estimated that Toulon would be captured by D + 20, and Marseilles three weeks later. He did not consider that mastery of the Rhône Valley, from Lyons to the sea, would be secured before D + 90.

De Lattre regarded the time-table as most pessimistic, and in his Personal Instruction No. 1, issued nine days before the landing, he emphasized, above all else, the need for speed in constantly seeking to outflank the enemy by manœuvring along the high ground north of the coast, and in the fearless exploitation of every favourable opportunity. Apart from other considerations, he was anxious quickly to capture Toulon and complete operations in the south, in order to effect an early junction with the French Resistance Groups in Savoy and the Dauphiné. He was also anxious for French troops to reach Lyons and Grenoble as soon as the Americans. When de Lattre put his views to Patch, the latter implied that the French were trying to get out of the task of taking Toulon and Marseilles. The insinuation caused a major outburst on the part of de Lattre, but it cleared the air, and thereafter there was complete comprehension between the Army Commander and his fiery subordinate.

Only those who have been concerned with the planning of a combined operation can visualize the magnitude of the task involved, and the meticulous attention to detail which it demands. In the First World War attempts to land on a hostile coast in the face of opposition had proved so expensive, that between the wars there had developed in England a school of thought that regarded such operations as impracticable. Only a limited number of officers, therefore, had seriously studied the problem, and it was only after

* As the French Army was now organized on an American basis, the American nomenclature has been retained. A "Combat Command" was the approximate equivalent of a "Brigade Group".

a succession of disasters that combined operations received the belated attention that had been their due. It is interesting to recall that de Lattre had always given thought to this matter; he had in fact read most of the literature on combined operations which had appeared in England. It well befitted him, therefore, to command the French forces participating in this difficult operation.

By August 1944, special craft for the transport of infantry and tanks, special craft to support them during those last difficult moments till they reached the shore, and all the other paraphernalia that human ingenuity could devise for the purpose, had sprung into being. Even so, Maitland Wilson described the preparation of "Dragoon" as the toughest bit of co-ordination with which he had ever been faced. In order that the Seventh Army should be ready to land on the 15th August, which was the date fixed for the operation, staffs had to work at full pressure. Troops and stores had to be embarked at ports that spread from Bari in the Adriatic to Oran in North Africa, and the airborne division had to be built up by collecting British and American parachute battalions from all over the Mediterranean. The complexity of the problem was not eased by a proposal from de Gaulle to land the airborne division in the Massif Central as a reinforcement to the Resistance Groups in that area. This was turned down on the grounds that it would have necessitated the diversion of aircraft from the main battle zone, and risked compromising the success of the landing. A variety of other modifications was suggested both from Washington and London.

If Maitland Wilson found the planning of this operation tough, de Lattre and his commanders also must have been not a little dismayed by the strange new problems which they had to solve. A proportion of de Lattre's army had gained experience of modern war in Italy, but, of the rest, many had been out of touch with the war since 1940, and others were young and inexperienced soldiers who had seen no fighting at all. But the enthusiasm and confidence of their commander was an inspiration to all.

In the very early hours of the 15th August, pathfinders took off from the Rome airfields. One hour later the main body of paratroops in 396 aircraft took off for their objective, an important road centre inland. Only thirty-seven aircraft missed their target. Then followed the effective covering bombardment by the naval and air forces, and by the evening of the 15th, the VI U.S. Corps was firmly established in the triangle Saint-Aygulf–Le Muy–Cap Negre, and in a small beach-head to the east of Saint-Raphael, which the resistance at that place had separated from the main beach-head. In the main beach-head, touch had been established with the airborne troops. Patch was quick to exploit success, directing VI Corps on Grenoble and the Rhône Valley.

De Lattre's turn was coming, and it was more fitting and congenial that his rôle should be exploitation rather than the establishment and consolidation of a bridgehead. He himself sailed from Taranto in the S.S. "Batory". As he stepped aboard, Admiral Jaujard handed him the special flag that he was entitled to fly at sea. To one who so loved *panache*, and who once had wished to be a sailor, the flying of this flag gave a special cause for pleasure, and rarely had he been prouder than when he beheld the great armada heading for the shores of France. With him was Bernard: he was only sixteen and a half, and the youngest soldier in his father's army. Before he was seventeen, as a corporal in the 2nd Dragoons, he was to be wounded, and decorated with the Military Medal.

Few men can have been so deeply moved as were those French crusaders as they drew closer to the motherland; and their Allies were not insensitive to the drama of the occasion. To those commandos who were to be the first to land, came the following signal: "The Admiral, officers and crews of the Allied Fleet salute Lieutenant-Colonel Bouvet and his men, who will have the honour of being the first to set foot on their native shores, and to liberate their land. May God guard and protect them." On the evening of the 16th August, the soldiers of France and her Empire, soldiers of all races and from many corners of the world, were united on the beaches of Southern France.

19. FATEFUL DECISION

ON the 17th, the landing of troops and unloading of equipment and stores continued. De Lattre had established his headquarters in the village of Cogolin, west of Saint Tropez, where he and his troops were the objects of a delirious welcome. The Municipal Council at once decided to make him a Citizen of Honour. There had been only one other, and that was Georges Clemenceau; and so in the book which he had to sign, de Lattre wrote after his name "Second Citizen of Honour of Cogolin, born in the same village as the first Citizen of Honour, Georges Clemenceau". It was a curious chance that Cogolin should have honoured these two sons of the little village of Mouilleron-en-Pareds, at the other end of France.

The scene in the Town Hall at Cogolin provided a pleasant little interlude while the troops were disembarking; but sterner work lay ahead. On the next day de Lattre was faced with one of the most fateful decisions of his life. The entrenched camp of Toulon was his immediate objective, but the garrison was known to comprise about 25,000 men, and the town was protected by a ring of thirty forts, and innumerable casemates and pill-boxes. Only a half of de Lattre's forces would be ashore within the first few days of landing; the remainder would not be landed until about ten days later. Either he could await the concentration of his whole force, and so advance at full strength, or he could strike at once at half strength, before the enemy recovered from his initial surprise. The latter course would risk the defeat in detail of each half of his army in turn, while the former would conform to the age-old principle of concentration, but forfeit the element of surprise. Could he risk, within a few days of landing, the defeat of that army which he had been at such pains to forge, and upon which the hopes of so many had been centred?

The simultaneous application of all the principles of war is rarely possible, but so great is the effect of surprise, that, if it can be obtained, some at least of the other principles may well be disregarded. De Lattre now decided to risk all in a rapid advance on Toulon. The advance was to be carried out in two columns. On the right, de Monsabert with his 3rd Algerian Division and attached troops was to move along the heights running parallel to the coast, and to outflank Toulon from the north. On the left Brosset, with his Free French Division and attached troops, was to move along the coast. In view of the hilly and rocky nature of the country, de Monsabert was given a detachment of General Guillaume's Goums, who had performed outstanding work in

Italy. Although de Monsabert had the more difficult country, Brosset, on the coast, would come up against the two belts of fortifications which protected Toulon from the east, and which were particularly strong round Sollies and Hyères. Of the 1st French Armoured Division, the 1st Combat Command had participated with the VI U.S. Corps in the initial landing, and was still directly under Patch. De Lattre, therefore, only had a part of the 2nd Combat Command immediately available. This he immediately ordered forward under du Vigier, with orders to protect the northern flank of his advance, to assure liaison with VI U.S. Corps, and to push on towards Aix and Marseilles.

De Monsabert and Brosset typified the contrasting elements of which de Lattre's army was composed. De Goislard de Monsabert, to give that gallant little Gascon warrior his full name, was short and stocky, and a neatly trimmed white moustache adorned his fresh and jovial countenance. He had not served with the Free French, and had remained faithful to the colourful general's head-dress of pre-war days. Brosset, who had served with the Free French, was tall and athletic, and had adopted that less formal dress which was the mark in general of those who had fought in the desert. Du Vigier typified all that was best in the French cavalry officer, and it was in large measure due to his initiative and dash that the impending operations were to achieve such rapid success.

Meanwhile the speed with which the disembarkation of the first half of de Lattre's force had been completed, had enabled the shipping to return to Corsica more quickly than expected, and the 9th Colonial Division, under Magnan, together with the "Choc" Battalion and Goums, already had begun to land several days ahead of the date fixed. Thus does fortune favour the brave. With the first battalion of the 9th Division to land, de Lattre formed a detachment which he interposed between de Monsabert and Brosset, and directed along the Saint-Raphael–Toulon road. The remaining units of the 9th Colonial Division would reinforce this detachment as they became available. Magnan's detachment, which would eventually comprise the whole 9th Colonial Division, de Lattre grouped with Brosset's southern detachment, and he deputed de Larminat to co-ordinate the operations of the two. De Larminat was one of those courageous Frenchmen who, in 1940, risked all, including his life, to repudiate the Vichy Government, and to throw in his lot with de Gaulle. Already, therefore, he had proved his strength of character, but by temperament he was not ideally suited to co-operate with de Lattre. For a short time he served as his deputy, but was later given command of a new army that was formed to invest Bordeaux.

Those whose privilege it was to serve on de Lattre's staff had to be possessed of the most robust constitutions; rarely a night passed when they could snatch the amount of sleep that men normally require. The more intelligent contrived to slip away at times from headquarters, and to build up their reserves with an hour or two of refreshing sleep. The night of the 18th August, which was the day on which de Lattre had decided to push on, was more than usually disturbed. Information reached him at about midnight to the effect that the Germans were working feverishly not only to reinforce the northern and eastern defences of Toulon, but also to destroy the buildings of the arsenal. The need to push on became imperative: he even contemplated an immediate raid into the heart of Toulon, with an armoured detachment. With that object in view he sent for du Vigier, commanding the protective detachment to the north. But in view of later information he abandoned the project.

On the 19th August, General Jacob Devers, Maitland Wilson's deputy, arrived at de Lattre's headquarters accompanied by Colonel Cabot Lodge, his liaison officer. In 1952, Cabot Lodge was to organize General Eisenhower's campaign in the Presidential Election. He made an immediate impression upon de Lattre, who summed him up not only as a man of exceptional intelligence, but of great uprightness of character. Cabot Lodge understood de Lattre better than most of his American compatriots, and was to render a great service, not only to de Lattre, but to the greater cause of Allied co-operation. On this day in particular, de Lattre had reason to be grateful to him. His decision to push on to Toulon without waiting was at complete variance with the timetable that had been laid down, but, as de Lattre was under command of the U.S. Seventh Army, he could not carry out his intentions without the approval of Patch. When he confided those intentions to Devers and Lodge, both were shaken, but were persuaded that the risk might be justified, and they agreed to put forward his views to Patch. The same morning de Lattre himself went to Patch's headquarters, where he had to deploy all his persuasive powers to obtain sanction for his project. After some hesitation, Patch agreed, and he also gave back to de Lattre the 1st Combat Command of the 1st French Armoured Division. In his book, "The History of the First French Army", de Lattre gives a moving account of this meeting with Patch:

> "Suddenly, those clear and serious eyes of the American Commander seemed to soften. With a gesture of hesitation that was full of modesty, he pulled from his pocket his wallet, and from it withdrew a little flower, whose petals were beginning to fade. 'Take this,' he said, breaking off one of the petals. 'It was given to me by a young girl on the slopes of Vesuvius on the eve of embarking. She told me it would bring me good luck. Let us each keep a part of this charm, and it may lead our two armies, side by side, to victory.' "

The greatest soldiers can be romantic.

All was now set for the adventure, and before dawn on the 20th, the army was moving westward. The 1st Combat Command was allotted to de Monsabert, and de Lattre, as always one jump ahead, made it clear to de Monsabert that he wanted the detachment not only to cover the capture of Toulon from the north, but also to help to secure the subsequent advance on Marseilles. The operations that followed comprised three main phases: the investment of Toulon, the penetration of its outer defences, and the capture of the town and port itself.

The success of de Lattre's plan depended in the main on the rapidity with which de Monsabert could encircle Toulon from the north and north-west. His confidence in the little Gascon had not been misplaced. De Monsabert had unleashed his Divisional Reconnaissance Regiment early in the evening of the 19th, and by the next day it had reached a point ten miles to the north-west of the city. But immediately north of Toulon a most remarkable feat was also accomplished by one of his detachments under Colonel de Linares. It was an advance over a wild and pathless country nearly 2,000 feet above the plain, lying between Belgentier and Montrieux. Led by the monks from Montrieux monastry, by dawn on the 20th, de Linares had reached the southern slopes of the plateau near Revest-les-Eaux, only a few miles north of Toulon.

Behind the story of the advance of de Linares there lies an interesting story. A few months earlier at a conference in Algiers, de Lattre had been discussing alternative methods for the capture of Toulon. Suddenly he turned to a naval officer who was present. "You ought to know the answer" he said, "with all your local knowledge." The officer reflected for a moment and suddenly remembered a novel by Claude Farrère, called "La Maison des Hommes Vivants". In it there is a detailed description of the wild country to the north of Toulon. "Get me a copy, at once" said de Lattre. A copy was procured and it is interesting to reflect that a novel of Claude Farrère, combined with the retentive memory of a naval officer, may have helped to inspire the manœuvre. During the day de Monsabert exploited his rapid advance. The divisional reconnaissance regiment now split into two halves: one half reached Bandol on the coast south of Toulon, while the other made contact with de Linares north of the town. Toulon was almost encircled.

To the east, de Larminat had to overcome very strong resistance before Hyères fell, and Magnan with his Colonial Division, and Brosset with his Free French, reinforced by commandos, had to contest every inch of the ground. Sollies and Mont Redon, with its observation over the whole surrounding country, proved particularly difficult nuts to crack, and in Hyères itself, the enemy offered strong resistance in the area of the Golf Hotel to the north-east of the town. But by the evening of the 21st, the French had reached La Valette on the outskirts of Toulon. The encirclement of the town was now complete.

Although there was little hope of help from outside, the Germans in Toulon obeyed to the letter the personal instructions of Hitler—to resist to the last. On the precipitous slopes to the north, were the forts of Le Faron and La Croix du Faron, and to the north-west was the fort of La Poudrière, to the perfection of which the Germans had devoted more than usual skill. With its labyrinth of underground corridors, it had been made almost impregnable. To the east also were a number of other strong positions, including the heights of Touar.

The Faron feature, and the two forts thereon, were taken by the commandos, but La Poudrière proved the toughest obstacle of all, and when de Linares finally captured it late on the night of the

22nd, 250 enemy corpses were counted within. There were only 180 prisoners, of whom sixty were wounded. De Lattre was the first to pay tribute to the heroism of the defenders, which recalled the exploits of his own compatriots at Forts Douaumont and Vaux in 1916.

On the left of de Lattre's front, near the coast, the heights of Le Touar were taken by Brosset on the 22nd, and in the centre Magnan too made progress. Indeed, the sight of Toulon spurred him on to the point of rashness, and he himself forged ahead in his jeep to the outskirts of the city. Going back to bring up the leading elements of his division, his excitement was intense. "Come along" he shouted, "I have kissed at least two hundred girls already."

The situation within Toulon had become extremely confused. Many of de Linares' men had infiltrated into the city, but the enemy continued to occupy strongpoints on the outskirts, and pillboxes and buildings in the centre, and it was evident that systematic mopping up would have to be organized. Meanwhile, de Lattre had refused to become absorbed by the operation at Toulon. Keeping in mind the larger picture, he had already, as early as the night of the 20th issued orders for the regrouping of his force with a view to the capture of Marseilles. De Monsabert with his 3rd Algerian Division was to be on the right, and Brosset with his Free French on the left. As de Monsabert with the bulk of his detachment was already outside Marseilles, and Brosset was meeting resistance near the coast east of Toulon, de Lattre entrusted the mopping up of that city to Magnan with his 9th Colonial Division.

By the 24th, although the Germans were still holding out in the naval arsenal and in the promontory to the south of the city, the major part of the city was in French hands. On that day de Lattre decided that the moment had come to enter the city, and beside him in his jeep was William Bullitt, former American Ambassador in Paris, who had obtained de Gaulle's permission to serve in the French Army, and had now joined de Lattre's staff. The situation was by no means ripe for the entry of the Army Commander, and de Lattre and Bullitt had frequently to descend from the jeep and lie flat on their stomachs.

The rest of the Toulon story is quickly told. On the 26th the last remnants of resistance were overcome and on the following day, eight days ahead of schedule, the victorious troops of de Lattre marched through the streets amid scenes of wild enthusiasm.

If the decision to move on Toulon, before his whole force had been concentrated, had been that of a great commander, the decision to launch part of his force on Marseilles, before Toulon had been captured, was almost the stroke of a master. It is only fair to record that it was a course that was urged by some of his subordinate commanders, including du Vigier, but the ultimate responsibility lay with de Lattre. Originally it had been de Lattre's intention merely to send a covering force to reconnoitre in the direction of Marseilles until the capture of Toulon had been achieved, but when de Monsabert and du Vigier made such rapid progress, he decided to engage his relatively small force simultaneously on two battlefields more than thirty miles apart. Again he had broken an elementary principle of war by this dangerous dispersion.

The garrison of Marseilles was comprised mainly of marines, reinforced by practically the whole of the 244th Infantry Division, and units of four other infantry divisions which had been split up by the surprise of the initial landing. At least 200 guns of various calibres were in support of the garrison. A double system of defences encircled the town, the outer of which comprised strongly defended localities astride the four main roads leading into Marseilles. These were respectively at the junction of the roads from Salon and Aix, on the road from Saint-Raphael in the La Pomme–Cadolive area, on the road from Toulon at Aubagne, and on the coast road at Carpiagne. Indeed, the opposition might well have proved formidable, and again there was an element of the gamble in the Commander's decision. Already by the 20th, de Monsabert had been ordered, while concentrating on the encirclement of Toulon, to push on with a portion of his mobile troops to Aubagne, which was the key to the eastern outer defences of Marseilles.

De Lattre's visit to Patch on the 19th had already been more than justified. Apart from the approval which he obtained for his daring design, it was the extra mobility given him by the 1st Combat Command under Sudre, and released by Patch, which enabled him to be so bold. De Lattre achieved much of his success in life through personal contact. He knew his powers of persuasion, and he knew the moment when it was important that he should leave his headquarters, and exercise those powers with his superiors.

By the evening of the 20th, when the battle for Toulon had hardly begun, Sudre with his Combat Command had reached the outskirts of Aubagne. Meanwhile, the remainder of Guillaume's Goums had disembarked. These were light infantrymen of the highest quality, who from 1940 until the Allies landed in North Africa had been kept in existence despite the Armistice Commission, largely through the energy of Guillaume himself in convincing the Commission that they were essential for the preservation of order in North Africa. They had been trained to move lightly equipped, relying mainly on mule transport, and to operate in mountainous country which would be almost inaccessible to the average infantryman. In Italy more than once, moving along the crests of hills, they had outmanœuvred the enemy armour which was tied to the plains. Now they were to prove their skill in dealing with the casemates and pillboxes that protected Marseilles. As soon as they landed, they marched to the sound of the guns and to the support of de Lattre's daring spearheads. In Guillaume they had a commander who was more than worthy of them: probably Guillaume was as fine an infantry commander as the war produced.

Sudre with his 1st Combat Command met heavy resistance at Aubagne and, near Cadolive. For the moment the armour had accomplished as much as could be expected of it, and the infantry now came into their own. On the right, de Monsabert launched two battalions into the almost impassable country known as the Chaîne de l'Étoile. These battalions reached respectively the areas Pilon-du-Roi and Allauch, and in the latter village made contact with a mixed body of Maquis composed of policemen, gendarmes, and labourers. Meanwhile the Goums had reached the scene of action, and one group successfully co-operated with the armour in capturing Cadolive and Aubagne.

With these two important centres in his hands, de Lattre might well have been tempted to push prematurely on Marseilles, but with all his audacity he could combine prudence. The events just briefly described took place on the 21st. Toulon had not yet fallen, and a request had come from General O'Daniel, commanding the 3rd U.S. Division, which had reached Aix, for de Lattre to cover his left flank and to extend his front northward to the Durance. Moreover, on the same day de Lattre was warned of the presence of the 11th Panzer Division west of Aix. The moment had come to take stock. His subordinates had been given their heads, and all obstacles had been taken in their stride. But, before the last fence, it would be wise to collect them.

On the afternoon of the 22nd, therefore, de Lattre assembled de Larminat, de Monsabert, and Guillaume at Gemenos. Brosset, with his Free French Division, was still heavily engaged east of Toulon, and therefore would not be available for the battle for Marseilles. He had no intention of penetrating into the heart of the city with insufficient means, or before the encirclement of the city had become tighter. Moreover, the more the enemy could be drawn towards the perimeter, the more chance there would be of avoiding street fighting and all the destruction that it would entail. He therefore traced an arbitrary line on the map, which corresponded roughly with the boundary between the suburbs and the main part of the city. Until that line was reached by the investing troops, no attempt was to be made to enter Marseilles.

The other main decisions reached at Gemenos were as follows: 1st Combat Command was to leave two squadrons of Shermans with de Monsabert for mopping up Marseilles, and immediately to send another detachment to relieve the 3rd U.S. Infantry Division near the Reservoir de Realtor, with the special task of protecting the aqueduct over which passed the water supply for Marseilles. Eventually du Vigier was to have both Combat Commands under him, so that the 1st Armoured Division would no longer be split. The Division was to relieve all American units west of the road Marseilles–Aix–Avignon, and to pave the way for the advance of the army to Avignon and the Rhône. For the final advance on Marseilles, de Monsabert's 3rd Algerian Division was to be in the centre while one group of Guillaume's Goums would operate on either flank.

On the 23rd, the leading elements of the 3rd Algerian Division reached the line beyond which de Lattre had forbidden any advance until further orders. The subordinate commanders on the spot now found themselves in a quandary. Beyond that line, groups of the Forces Françaises de l'Intérieur (F.F.I.) and indeed the whole civil population were urging the French to come on, but their orders were quite definite—they must halt where they were; and yet the spirit behind de Lattre's original instructions issued before the operations started had been equally clear—there was need for speed in the fearless exploitation of every favourable opportunity. The loop-hole was there, and Chappuis, the local commander, did not hesitate to exploit it; the urge was too great, so on he went. De Monsabert himself was equally hard to restrain. Before even the mopping up had started, he installed himself in the heart of the city. By all the books he was wrong, and liaison officers and others had precarious moments in trying to reach him—"It was quite a game," said de Lattre, "to reach de Monsabert: one had more often than not to crawl on one's stomach." In theory de Monsabert may have been wrong, but there are always moments when the presence of the commander in the fore-front of the battle can be fully justified. The moral effect upon the hesitant can be immeasurable.

From the 24th to 26th August, there took place at Marseilles two operations, each with an entirely distinct character. There was the battle to clear up the heart of the city, and the battle outside to subdue those many defence works which the Germans had strengthened with such devoted labour. The task of clearing up the inside of the city fell mainly upon Sudre, with his Shermans and a battalion of Algerians. The character of the fighting presented extraordinary contrasts. In one street, which had fallen to the French, their tanks and armoured cars would be greeted by groups of girls showering flowers and kisses upon the victors. Round the next corner, the French would come into a street where the enemy were still holding out. When de Monsabert's spearhead reached the Old Port, there was in effect behind him only a long thin line of troops with no depth, stretching back to Aubagne. North and south of it, the Germans were still ensconced all over the city. Fortunately the enemy were slow to grasp a situation which might easily have turned to their advantage, and, as the precious moments slipped by, groups of F.F.I reinforced de Monsabert's leading elements and played an invaluable part in the final reduction of the city.

As early as the evening of the 22nd, de Monsabert had established contact with Schaeffer, commanding the Marseilles sector, but the latter refused to accept de Monsabert's conditions, and the fight continued. The main objective within the city was the extensive dock area, about four miles in length, but the key to that area was the forbidding feature of Notre Dame de la Garde which the Germans had not failed to strengthen. It needed a full-scale assault with the maximum artillery support to capture it.

It will be remembered that on either flank of the 3rd Algerian Division were groups of Guillaume's Goums, and it fell to their lot to clear up the defences north and south of the city. These works had absorbed the energies of the "Todt" organization for two years, and the one which gave the most trouble was in the area of the road junction at Gavotte, where the road from Aix joins that from Salon. Here the Germans had constructed defence works composed of concrete as much as twelve feet thick. This formidable redoubt, with its garrison of 11,000 and its inexhaustible supplies of food and ammunition, held out for four days, and inflicted heavy casualties upon the attackers.

By the 26th, Toulon had fallen, and reinforcements were hurried west to support the final efforts in Marseilles. On the 27th Marseilles fell. Schaeffer had refused to surrender until the very end, and, in recognition of his gallantry, de Lattre allowed him to retain his personal weapons.

While the struggle for Marseilles reached its concluding phases, the stage had been set for the next advance. Du Vigier had not wasted his time. In addition to his own division he now had Brosset's Free French Division under him. On the evening of the 24th he reached Arles and Tarascon, and on the 25th was at Avignon.

It had been a memorable and breath-taking gallop. Under the impulsion of their leader, cavalrymen, infantrymen, gunners, and everyone, had been determined to push on, and had reached the port a month sooner than had been expected. Allied Force Headquarters had contributed a full and difficult share, for the landing had been planned in a short time, and in the face of continued uncertainty. With superb efficiency, the Allied navies had put the Seventh Army ashore, and Patch had exploited his initial success with befitting energy. To Patch also is due no small measure of credit for deciding to give de Lattre his head, for he too was sharing the risk.

The operations had provided a refreshing contrast to those in which the 14th Infantry Division had been engaged four years earlier, and yet they had one characteristic in common. In both campaigns de Lattre had committed his forces piecemeal into action. The military pedant might well argue that he broke the principle of concentration, but blind and rigid adherence to principles will never make a great leader, and the timely arrival of a platoon can often be more effective than the belated arrival of a division. Risks he certainly took, but they had been calculated. If ever a commander practised what he preached, it was de Lattre during those stirring days between the 17th and 27th August, 1944. Speed in exploiting opportunities had been the keyword in his instructions, and he himself set off at full gallop.

The quick decision to carry out simultaneously the attacks on Toulon and Marseilles was one of the most masterly which he ever made, and it needed more than ordinary confidence in his own capacity to go through with it in the face of his doubting superiors. He had faith in himself, faith in his troops, and faith too in the part which the F.F.I. might play in the interior of Toulon and Marseilles. The speed with which he acted maintained the effect of the initial surprise, and prevented the timely reaction of the enemy. Almost before they realized that Toulon was threatened, the Germans in Marseilles found themselves pinned, and unable to move to the help of their comrades in the other city. In one fell swoop they had been immobilized.

Apart from the loss of several thousands killed, the enemy left 37,000 prisoners in the hands of the French, including 700 officers. The French had a total of about 4,000 casualties. It was not that the enemy did not fight—he fought magnificently, and when it became necessary to assault his defence works the French losses were heavy. But the speed and skill of manœuvre, particularly on the part of the armour and of Guillaume's Goums, reduced losses to the minimum, as did the policy of bold infiltration.

The effect which the early fall of Toulon and Marseilles had on the subsequent course of the campaign is not easy to calculate. The speed of events had prevented the complete demolition of the harbours, but even so, they presented a shambles that looked like

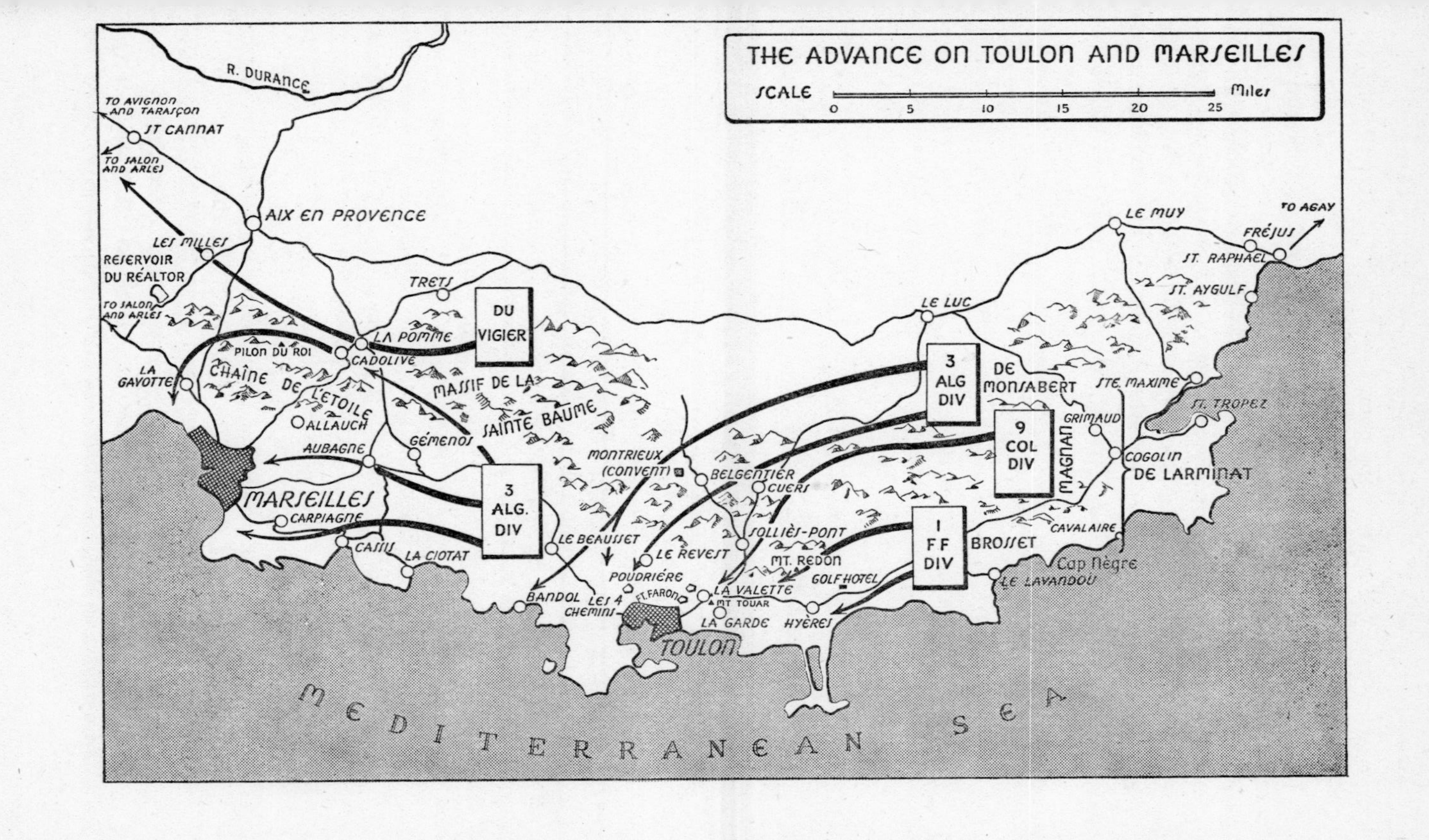
THE ADVANCE ON TOULON AND MARSEILLES
SCALE
0
5
10
15
20
25
Miles
R. DURANCE
TO AVIGNON AND TARASÇON
ST CANNAT
TO SALON AND ARLES
AIX EN PROVENCE
LES MILLES
RESERVOIR DU RÉALTOR
TO SALON AND ARLES
TRETS
DU VIGIER
LA POMME
CADOLIVE
PILON DU ROI
LA GAVOTTE
CHAÎNE DE L'ETOILE
ALLAUCH
MASSIF DE LA SAINTE BAUME
GÉMENOS
AUBAGNE
MARSEILLES
CARPIAGNE
CASSIS
LA CIOTAT
3 ALG. DIV
LE BEAUSSET
BANDOL
LES 4 CHEMINS
FT. FARON
POUDRIÈRE
LE REVEST
MONTRIEUX (CONVENT)
BELGENTIER
CUERS
SOLLIÈS-PONT
MT. REDON
LA VALETTE
MT TOUAR
LA GARDE
TOULON
HYÈRES
GOLF HOTEL
LE LUC
3 ALG DIV
DE MONSABERT
9 COL DIV
MAGNAN
1 FF DIV
BROSSET
CAVALAIRE
Cap Nègre
LE LAVANDOU
GRIMAUD
COGOLIN
DE LARMINAT
STE. MAXIME
ST. TROPEZ
LE MUY
FRÉJUS
TO AGAY
ST. RAPHAEL
ST. AYGULF
MEDITERRANEAN SEA

taking months to repair. In the event, the first Liberty ship was able to dock on the 15th September, and from then until the end of the war, several divisions were disembarked at ports in the South of France, and an average of 18,000 tons of stores a day. But it was upon de Lattre's army itself that the effect was so pronounced. In a few days it had acquired a spirit that has rarely been equalled, and never surpassed.

20. NORTHWARD

MEANWHILE, the U.S. VI Corps, moving on Grenoble, and extending its front westward, had reached the Rhône, where it threatened to cut off remnants of the Nineteenth German Army withdrawing northward (see map on p. 159). These were receiving full punishment from the air, as they streamed back along that road which so many have travelled on their way to the French Riviera. De Lattre was now ordered to find garrisons for Toulon and Marseilles, and also to protect the right flank of the Seventh Army facing the Alps, and to carry out reconnaissances west of the Rhône. He had always feared that the operations for the capture of the two great ports would result in his being "trapped", as he called it, and only being able to follow up behind the Americans, instead of abreast of them. The orders which he now received confirmed his worst fears. Indeed they were most distasteful, for the eyes of the whole army were on Alsace.

De Lattre's impatience knew no bounds. He foresaw the Americans linking up with that other difficult and impatient subordinate, George Patton, commanding the Third U.S. Army advancing from Brittany, before his own would have a chance. Once again, therefore, he decided to harass his superiors. Hastening to Patch's headquarters, where he found Maitland Wilson and Devers, he put forward his own views with his usual force. The visit was not ineffective. He persuaded Patch to allow the main body of his army to follow up the U.S. VI Corps to Grenoble with a view to slipping in later between the right of that corps and the Swiss frontier.

The arrangement which de Lattre made with Patch was not an entirely satisfactory compromise, for initially it would involve the splitting of his army into two groups, separated by the U.S. VI Corps in the centre. On the right would be his main force, comprising de Monsabert's 3rd Algerian Division, Magnan's 9th Colonial Division, and Dody's 2nd Moroccan Division, which was just disembarking. On the left would be du Vigier, with the 1st Armoured Division, who had been directed to cross the Rhône at Avignon, and also Brosset's Free French Division. The ultimate intention of de Lattre after the capture of Lyons, was for du Vigier to side-step to the right, and join the main group of the Army, which would then become responsible for the front between the Swiss frontier and the River Saône, its axis of advance being Besançon–Belfort–Alsace.

De Lattre retained his headquarters at Aix, where he would be in touch not only with Patch but also with du Vigier, for it was the progress of du Vigier at that moment which interested him most. The sooner du Vigier was on the move, the sooner would French troops be in action again, and be able to share the honour of capturing Lyons. Before du Vigier's force could be unleashed or even begin its northward move, it would have to cross the Rhône, which in the Avignon area is at least 250 yards wide. Every bridge had been destroyed, and no provision had been made for any heavy bridging equipment to be available so soon after landing: in fact, no crossing of the Rhône had been envisaged for several weeks. But with de Lattre it was useless for his engineers to raise technical difficulties. The impossible had got to be achieved, and de Lattre himself spent many hours at the three crossing places selected at Arles, Vallabrègues, and Avignon. Every conceivable means of fortune was brought into use, and by superhuman improvisation on the part of Dromond, Chief Engineer of the Army, du Vigier was across the Rhône in forty-eight hours. Of all the people whom de Lattre drove hard during the course of his life, none were driven harder than his engineers. The crossing of the Rhône was not the only difficulty that delayed du Vigier. If bridging equipment was lacking, so also were fuel and transport, but the French capacity for improvisation triumphed, and du Vigier swept northward.

Under the threat of envelopment from the east and the west, and under pressure from the F.F.I. within the city, the Germans withdrew to Dijon, and Lyons fell on the 3rd September. With a delicacy and grace that pleased de Lattre, the Americans conceded to the Free French Division the honour of entering the city first. Meanwhile du Vigier's armour, which had moved round Lyons to the west, cut off a number of Germans to the north, and apart from killed, the Germans lost 2,000 prisoners.

De Lattre tended to regard this stage of the operations as a race between his own main group on the right, the VI U.S. Corps in the centre, and du Vigier on the left. By the 3rd September, partly as a result of a strong counter-attack by the 11th Panzer Division against the U.S. VI Corps near Bourg, the competitors were level, and de Lattre's right group, headed by the 3rd Algerian Division, forged slightly ahead.

Although de Lattre's attention was focused on Alsace, he could not neglect the reconnaissance which he had been ordered to make south-west from Avignon into the Languedoc. No threat materialized from that area, but a fleeting visit which he made to the detachment carrying out the reconnaissance gave him an opportunity of living again those dramatic moments at Montpellier, when, two years before, his efforts to save the honour of the French Army had landed him in prison.

By the beginning of September, de Lattre had reorganized his divided army into two corps. The right group became I Corps, and was given to Bethouart, who had arrived from Italy; the left group under du Vigier became II Corps and was given to de Monsabert, who handed over his beloved 3rd Algerian Division to Guillaume, who in turn did not leave his Goums without much heartburning.

Early in September, another change of plan was again to displease de Lattre. The U.S. VI Corps was to change direction north-east, and make for Belfort, with a view to cutting off the remnants of the German Nineteenth Army and other German troops retreating on Alsace. The French, in turn, were to be switched from their original axis of advance, and to move on Macon–Dijon–Épinal–Strasbourg. The proposed plan would mean that the leading elements of the 3rd Algerian Division, which had so successfully forged ahead on the right of VI U.S. Corps would be deprived of the opportunity of exploiting their success. To withdraw them at that moment, and switch them over to the left, would involve a most inopportune delay. Truscott, commanding the U.S. VI Corps, with a comprehension that de Lattre fully appreciated, allowed him to exploit the advance of the 3rd Algerian Division, and I Corps was now directed east of Besançon on Belfort, while II Corps was to move on Dijon and Épinal. At the same time, that corps was to establish touch with the right of Patton's army advancing from Brittany. Thus the two corps of de Lattre's army were still on either flank of the U.S. VI Corps.

After the loss of south-eastern France, the main preoccupation of the Commander of the Nineteenth German Army was the defence of the Belfort Gap, which was the gateway to Alsace and the Rhine. He was anxious, therefore, to delay the Allies round Dijon and Beaune, with a view to being able to withdraw to Belfort not only as much as possible of his own army, but also elements of the First German Army retreating from the West. Wiese's task would be eased by the fact that the Franco-American forces were still being supplied from the beaches of southern France. Indeed, their administrative machinery, which was being taxed to its extreme limits, dictated a halt. Wiese, on the other hand, was falling back on vast stocks which had been accumulated in Alsace during the occupation, and he was able effectively to delay Bethouart.

On the left, de Monsabert continued to impart to the newly-formed II Corps the same vigour with which du Vigier had driven forward the 1st Armoured Division. After a hard fight for Autun, by a detachment under Demetz, later to be de Lattre's Chief of Staff, Dijon was outflanked, and it was in that fight that Bernard de Lattre was wounded. On the 12th September, the left flank of the Franco-American forces, which had landed on the Riviera, linked up with the right of Eisenhower's armies who had landed in Normandy. For the French it was a great moment, for near the right of Patton's Third Army was General Leclerc's 2nd Armoured Division. The nucleus of that famous Division had marched from Lake Chad in West Africa, and across the desert to

North Africa, where it had linked up with Montgomery's Eighth Army. Then it had been moved to England, and, after landing in Normandy, had been the first to enter Paris.

The Higher Command was now reorganized. Devers, until now deputy to Maitland Wilson, was given command of the new 6th Army Group, which was to include Patch's Seventh Army and de Lattre's army, which now gained its independence from the Seventh Army, and was to become the First French Army. The new Army Group was to come under Eisenhower. Except for certain administrative purposes, the link with the Mediterranean had been severed.

The rôle of the First French Army would be to operate on the extreme right flank of Eisenhower's Army, and its line of operations would now be eastward, and not northward. At the time these decisions were reached, Bethouart's I Corps on the right was held by the enemy south of Belfort, and away on the left, beyond U.S. VI Corps, was de Monsabert's II Corps advancing north-eastwards, and in contact with the enemy west of Vesoul and north of Langres. To switch that corps east, so that it could operate immediately on the left of I Corps, would necessitate crossing the line of advance of U.S. VI Corps, itself in contact with the enemy and advancing north. To effect this awkward reshuffle in contact with the enemy was by no means easy.

By the 12th September, when the junction had been effected with Eisenhower's right wing, de Lattre had covered the four hundred miles from the shores of the Mediterranean to the foothills of the Vosges in three weeks. His transport resources had not been lavish; indeed he had been continually improvising, and incurring a measure of unpopularity by depriving one formation of its lorries to give greater mobility to another, whose speed of advance was more important. Engineering and other equipment also was lacking, and when due account is taken of these handicaps, the performance of his army may be regarded as remarkable. It was weeks ahead of the time-table. But bigger fences loomed ahead.

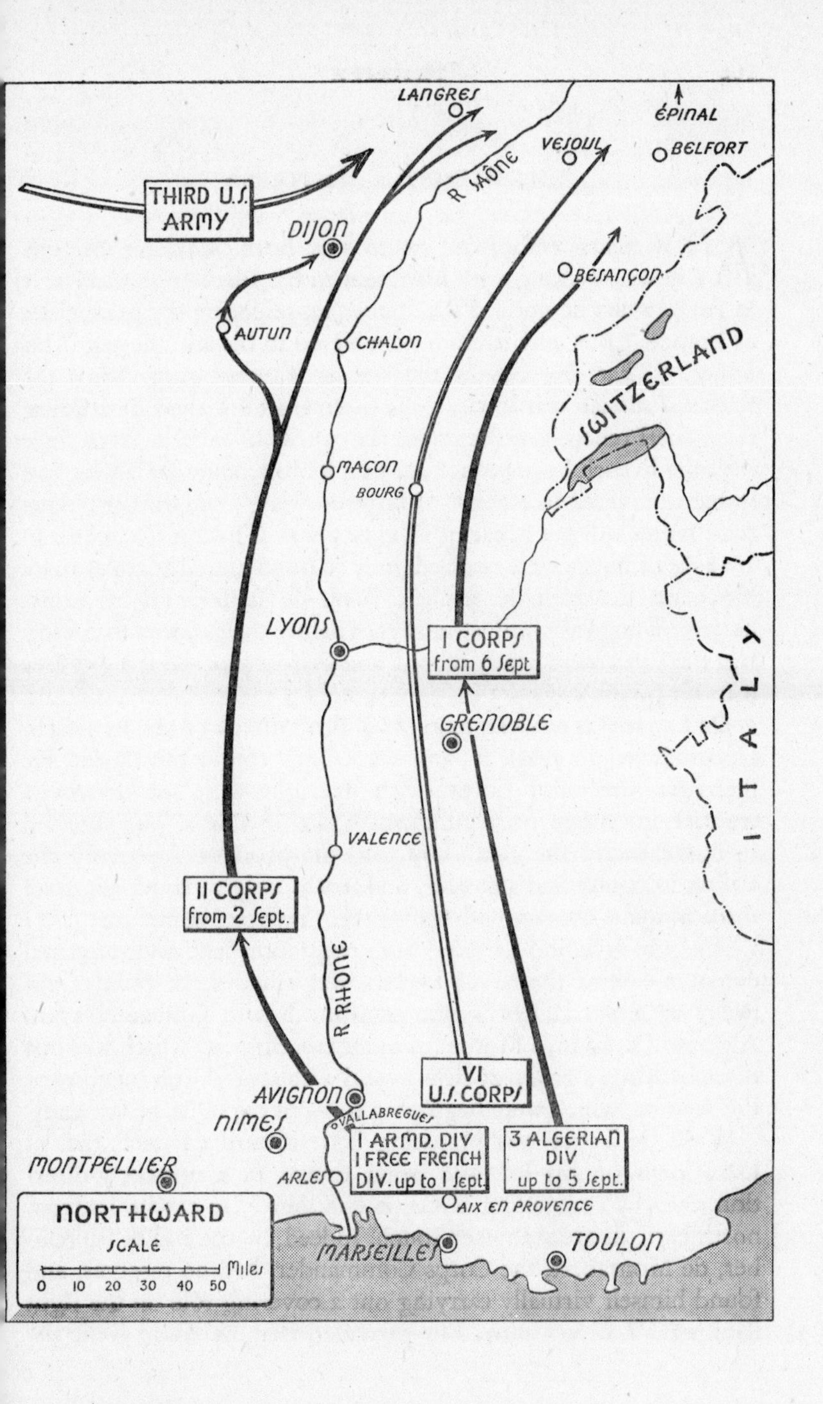
LANGRES
ÉPINAL
VESOUL
BELFORT
R SAÔNE
THIRD U.S. ARMY
DIJON
BESANÇON
AUTUN
CHALON
SWITZERLAND
MACON
BOURG
LYONS
I CORPS from 6 Sept
GRENOBLE
ITALY
VALENCE
II CORPS from 2 Sept.
R RHONE
VI U.S. CORPS
AVIGNON
VALLABREGUES
NIMES
I ARMD. DIV I FREE FRENCH DIV. up to 1 Sept.
3 ALGERIAN DIV up to 5 Sept.
MONTPELLIER
ARLES
AIX EN PROVENCE
NORTHWARD
SCALE
0 10 20 30 40 50 Miles
MARSEILLES
TOULON

21. BIGGER FENCES

A FEW years before de Lattre was born, a young English boy was walking with his father in the Place de la Concorde in Paris, when he noticed the statues representing the great cities of France. "But why is that one covered in black?" he asked his father. "That, my boy is the statue of Strasbourg. After the Franco-Prussian war in 1871, the Germans took away Strasbourg from the French, together with the whole of Alsace. Ever since then the French have been mourning its loss, and that is why that statue is covered in black." "I hope one day," said the boy, "that the French will get it back." The boy was Winston Churchill. In 1918 those hopes were realized, only to be shattered again in 1940. Now, on the 20th September, 1944, de Lattre and his army, having swung eastward, stood again before the gateway to Alsace. But the gates were firmly barred, and Belfort blocked the way (see map on p. 167).

De Lattre was anxious to avoid a direct attack on the fort itself. He preferred to mask it, and manœuvre round the flanks. He therefore directed I Corps, with its right wing on the Swiss frontier, to move on Mulhouse, while II Corps was directed to move round the north and into the plain of Alsace by the Ballon D'Alsace and Bussang, and it was only to employ a small force to make contact with the western defences of the fort. To I Corps, which would be faced with continuous and well-prepared defences east of the River Doubs, was allotted the bulk of the heavy artillery. II Corps was reinforced with Guillaume's 3rd Algerian Division, a Moroccan mountain division which was just disembarking, a group of Goums and with several Commando and F.F.I. units, which were beginning to swell the ranks of the army.

While de Lattre was preparing his eastward advance, the VI U.S. Corps on his left was being drawn in a northerly direction, thereby compelling II Corps continually to extend its front northward, in order to keep touch. Indeed, by the end of September, de Monsabert, the Corps Commander, had no reserves, and found himself virtually carrying out a covering rôle on the right flank of VI U.S. Corps. But provided that he could limit the extension of de Monsabert's front, de Lattre was anxious still to make his main effort with that corps. He was encouraged by the fact that the Americans seemed hopeful of capturing Gerardmer, and also by the optimism of de Monsabert. Moreover, the supply problem was beginning to cause anxiety, and he was hoping that the project for I Corps on the right, which would entail heavy expenditure of ammunition, might be avoided. His dispositions, however, were still flexible, and if de Monsabert failed on the left, the Army Commander could still switch his main effort to the right.

The fence now in front of him was to prove the biggest he had yet encountered. The enemy was determined to deny access to Alsace. If anyone could succeed in this hilly country, it was Guillaume, but the enemy was not to be displaced. De Monsabert suffered heavy casualties, and his difficulties were increased by the exceptional severity of the weather. But a few weeks before, the men had been sweltering in the heat of a Mediterranean sun: now they shivered and suffered, particularly the native troops, in soaking rain and bitter cold. To be checked at the very gates of Alsace was a great disappointment. At the end of October, with extreme reluctance, de Lattre called off the attack. But if he could not jump the fence to the north, then he would jump it to the south.

In addition to his other difficulties, de Lattre had frequent differences with the Americans at this time, for they tended to assign him a covering rather than an offensive rôle. At the end of October, General Eisenhower's plan for the continuation of the Allied offensive was for the 6th Army Group on the right to take Strasbourg, 12th Army Group in the centre to advance on the Rhine between Mainz and Düsseldorf, and 21st Army Group on the left to advance on Antwerp. It would fall to Patch's Seventh Army to take Strasbourg, so that the task of the First French Army would be limited to protecting the right flank of its American neighbours De Lattre was again dissatisfied, and strongly urged support for his projected advance through the Belfort Gap. Devers showed great comprehension of his subordinate's viewpoint, and preparations for the attack were completed.

Standing at Fort Lomont, near the Swiss frontier, about thirty miles south of Belfort, with its magnificent view to the north-east, de Lattre conceived the outline plan for the impending operations which he divulged to Bethouart, commanding I Corps. The succession of wooded slopes to the north-east struck him as admirably suited to the manœuvre of infantry, who would pave the way for the armour. The main front of the attack would be between the bend in the River Doubs immediately south of Belfort and the forest of Grange. Success would be exploited simultaneously by the reduction of Belfort, after it had been outflanked, and an advance on Montbeliard and the Rhine. The right flank would march with the Swiss frontier.

The attack was to be carried out by I Corps, while II Corps on the left was to remain as aggressive as possible in order to deceive the enemy as to the point of attack. A very thorough cover plan was prepared and de Lattre himself drafted a Personal Instruction, ordering the main effort to be continued on the front of II Corps. Unfortunately the agent who was supposed to pass through the lines and ensure this document falling into the hands of General Wiese, was seized by an over-zealous Moroccan soldier.

Early in November, while his preparations were nearing completion, de Lattre was told by Devers that he was to lose his 1st Armoured and Free French Divisions, which were required for an independent operation for the reduction of Bordeaux. Fuming with anger, he rushed off to Devers, and placed before him the disastrous effect which the loss of these formations would have on his own impending offensive. Devers again gave his angry subordinate a patient hearing, and agreed to the transfer of these formations being deferred.

Appalling weather conditions continued, and some of his subordinate commanders were in favour of the operations being postponed. De Lattre, however, was determined to go through with it on the date decided, the 13th November. He visited Bethouart a few days before, and explained with conviction his reasons for proceeding with the offensive on the appointed date, and infused a little of his own faith into all with whom he came in contact. When dawn broke on the 13th, snow was falling thickly, and to attack was out of the question.

It was curious that the boy who years before, in the Place de la Concorde, had expressed the hope that the French would get back Alsace, should have visited the French Army on the eve of its liberating that province for the second time in thirty years.

During the 13th, in fact, Mr. Churchill, with General de Gaulle, General Sir Alan Brooke, General Juin, and Monsieur Palewski, arrived by train at Besançon, where they were met by de Lattre, and escorted forward towards the battlefield. The blinding snow continued. "You are surely not going to attack in this weather?" asked Mr. Churchill. But de Lattre was determined to keep secret, even from the British Prime Minister, his intention to proceed with the attack, despite the weather; and so he quickly reassured him that it was out of the question.

One of those who had accompanied Mr. Churchill from England on that occasion wrote vividly at the time, not only of the arctic conditions that prevailed, but also of the inspiring morale which animated the First French Army. "As we climbed," runs the account, "the snow thickened and it got colder and colder. . . . I was so proud to be present on this occasion, in this snowbound village, and to be able to drink with all my heart to resurgent France. May God speed and prosper the forthcoming attack. . . . Most of the troops were completing their training. I thought they looked splendid . . . and animated by one desire—to confront the enemy."

Mr. Churchill lunched with de Lattre at his headquarters, and, after luncheon, he proposed the health of the First French Army and its Commander, "Ce Général rusé". At the same luncheon, General de Gaulle spoke also, and paid an unusually generous tribute to Mr. Churchill, whom he described as "Le Clemenceau de cette Guerre".

At midday on the 14th, despite little improvement in the weather, I Corps went forward to the attack. The 338th Volksgrenadier Division was holding the front between the Swiss frontier and the Besançon–Belfort road, and it was upon that division that the weight of the French artillery bombardment fell. The divisional commander was killed, and upon him were found the complete dispositions of his division. This greatly helped the French. After three days fighting, they had by the evening of the 17th captured Montbeliard, Hericourt, and other important centres.

Although Belfort itself was still held, de Lattre decided that the moment for exploitation had come. Du Vigier's 1st Armoured Division was therefore placed under command of Bethouart, and ordered to exploit towards the Rhine at Huningue. De Lattre now had the 5th Armoured Division under his own hand, and it was his intention, if du Vigier succeeded, to push that division behind him with a view to wheeling northward, and exploiting towards Colmar and the Rhine crossings at Brisach. The right of II Corps was also now ordered to advance through Giromagny on Rougemont.

The Army Commander's orders for the 18th entailed the putting into effect simultaneously of three distinct operations on the front of I Corps: the reduction of the Belfort fortress by the infantry, the exploitation eastward to the Rhine by the 1st Armoured Division, and the initial move of the 5th Armoured Division with a view to eventual exploitation northward. The formations concerned needed little driving, and at six-thirty on the evening of the 19th October, the leading elements of du Vigier's 1st Armoured Division reached the Rhine, ahead of all the Allies on that front. For the officers and men of that division the moment must have been the proudest in their lives. "Bravo with all my heart", wrote de Lattre to du Vigier.

As Belfort still held out, de Lattre now relieved I Corps of any responsibility for its capture. A special group, acting directly under Army would become responsible for this task. Bethouart was to apply all his energy to enable the 5th Armoured Division to debouch northward. The key for this movement was the establishment of a bridgehead across the canal at Fontaine, and de Lattre laid special emphasis on the importance of this being achieved at the earliest moment. Bethouart's ultimate rôle was to capture Mulhouse and secure a footing on the banks of the Rhine. In the event, this ambitious project could not be realized. The bottleneck east of Belfort would not take the mass of vehicles belonging to the tail of du Vigier's division, as well as those of the 5th Armoured Division. There was an appalling traffic jam, which was only disentangled after valuable hours had passed.

It was only on the 25th that Belfort was completely in French hands, and it was from the north that it was eventually taken. Meanwhile II Corps, reduced to two divisions, was holding a front of forty miles, and making difficult progress. By the 22nd November, therefore, the First French Army had become dangerously extended, and extremely vulnerable. It was virtually disposed in the shape of a U, of which the eastern branch, running from Mulhouse to Altkirch was the shorter. The longer branch to the west ran along the Vosges. At the bottom, the two branches of the U were joined by an ill-defined line adjacent to the Swiss frontier. The enemy commander saw his opportunity, and decided to move swiftly south, with a view to splitting the First French Army in two at the bottom of the U. This move by Wiese coincided with the difficulties of the French 5th Armoured Division, and might well have had serious consequences if it had been pushed with greater vigour. But if de Lattre was vulnerable, Wiese also might be made vulnerable. His forces moving south might well be encircled and trapped if the French could close the top of the U by effecting a junction between I and II Corps near Burnhaupt.

Meanwhile, to the north, General Leclerc with his 2nd Armoured Division had captured Strasbourg. If only the Americans had now had available a large enough force to move south from Strasbourg, the encircling manœuvre which de Lattre was planning might have been effected on an even grander scale. Moreover, the securing of the Rhine between Switzerland and Strasbourg would have permitted considerable economy of force. But this was not to be. An equally determined cavalryman, who had galloped across France from west to east, was exploiting success to the north, and more interest centred on his front than on Alsace. The First French Army must therefore act alone.

By the 28th November, the junction between the I and II Corps was effected at Burnhaupt, but only fractions of the German LXIII Corps were cut off. However, in the last three weeks, the French had captured 17,000 prisoners, and 120 guns, while several thousand of the enemy had been killed. They were still fighting well, and the defence of this front, which was the left flank of the German Armies opposing Eisenhower had now been entrusted to Himmler.

At the beginning of December, the situation in Alsace was briefly as follows. To the south, de Lattre had forced the Belfort Gap and reached the Rhine, while to the north, the Americans and Leclerc's division had forced the Saverne Gap and reached Strasbourg. Between them, there bulged westward into the Allied line a strong German pocket that came to be known as the Colmar pocket. Himmler's orders were to retain this bridgehead to the west of the upper Rhine at all costs. If the low priority which SHAEF (Supreme Headquarters Allied Expeditionary Force) accorded to the reduction of this pocket was a bitter blow to de Lattre, who had made such prodigious efforts to reach the Rhine, the American viewpoint is easy to understand. The Colmar pocket could be mopped up later, and should not prove difficult, for the enemy appeared to be in a most vulnerable salient, and his supply lines across the Rhine would offer an excellent target to the Allied Air Forces. But already in Italy, under similar conditions, with their communications across the Po being continually bombed, the Germans had successfully clung on for many weeks to their positions south of that river. Indeed, their position at Colmar was not so weak as would appear, for while they had the advantage of interior lines, the ability of the Allies to move troops from one point to another was handicapped by the Vosges. These advantages fully justified the German attempt to stand at Colmar. No less than nine infantry divisions, many of them relatively fresh, and two armoured brigades were poured into the pocket. Only in armour were the Allies superior, but that advantage was offset by enemy demolitions and also by extensive flooding in the area.

In face of the new situation, Devers decided to give de Lattre command of the whole of the Colmar sector. This necessitated a considerable extension of his front, and Devers therefore placed the 36th U.S. Infantry Division and Leclerc's 2nd Armoured Division under the command of de Lattre. Even so, the First French Army was much extended.

Proud as de Lattre was that Devers should have sufficient confidence in him to place American troops under his command, he was beginning to feel anxious about morale, which is ever vulnerable, even when it has reached those heights to which de Lattre had brought that of the First French Army. Few commanders could raise morale as he, but he quickly sensed when it was in danger. The spectacular successes which for more than three months had marked the campaign had only been achieved through superhuman efforts. The limit of human endurance had almost now been reached, and the check before Colmar, combined with the increasing fall of snow began to take toll. Moreover, a

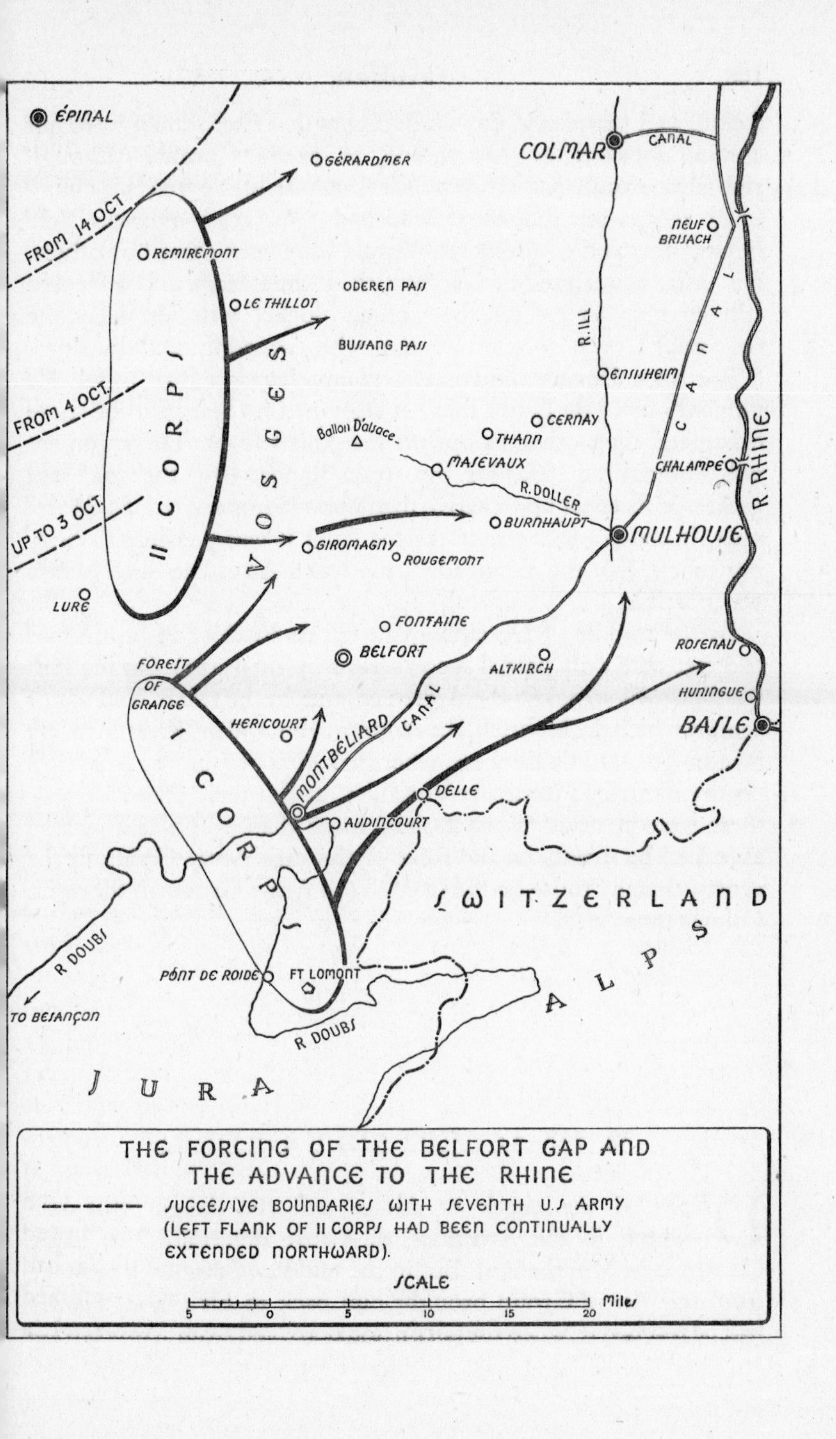

THE FORCING OF THE BELFORT GAP AND THE ADVANCE TO THE RHINE

– – – – – SUCCESSIVE BOUNDARIES WITH SEVENTH U.S ARMY (LEFT FLANK OF II CORPS HAD BEEN CONTINUALLY EXTENDED NORTHWARD).

feeling had permeated the whole Army that Frenchmen were not coming forward, as they should, to swell its ranks. Although resistance groups of every political colour had given a helping hand, it was felt that those who had come from overseas were bearing the whole burden that should have been shared by others. De Lattre acquainted de Gaulle with all these fears, and as he was still anxious to reduce the Colmar pocket without delay, he requested Devers to reinforce him with two additional divisions.

For once Devers showed less comprehension than usual. He pointed out to de Lattre that his army had no reason to be more exhausted than other troops on the Allied front. The argument was not entirely fair, for the strain imposed by the cold was greater in its effect upon native than upon European troops. Moreover, in many other sectors of the front it was possible to carry out reliefs. For the extended First French Army, no such luxury was possible.

By the middle of December, the efforts to close in on Colmar had met with only partial success (see map on p. 183). On the 18th the Germans struck in the Ardennes, and, in the thinly held sector against which the blow fell, the enemy made rapid progress. Anxiety is often greater at a distance, where rumours accumulate, than it is on the battlefield itself. At Versailles, at Supreme Headquarters, there were anxious moments, and more than ever was attention absorbed by events on the front of the 12th Army Group in the centre, than by those on the front of 6th Army Group on the right. Colmar must wait.

22. UNACCEPTABLE ORDERS

DESPITE the check in Alsace and the danger that still hovered in the Ardennes, de Lattre determined to enjoy Christmas at Montbeliard. But in the middle of dinner, a message from 6th Army Group brought him back to his office. Hardly had he reached it, when the tall du Souzy arrived from Army Group

Headquarters. Du Souzy in his youth had been a member of that imposing team of officers that always adorned the entourage of Lyautey in Morocco. Now he was acting as de Lattre's liaison officer at Devers' headquarters. Du Souzy and Senator Cabot Lodge were frequently called upon during those momentous days to smooth over difficulties that arose between Devers and his difficult and temperamental subordinate. Referring to these moments after the war, Devers wrote:

> "General de Lattre never spoke a word of English to me, although I believe he understood English much better than I realized. I cannot speak French, and in a heated discussion understood it not at all. My interpreter was Colonel Cabot Lodge, and de Lattre's was Colonel Édouard du Souzy. Both of these men were excellent soldiers and politicians, and each understood the language of the other as well as he understood his own. We made an excellent team. General de Lattre and I both understood that common language, the gesture and the smile. It is wonderful what your ancestors give you as weapons for solving the difficult problems of life."

This is a most modest account, giving no hint of the extreme patience and comprehension that Devers so often showed, and to which French officers on de Lattre's staff at the time have often testified. Senator Cabot Lodge had a great admiration for de Lattre: he said he had never met a man he liked more, and described him as one of the great men of his life.

De Lattre saw, as soon as du Souzy entered his office, that all was not well at Devers' headquarters. Briefly, the situation was this. Patton, commanding the Third U.S. Army on the left of Devers was to attack the southern flank of the bulge created by the enemy thrust in the Ardennes. In order to give Patton the required strength for his counterstroke, his own front was to be reduced, while that of Devers was to be extended. The anxiety which this project gave Devers may well be imagined, for he himself had reason to believe the enemy was preparing to attack his own front in the neighbourhood of Bitche (see map on p. 187). Acquainted with this anxiety, Eisenhower made it clear that rather than risk another enemy penetration, the 6th Army Group must be prepared, in the event of heavy pressure, to carry out a withdrawal.

The information which du Souzy gave de Lattre made it clear

that the abandonment of a part of Alsace, so recently and dearly won, was already in the minds of his superiors. With that anxiety weighing heavily on his mind, he attended midnight mass. Afterwards he assembled some of his staff, and with them, as was his custom, he thought aloud until the early hours. If the attack which Devers feared to the north of his front were in fact to develop, it was more than probable that it would be combined with a northward thrust on the part of the enemy from the Colmar Gap. More than ever, therefore, was it imperative to reduce the Colmar pocket, and, as the dawn broke, de Lattre traced the outline plan for its reduction. Although grim events were to delay its execution, the plan as then traced was to stand.

Devers visited de Lattre on the 26th December, and confirmed the information which du Souzy had given him the previous day. De Lattre put forward with his usual force his argument in favour of the immediate reduction of the Colmar pocket, but Devers could give him little assurance, beyond a promise to reconsider the project as soon as the crisis had passed. The crisis did not quickly pass; a few days later it was to reach its climax.

Devers followed up his visit with written instructions to prepare for a withdrawal to the Vosges. Unhappy as de Lattre was with the turn of events, he tried to remain loyal to the spirit, if not to the letter, of Devers' orders. In his own instructions, he refused to refer to withdrawal, or indeed to mention anything that might create a defeatist atmosphere. He made it clear that the task of the First French Army was to maintain intact the present front, with a view to covering, on the right, the Belfort Gap, and, on the left, Strasbourg and the right flank of the Seventh U.S. Army. De Lattre sent a copy of these instructions to Devers, together with a personal letter setting out once again his own views, and emphasizing in particular his anxiety to resume the projected offensive at an early date.

One hour before the New Year, the Germans struck north-west of Strasbourg, with a view to seizing the Saverne Gap. The Americans gave ground, but the enemy was held. On the afternoon of New Year's Day, Eisenhower instructed Devers on the telephone, in order to prevent VI U.S. Corps on the right of his Seventh Army being trapped in a salient, to withdraw at once to the Vosges. In fact, Alsace and Strasbourg were to be abandoned.

For various reasons, news of the above decision did not reach de Lattre until late on the 2nd January, but his own intuition, reinforced by suspicions on the part of du Souzy, had already caused him to write to Devers. Strasbourg, he argued, was a symbol of the resistance and grandeur of France. To abandon it now would create throughout France doubts about victory. Throughout the world, too, there would be repercussions, and in Germany, on the verge of defeat, morale would be exalted. Despite his limited resources, he would do all in his power to cover Strasbourg to the south. He therefore begged Devers to order the Seventh U.S. Army to hold on to that city at all costs, drawing his attention to the reprisals to which its inhabitants would be subjected if it were abandoned. The military honour and prestige of the Allies were at stake.

But the worst had already happened. Just before midnight on the 2nd January, de Lattre received orders to withdraw his left to the Vosges by the morning of the 5th. The forward defences of his present position were to be lightly held with highly mobile troops, capable of hasty withdrawal. "Ça, non!" was de Lattre's reaction. He was white with anger. The execution of such an order would spell disaster of unpredictable magnitude. Often in war, the military and political factors dictate opposing courses, but rarely have they so dramatically conflicted as they did in those opening days of the year 1945, on the battlefield of Alsace. On purely military grounds, the holding of Strasbourg was hard to justify. If the new German thrust should reach the Saverne Gap, the withdrawal of all the Franco-American forces in northern Alsace would be cut off. In short, the retention of Strasbourg would invite a major diaster. It is difficult to criticize Eisenhower for his decision. He and others at Supreme Headquarters fully appreciated all that Strasbourg meant to France, but at so critical a juncture, it would have been difficult for anyone but a Frenchman to give the same weight to considerations of sentiment, as to the hard indisputable military factors that dictated a withdrawal to the Vosges. But sentiment on this occasion was inextricably interwoven with morale, and it was not only the morale of the First French Army which would be affected; it went deeper than that. De Lattre had not overstated his case. The Allies were championing the cause of freedom: to have abandoned the inhabitants of Alsace, so recently freed, to a fate the cruelty of which is hard to imagine, would have caused the free and trusting world to doubt.

Never was de Lattre more determined than he was at that moment. Only over his dead body would Strasbourg fall. He himself would take on the defence of the city. He would send one of his best divisions, Guillaume's 3rd Algerian Division, to hold it. That division was about to enjoy a long-promised rest. But on the 3rd January, de Lattre sent for its commander. He and Guillaume had known each other intimately since Morocco. Guillaume, blunt and frank, feared less than most to speak his mind. He had a difficult journey over the ice-covered roads to de Lattre's headquarters at Montbeliard, and did not arrive until late at night. For once, de Lattre was in bed, for he had a chill. When given his orders, Guillaume protested that his division had been fighting without a pause since the 6th October, and that some units had even been fighting since the 15th August. Already his front was very extended, and he only had one battalion in reserve. "Never mind" said de Lattre, "I am counting on you. The thing is to get off to Strasbourg at once yourself, and get as much of your division as possible to follow immediately. Later we will see what we can do to relieve some of your units. But it is essential to act quickly. You will have the honour of saving Strasbourg, so don't grumble."

Describing the scene later, de Lattre said that Guillaume groused a little, like the "grognards" (grumblers) of Napoleon's guards, but that he went off, and, as usual, did his job superbly. Guillaume has written of these events as follows:

> "The instantaneous decision of de Lattre, the direct and human contact with the commander responsible for the operation, and the rapid execution of his orders that resulted, were the basic reasons for the failure of the last attacks of the enemy on Strasbourg, and the unequalled valour of the troops was once more to justify the most audacious conceptions of the Army Commander."

De Lattre brought pressure to bear through every source he knew, to ensure the cancellation of the orders to abandon Strasbourg. Allies were not lacking. Already in Paris both de Gaulle and Juin had taken up the cudgels, and Mr. Churchill too flew over from England. At a conference at Supreme Headquarters on the 3rd January, it was agreed that Strasbourg should be held, and de Lattre was informed of this decision. "I think we did the right thing," said Mr. Churchill, as the meeting broke up.

De Lattre took on the sole responsibility for the defence of Strasbourg from the 5th January. The first essential was to move the 3rd Algerian Division, which involved a long and difficult journey round the west of the Vosges, and along roads that were for the most part covered with a sheet of ice. The arrival of Guillaume's division was only just in time. To the north of Strasbourg, the Germans were already probing forward, and there was only precarious liaison with the Americans on the left. As the first regiment of Guillaume's division reached Strasbourg, Guillaume himself was there to meet it. There was no time for detailed orders. One battalion was directed south of the city, one north, and one to the port and the city itself. Strasbourg at least was now defended by something, and, in addition to Guillaume's division, there were various F.F.I. units, and some garrison detachments which were just beginning to be organized.

The personal action of de Lattre during these critical days was typical. The more threatening the situation, the more difficult it always was to find him at his headquarters. He preferred to be in the danger area, where he knew that his mere presence would stimulate the will to resist. To one of his staff, who warned him that the Germans might well be in Strasbourg first, de Lattre merely replied, "All the more reason for going off there now." Valluy, the General's Chief of Staff at the time, has given the following graphic description of de Lattre's arrival in the city:

> "He rushed to the office of the Commissioner of the Republic, who was packing up to go, cursed everyone with whom he came in contact, from the humblest employee to the Commissioner himself, collected the few officials who remained, fell into the arms of the Mayor, Monsieur Frey, an old friend of his, cancelled all orders for evacuation, ordered back to their posts a group of gendarmes who were just leaving, harangued the odd Maquis patrols and everyone else he met in the streets, and himself organized a line of resistance that was to be held by the next morning. Then he went and had a well-earned

drink with the Mayor, went back to the Commissioner's office, took off his gloves, and made a stirring speech to those present. It was now four o'clock in the morning."

Such were the moments that de Lattre enjoyed most. It had been the same at Rethel in 1940. In the hour of crisis, he seemed possessed of superhuman power.

Meanwhile, the barometer that showed the state of his relations with Devers moved irregularly up and down. For Devers there was often much provocation, but nature had endowed him with a store of patience that seemed inexhaustible. At the beginning of January, Devers wrote de Lattre a most courteous letter, in which he expressed his profound appreciation of the sincerity with which he had put forward his views in regard to Strasbourg. A few days later, on the 6th January, de Lattre was again on the warpath. He was worried about the VI U.S. Corps on his left, and its ability to protect his own left flank. He visited Devers and expounded his fears. It seems that the patient Devers on this occasion was not best pleased. Recounting the interview later, de Lattre wrote: "Our conversation at once became vigorous and frank. The man is direct, but this realist hides under an exterior that is sometimes hard, a warm and sensitive heart." At the end of the talk, Devers assured de Lattre that despite the risks the U.S. VI Corps would continue to cover his left flank.

The arrangements which de Lattre had so vigorously put in hand for the defence of Strasbourg were completed just in time. On the 7th January, the day after de Lattre's visit to Devers, Hitler launched a major offensive for the recapture of the city. The operations took the form of a southern thrust by the First German Army in the general direction of Wissembourg–Strasbourg, combined with a northward thrust by the Nineteenth German Army debouching from the Colmar pocket and directed on Molsheim. It was the form that de Lattre had predicted. It was one of the enemy's final attempts to reverse his misfortunes. On the evening of the battle, the enemy commander launched this appeal: "I count on you to enable me within a few days to announce to the Führer that the swastika flag flies once again from the cathedral of Strasbourg."

The attack was pressed with all vigour. To the south it was the

Free French Division that was to take the main shock, to the north it was the VI U.S. Corps, now commanded by Brooks. The Free French Division was dangerously extended, and at the outset the German thrust gained considerable ground, the enemy armour reaching Krafft, about ten miles only from Strasbourg. For four days the battle raged. It is invidious to refer to the gallantry of one unit only, but the tenacity of the 24th Battalion at Obenheim should not pass unnoticed. On the 10th January, five enemy infantry battalions and several tanks, under drenching artillery support, were hurled at this battalion, which had fought continuously with the Allies since 1940. On the day following the attack, a few posts still held out, but the battalion had been virtually overwhelmed. Only two officers and twenty men survived.

This great fight on the part of the Free French Division enabled de Lattre to secure the front south of Strasbourg. On the 11th he again went to Devers, to thank him for the whole-hearted help he had received in those critical days from the American Air Force. The 12th Tactical Air Command which was in support of the Seventh U.S. Army, had in fact been wholly diverted to the support of the hard-pressed French Division. But de Lattre did not miss the occasion again to press for the resumption of operations to reduce the Colmar pocket. In his view, it was the only way of eliminating once and for all, the threat to Strasbourg and to the right flank of the Allies. But to carry out his intention, de Lattre needed at least another infantry and another armoured division. Devers promised his support, and he was to prove true to his word.

To the north, the VI U.S. Corps beat off the enemy continuously for eight days in the Haguenau Forest, and the enemy then switched his efforts to the bridgehead which he had established at Gambsheim, just north of Strasbourg, where de Monsabert and Brooks had already been struggling to throw him back. On the 17th, another effort was made against the extreme right of the VI U.S. Corps towards Weyersheim. This advance was fully observed by French artillery observation posts, and the French gunners were able to repay a little of the help which the American Air Force had given in repelling the enemy south of Strasbourg. In the evening, the 12th Tactical Air Command also intervened, and the enemy was wholly checked, but Brooks, with the consent of Patch, wisely withdrew south of Haguenau Forest.

Failing in his thrust westward towards Weyersheim, the enemy decided to break southward from his bridgehead, towards Kilstett, on the night of 21st/22nd January. By dawn on the 22nd, the French battalion holding Kilstett had been encircled, and the enemy had reached a point only ten miles from the centre of Strasbourg.

Meanwhile, du Vigier had been appointed Military Governor of Strasbourg, and with this function he combined that of deputy to de Monsabert. On the evening of the 21st, du Vigier had been in touch with Leclerc and his 2nd Armoured Division, and the latter at once agreed to make one of his Combat Commands available to operate in the northern sector of the II Corps Front. By a rapidly mounted counter-attack Kilstett was relieved. The heroic garrison, which had defended it, lost a third of its effectives. The situation was now in hand, and although the enemy made a final effort on the 25th, and continued to exert pressure against the VI U.S. Corps on the left, Strasbourg was safe.

There were many in the highest places who had contributed to the reversal of the decision to abandon Strasbourg, but it was to de Lattre that the credit was mainly due. On his own initiative he had decided to defend the city, and in putting that decision into effect, he had virtually acted in defiance of superior orders, for it was only later that the decision to evacuate Strasbourg was reversed. De Lattre had staked his whole reputation on a decision that incurred supreme risk, for he had not the resources to cover Strasbourg. The extension of his front, which his action involved, made him vulnerable everywhere. Not only did he take the risk, but, when the crisis was at its height, he never lost sight of the offensive which he had planned on Christmas night.

If de Lattre had made one of the boldest decisions of his career, it would be less than fair to withhold credit from Devers, who was faced with a situation that was most unenviable. As Army Group Commander, it was inevitable that he should be able to view the situation more dispassionately, and that he should be more in sympathy with the views of the Supreme Commander than with those of his French subordinate. To his exceptional comprehension of the situation, and to the whole-hearted support which he gave to de Lattre, after the initial decision of Supreme Headquarters had been reversed, is due not a little of the credit for averting a disastrous set-back.

23. COLMAR

"THERE must never be a French soldier content to rest so long as there is one German on this side of the Rhine." So had spoken Marshal Turenne nearly two hundred years before. De Lattre was now to play his part in driving that last German soldier across the Rhine. But once again the weather was against him. For three weeks his troops were to fight their way forward, mostly in blinding snow. It was not only the men in the forefront of the battle, particularly those in the Vosges, who were called upon to endure the rigours of those weeks. The roads, both in the hills and in the plain of Alsace, were covered with ice or snow, and herculean efforts were often required to supply and move the army. But to the defenders of the Colmar pocket, those cold and biting storms were a precious ally.

It was on the 15th January that de Lattre assembled his staff and subordinate commanders at Montbeliard, and confirmed the outline plan, which he had conceived on Christmas night, for the reduction of the pocket. Colmar itself was to be cut off, by Bethouart's I Corps in the south, and de Monsabert's II Corps in the north, converging on Brisach. The attack of I Corps was to precede that of II Corps by two days, thereby drawing off reserves from the front of II Corps. Billotte's division, which had now joined the First French Army, was to contain the enemy in the Vosges by large-scale raids. De Monsabert now had the 3rd U.S. Division under his command; it had replaced the 36th U.S. Division.

In the pocket was a determined enemy comprising the LXIII and LXIV Army Corps, and totalling seven infantry divisions and one armoured division. There was one infantry division also in reserve. The French had only seven infantry divisions, but their three armoured divisions gave them a superiority in armour. Their superiority in artillery and in the air was largely nullified by the appalling weather.

The objective of I Corps was limited to the line Mulhouse–Thann. The right of the attack was to rest on the River Ill, and the left on the Vosges. The objective of II Corps to the north was, firstly, the line Jebsheim–Grusenheim, and eventually the Rhine at Brisach.

For de Lattre the double battle would be particularly difficult to control. He liked, during battle, to be able to move quickly from one corps headquarters to another, and often to move further forward still. But the obstacle of the Vosges necessitated a 100-mile detour, to enable him to move between I and II Corps Headquarters.

By the middle of January, the situation in the Ardennes had been re-established, and it was now Supreme Headquarters who were anxious to reduce the Colmar pocket as early as possible. De Lattre decided to launch I Corps on the 20th January, and II Corps on the 23rd. The I French Air Corps was to support him. Few things can uplift the hearts of an attacking army more than the sight of its own aircraft dominating the skies, but of this heartening spectacle, the men of I Corps were to be deprived. On the morning of the 20th, once again they went forward in the face of driving wind and snow.

Slight progress was made on the first day, but on the next day the resistance of the enemy stiffened, and a counter-attack by his armour brought the attackers to a standstill. The weather had deteriorated, the men were exhausted, and the casualties had been heavy. Very reluctantly, for there could be few more stout-hearted soldiers than he, Bethouart went to Army Headquarters, and proposed that the continuation of the offensive be deferred until the advent of more propitious weather.

For de Lattre it was a difficult moment. To react against the depressing effect upon morale exercised by driving wind and snow demanded a supreme effort of will. Moreover, to disregard the advice of so sound and courageous a commander as Bethouart required unusual conviction and determination. But he did not hesitate. Strasbourg was still in danger: at that very moment, the enemy was beginning to attack again north of the city. Whatever the losses, whatever the fatigue, and whatever the weather, the attack must proceed. It did not take long to convince Bethouart, but de Lattre felt that the moment was opportune for him to go forward himself, and infuse some of his own determination into his divisional commanders. Into the night, therefore, and into the howling gale, he and Bethouart set off.

First they went to Mulhouse, where they met Morlière, commanding the 9th Colonial Division on the right. Despite the conditions, he seemed ready to proceed. Thence they set off for the headquarters of Carpentier, commanding the 2nd Moroccan Division, at Soppe-le-Bas. The precariousness of that midnight drive can only have been rivalled by de Lattre's drives long ago, in his father's carriage, to catch the train at Mouilleron. De Lattre himself described as "hallucinating" those three hours that it took to cover the few miles that separated the two headquarters. The conditions were enough to shake the confidence of any commander in the wisdom of his decision to continue an offensive. He himself was beginning to tire after an exhausting day and night, and would have to muster all his strength to maintain the morale of his subordinate, for the 2nd Moroccan Division had suffered very heavy losses. But its intrepid commander, Carpentier, was not dismayed, and leaving Bethouart to arrange things with the Divisional Commander, de Lattre went on to the headquarters of the 4th Moroccan Division at Masevaux. He arrived there at five o'clock in the morning, and again explained the reasons that compelled him to continue the offensive. It was not the best hour of the day at which to try and raise morale, but at Masevaux he found Lieutenant-Colonel Beaufre, the Chief of Staff, hard at work, and full of hope. The optimism of a subordinate at such a time can do much to strengthen the determination of his superiors, and the attitude of Beaufre on that occasion made a deep impression upon the Army Commander, and later Beaufre was to become one of his most able collaborators. Invigorated by the faith of its commander, I Corps struggled on, and, although progress was not marked, it exerted continuous and heavy pressure upon the enemy in the southern part of the pocket.

To the north, de Monsabert had attacked with O'Daniel's 3rd U.S. Division on the right, and the 1st Free French Division, now under Garbay, on the left. Leclerc's 2nd Armoured Division, now also under his command, was to cover the left flank of the attack, and be available to exploit northward. Guillaume's 3rd Algerian Division remained responsible for the immediate defence of Strasbourg. Corps zero hour was seven-thirty on the 23rd January, but O'Daniel with his 3rd U.S. Division had decided to start in the hours of darkness. De Lattre had a high opinion of O'Daniel—"that warrior", as he described him, "with his face scarred as if by blows from an axe, and revealing in every line, dynamic will-power and energy to an uncommon degree".

As with I Corps, so with II Corps, initial successes were followed by a stiffening of the enemy resistance. Strong German counter-attacks were helped by the collapse of a bridge over the river Ill, which had prevented the timely arrival of the Allied armour. Indeed, by the evening of the 24th, the situation was not encouraging.

De Lattre had always let it be known that to ensure the success of his operations he needed two more divisions, and on the eve of the attack he had urged Juin, who was de Gaulle's Defence Chief in Paris, to press for the reinforcement that he needed. Juin was most sympathetic, but the losses suffered by I Corps at the outset of its attack determined de Lattre again to press his claims with Devers, and, with that object in view, on the 21st January he sent de Linares to Headquarters 6th Army Group.

The gravity of the situation on the 24th caused de Lattre to summon a conference in the evening at the headquarters of the 3rd U.S. Division, at Ribeauville. It was attended by corps and divisional commanders, and du Vigier, the new Military Governor of Strasbourg, and General Barr, Chief of Staff to Devers, were also present. De Lattre allotted a variety of tasks to du Vigier, whose duties at Strasbourg for the moment were being undertaken by Guillaume. Du Vigier has given the following account of this conference, which opened in an atmosphere of considerable depression:

"The Chief started by asking divisional commanders in turn, what was the state of their divisions. From each came a similar reply, 'The men are exhausted; many have got frostbite; the weather and ground are impossible, and casualties have been heavy.' Having heard their depressing story, de Lattre turned to General Barr. 'You see,' he said. Everyone imagined that de Lattre was going to tell Barr that, in view of the exhausted state of his troops, the operations must be halted. But with de Lattre it was always the unexpected that happened. He continued, 'That is the situation: none the less, I am going on with the battle—but I need two more divisions. What about your XXI Corps which is doing nothing at Sarreguemines? Give me that, and you will see.' Barr then asked de Lattre how long he would take to bring the operations to a successful conclusion if he got this corps. Without a moment's hesitation de Lattre drew various arrows and phase lines on his map, and with an air of supreme conviction, said, 'The 10th February.' In the time he could have based that date on no calculations, but it was a remarkable and most impressive and convincing shot in the dark."

Barr may have wondered, when he first went to that conference, whether all was well with the First French Army. It was his privilege to see de Lattre towering proudly above the difficulties and discouragements that surrounded him. He went away convinced that, given the resources, de Lattre could bring the battle to a triumphal conclusion.

In the early hours of the following morning, de Lattre received a telegram from Devers to the effect that XXI U.S. Corps under Milburn would be placed forthwith under his orders. If ever a commander deserved such a telegram, it was de Lattre at that difficult moment, and his delight was the greater to feel that Devers had sufficient confidence in him to place an American corps under his command. With three army corps, he knew that the First French Army had victory within its grasp. Milburn made the same good impression on de Lattre as O'Daniel had done. He struck him as a man of honesty, energy, and determination, and above all as a subordinate upon whose loyalty he could count. In this he was not to be deceived.

It was a most courageous decision on the part of General Devers to entrust first an American division and then a whole corps to the command of de Lattre. At the staff conference, at which Devers mentioned this project, there was strong opposition on the part of all the senior American officers present. They felt that General Devers would never be able to explain to the War

Department at Washington how he had been able to agree to an entire American corps coming under a French general, who belonged to an Army still under the cloud of the defeat of 1940. Although he was a relatively junior officer, one of the few who supported the project was Cabot Lodge. He argued that de Lattre was universally recognized as a competent professional soldier, and that by giving him command of American troops he would have the strongest possible incentive for driving his own French troops hard. If the worst came to the worst, the American troops could be removed from de Lattre's command. It is a tribute to the imagination and courage of Devers that he persisted in his decision. It is a reflection also on the high regard which he had for de Lattre, despite the differences that had sometimes marred their relations.

Meanwhile, the south-easterly advance of II Corps had continued in the face of determined resistance. Two waterways, the Ill and the Colmar Canal, had to be crossed before the armour could be launched. The struggle for Jebsheim and Grussenheim was particularly desperate, but the combined efforts of the 3rd U.S. and the 1st Free French Divisions brought about their capture. The streets of Jebsheim were strewn with the bodies of 500 of its desperate defenders.

Now that the centre of gravity of the battle had switched to the north, de Lattre held a conference every night at nine o'clock at the headquarters of the 3rd U.S. Division in Ribeauville. He retained control of the battle on the front of I Corps through de Linares, who acted in a liaison capacity.

The XXI U.S. Corps now took under its wing the 3rd U.S. Division, and took over the sector of the battle-front between Billotte's 10th Infantry Division on the right, and de Monsabert's II Corps on the left. The reinforcement by XXI U.S. Corps made little difference to the initial plan by which Colmar was to be cut off by a combined advance of I and II Corps towards Brisach. The XXI U.S. Corps was now to move with its left on Brisach, while its right was to try and make contact with I French Corps near Ensisheim. If opportunity offered, the attack on Colmar itself might be launched before the junction between the I Corps and XXI U.S. Corps had been effected. II Corps was to concentrate on clearing up the northern area of the pocket.

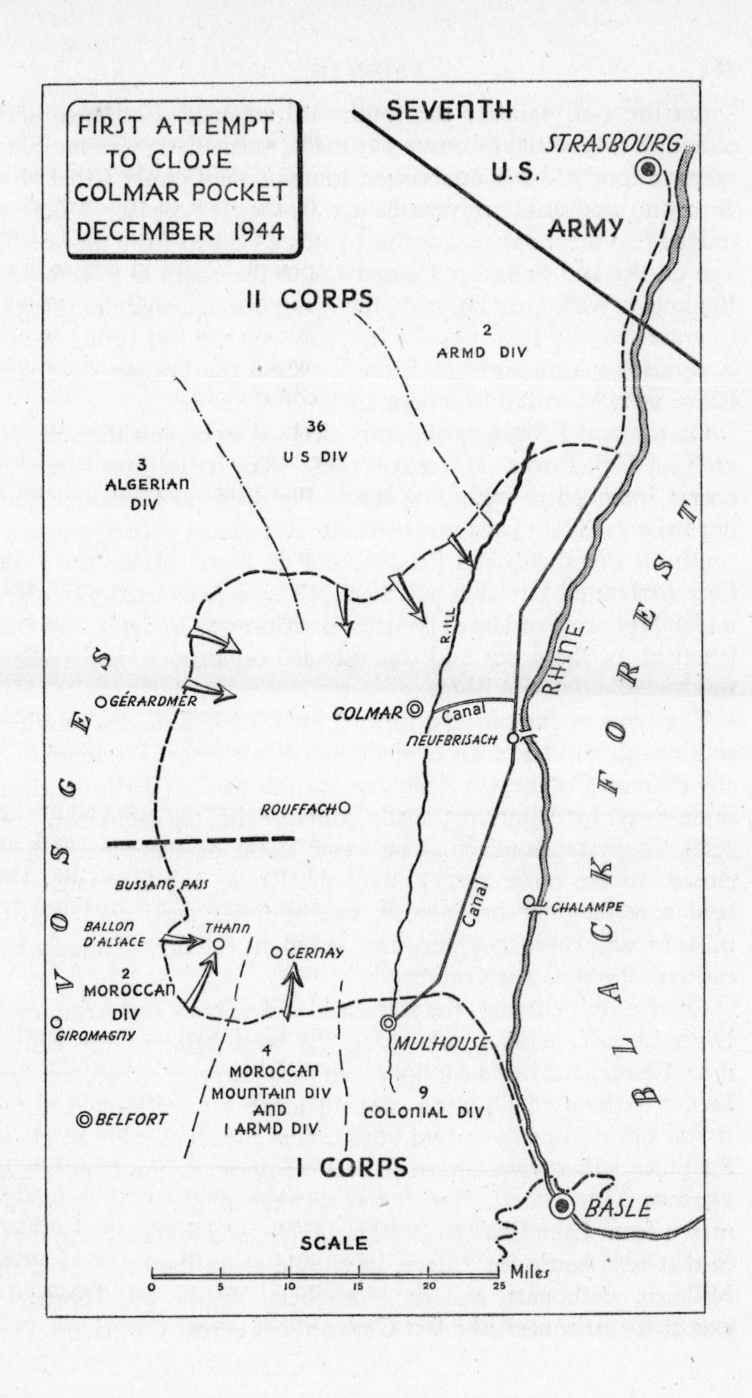
FIRST ATTEMPT TO CLOSE COLMAR POCKET DECEMBER 1944
SEVENTH U.S. ARMY
STRASBOURG
II CORPS
2 ARMD DIV
36 U S DIV
3 ALGERIAN DIV
VOSGES
BLACK FOREST
R. ILL
RHINE
GÉRARDMER
COLMAR
Canal
NEUFBRISACH
ROUFFACH
BUSSANG PASS
CHALAMPE
Canal
BALLON D'ALSACE
THANN
CERNAY
2 MOROCCAN DIV
GIROMAGNY
MULHOUSE
4 MOROCCAN MOUNTAIN DIV AND I ARMD DIV
9 COLONIAL DIV
BELFORT
I CORPS
BASLE
SCALE
0 5 10 15 20 25 Miles

On the 29th January the southward advance continued, and although substantial progress was made, particularly on the right, where a foothold was established south of the Colmar Canal, the enemy resisted stubbornly on the left. By the 1st February, Milburn judged that the moment was ripe to attack Colmar from the north, and on the 2nd February Colmar fell to the 109th U.S. Infantry Regiment. With great chivalry, the Americans allowed the French to enter the city first. On the left, the advance had brought the Americans within sight of Brisach, where the bridges over the Rhine were obscured by a permanent smoke screen.

On the 2nd February, de Lattre decided to exploit the success of XXI U.S. Corps. Moreover, there were indications that the enemy intended to withdraw across the Rhine at Chalampe and not Brisach. XXI Corps was therefore directed at once to advance south on Ensisheim and Brisach, and de Lattre placed the 12th U.S. Armoured Division and Leclerc's 2nd Armoured Division under Milburn's orders. The latter division was to deploy on the left flank of the corps and was directed on Brisach, and thence southward along the Rhine.

The arms of the pincers, formed by XXI U.S. Corps moving southward, and I French Corps moving northward, were gradually closing. On the 5th February, the left flank of I Corps, after three days' hard fighting, made contact with the right flank of XXI Corps at Rouffach. The inner circle of the pincers had closed. In the outer circle, along the Rhine, the Germans still held a rectangular bridgehead, twelve miles deep and twenty miles broad, where they were exposed to the full fury of attacks by the 12th Tactical Air Command.

On the 8th February, the spearhead of Leclerc's 2nd Armoured Division, advancing south along the west bank of the Rhine near Fessenheim, picked up a wireless message from the 1st French Armoured Division moving north on the same village. A few hours later these two outstanding divisions were to close the pincers that were almost to seal the doom of the Nineteenth German Army. For Leclerc it was another milestone in that epic march from Lake Chad to Berchtesgarten, and it was fitting that, in that final battle for Alsace, he should share the honours with Milburn, Bethouart, and de Monsabert. By the 9th February, except for prisoners, the last German was across the Rhine. For all it had been a hard fight, but for none had it been harder than for the men of Bethouart's Corps.

If the men of the First French Army had endured hardships, unsurpassed on any field of battle, it was the unflagging determination of its commander, and his domination of difficulties and discouragement of every nature, which had ensured success. Well might he feel proud, when on the 11th February, at Colmar, de Gaulle invested him with the Grand Cross of the Legion of Honour. From Devers and Eisenhower too he received the congratulations that were his due.

24. VICTORY

A BRIEF respite—the first which the Army had enjoyed since landing in France six months before—was now to follow, and while formations and units refitted and re-organized, de Lattre himself devoted his main attention to the establishment of a training centre at Rouffach. These training centres were an essential part of his technique of command. There, more effectively than by any other means, he could make himself known to all those young officers and non-commissioned officers, of whom he was to ask so much. His faith in his own magnetic powers was absolute. In those frequent visits that he paid to Rouffach, he believed in his ability to inspire, and for that reason he devoted to these training centres a degree of attention that to many seemed exaggerated.

At the beginning of March, de Lattre found time to slip away for a few days to see his old father at Mouilleron. The victor of Colmar received a warm welcome. At the village inn, the "Hotel du Tigre", a few yards from his father's house, the charming *patron* had prepared a superb dinner one night for the small staff which had accompanied him. The *pièce de résistance* was to be a delicious cake. But, in the meantime, de Lattre had made one of his rapid decisions. Hardly had they sat down to dinner, when a message came from the Chief, to say that they were to move in five minutes' time. They had to leave the cake. He had decided to accede to the request from a neighbouring village to go and give a lecture. Already he had lectured to other villages in the neighbourhood, and he did not want to disappoint them. It was very late at night before they got back and were able to eat the cake. Although they were far from the front, the tempo had not changed.

In the golden book at the "Mairie", a quarter of a century earlier, Georges Clemenceau had written "To the great dead of the Great War—homage from their compatriot of Mouilleron—Georges Clemenceau." Beneath it, on the 6th March, 1945, de Lattre now wrote as follows: "In the shadow of Père la Victoire, his little compatriot, of whom he was so fond, is so proud today to be able to sign as a child of Mouilleron—J. de Lattre." And as a postcript he added: "A pious homage also to my venerable father, Mayor of Mouilleron for 34 years, and to my grandfather and great-grandfather, Mayors of our dear Commune for 128 years."

Now that the fences of Belfort and Colmar were behind him, de Lattre could begin to think of getting over the water jump, but before the Rhine could be jumped there were difficulties of a different kind that would have to be surmounted. Eisenhower's plan for the advance into Germany was to move on a broad front and encircle the Ruhr. Montgomery had felt that a concentration of force to the north and one strong punch on that flank would be more profitable. But whichever view was to prevail, the concentration of force necessary to ensure success on the front of attack would necessitate economy elsewhere, and, now that the Colmar pocket had been liquidated, the one sector in which economy could be effected was the upper Rhine from Switzerland to north of Strasbourg. This front was held by the First French Army, and, for the furtherance of Eisenhower's plan, the obvious and simple solution was for de Lattre to extend his front north of Strasbourg and for the moment to remain passive, but ready to follow up the Seventh U.S. Army.

Even if he had the resources, an attempt to jump the Rhine in his sector would have been the height of folly. In the plain beyond the far bank, the Siegfried defences were strong and continuous, and beyond them to the east rose the Black Forest (see map on

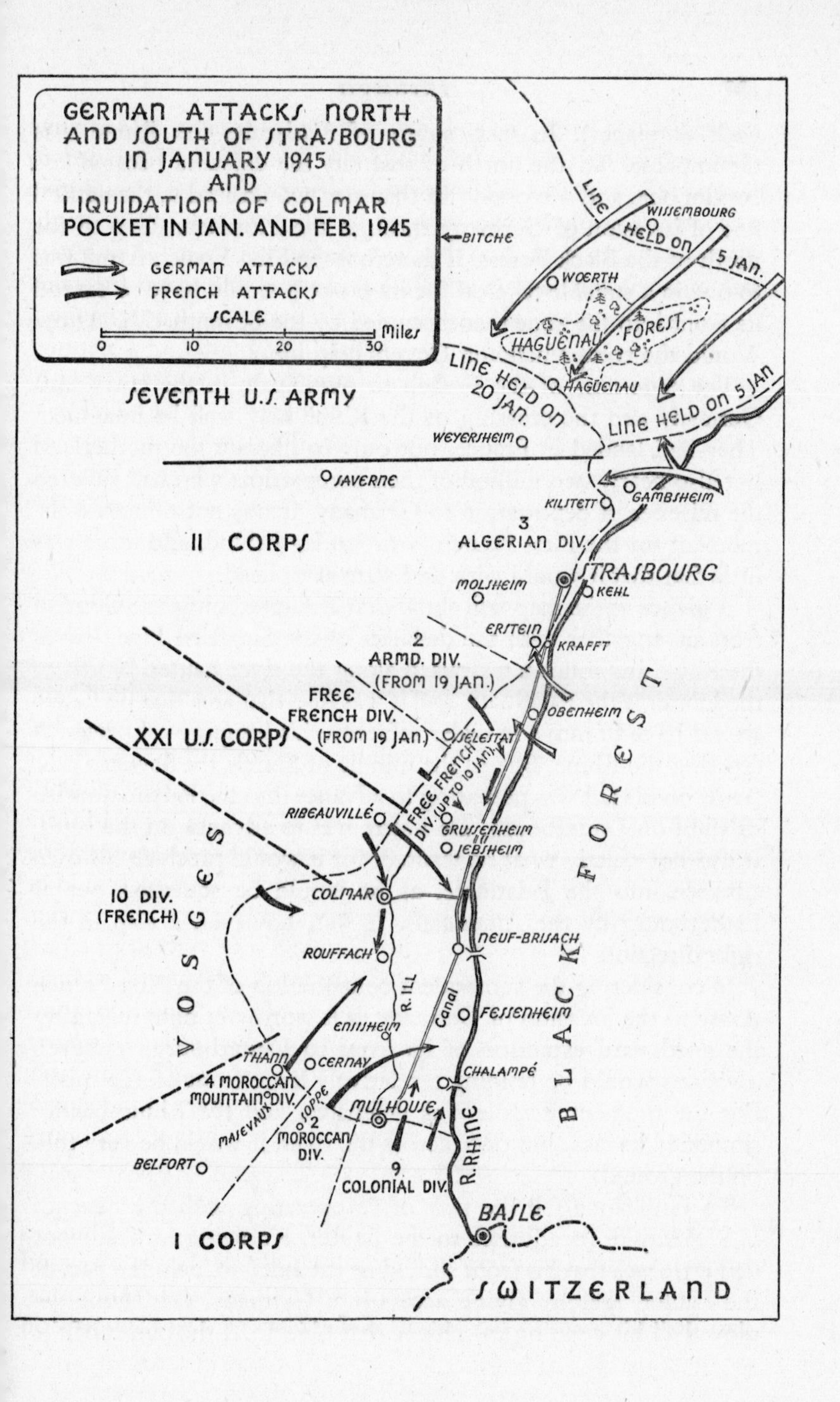
GERMAN ATTACKS NORTH AND SOUTH OF STRASBOURG IN JANUARY 1945 AND LIQUIDATION OF COLMAR POCKET IN JAN. AND FEB. 1945
GERMAN ATTACKS
FRENCH ATTACKS
SCALE
0
10
20
30
Miles
BITCHE
WISSEMBOURG
LINE HELD ON 5 JAN.
WOERTH
HAGUENAU FOREST
HAGUENAU
LINE HELD ON 20 JAN.
LINE HELD ON 5 JAN
SEVENTH U.S. ARMY
WEYERSHEIM
SAVERNE
KILSTETT
GAMBSHEIM
II CORPS
3 ALGERIAN DIV.
STRASBOURG
MOLSHEIM
KEHL
ERSTEIN
KRAFFT
2 ARMD. DIV. (FROM 19 JAN.)
FREE FRENCH DIV. (FROM 19 JAN.)
OBENHEIM
XXI U.S. CORPS
SÉLESTAT
I FREE FRENCH DIV. (UP TO 10 JAN.)
RIBEAUVILLÉ
GRUSSENHEIM
JEBSHEIM
VOSGES
10 DIV. (FRENCH)
COLMAR
NEUF-BRISACH
ROUFFACH
BLACK FOREST
R. ILL
Canal
FESSENHEIM
ENSISHEIM
THANN
CERNAY
CHALAMPÉ
4 MOROCCAN MOUNTAIN DIV.
SOPPE
MASEVAUX
MULHOUSE
2 MOROCCAN DIV.
R. RHINE
BELFORT
9 COLONIAL DIV.
BASLE
I CORPS
SWITZERLAND

back endpaper). In fact, south of Karlsruhe the Rhine was unjumpable. To the north of that city the defences became less continuous, and a crossing in that area would lead to the natural line of invasion of Germany through the Pforzheim Gap to the north of the Black Forest. If therefore the First French Army was to obtain a suitable take-off for its jump, it would have to extend its front into the zone then occupied by the Seventh U.S. Army. Would the comprehending Devers help him?

The eagerness of the French to participate in the entry into Germany and the crossing of the Rhine may well be imagined. They had landed in France, not only to liberate the motherland but also nearly two million of their compatriots who had suffered the miseries of deportation to Germany. It was not therefore the moment for the First French Army to lag behind, and there was little fear that it would with de Lattre at its head.

A glance at the map will show that at Lauterbourg the German frontier, together with the defences of the Siegfried Line, leaves the Rhine and follows westward along the river Lauter. North of the Lauter is the Palatinate, and it was into that area that de Lattre would have to move in order to secure his jumping-off place for crossing the Rhine. But, in the middle of March, the Seventh U.S. Army on his left was preparing to advance into the Palatinate with its right on Lauterbourg. De Lattre was to advance on the right. It was not exactly what he wanted, for it would preclude his own advance into the Palatinate, as he would be squeezed out at Lauterbourg by the Americans. It was, however, a step in the right direction.

In considering the subsequent contribution of the First French Army to the invasion of Germany, it is worthy of note that, after the northward extension of its front to Lauterbourg, its seven divisions would be holding a relatively large front of 120 miles. For the moment its rôle was defensive, and the Rhine barrier simplified its task, but once across the river, it would be very thin on the ground.

To Guillaume fell the task of co-operating with the Seventh U.S. Army in its advance to the Lauter. Knowing how anxious de Lattre was that his front should be extended to include a part of the Lauter, thereby giving access into Germany, Guillaume deployed all his cunning to achieve that object. At the outset of the attack, the Forest of Haguenau was outside his left boundary, but, as the American decided to by-pass it to the left, Guillaume felt justified in sending his Goums through the forest in order to secure his left flank. They therefore emerged to the north of the forest, well to the left of the divisional boundary, and, owing largely to the comprehension of the friendly American unit on his left, Guillaume continued to advance with his left well inside the American boundary, until, after hard fighting, the Lauter was reached. De Lattre was delighted. His army was now abreast of the Seventh U.S. Army, and along the Lauter, instead of being pinched out at Lauterbourg. It had been a forgivable piece of poaching, but a few weeks later the poacher was to go too far.

De Lattre now felt that the moment had come to go and see Devers, and to place before him frankly his fears in regard to the future employment of his army. He begged Devers to allow him to enter Germany by the side of the Seventh U.S. Army, and pointed out all the advantages if he could be allowed to cross the Rhine north of Karlsruhe, instead of remaining idle on the banks of that river in Alsace. As regards the proposal to enter Germany, Devers gave his full accord, but it was beyond his competence to make any promise in regard to crossing the Rhine. It was agreed that for the initial advance into the Palatinate, which involved an assault against the Siegfried Line north of the Lauter, de Monsabert should form a Task Force, which in the first instance would be under command of the VI U.S. Corps. Events were evolving in the direction that de Lattre wished.

For de Monsabert's Task Force, of which the main components were Guillaume's 3rd Algerian Division and Carpentier's 2nd Moroccan Division, transferred from I Corps, the 19th March was a memorable day. On that morning they crossed the Lauter into Germany, and by the 25th March, after hard fighting, de Monsabert had pierced the Siegfried Line and was established along the left bank of the Rhine, with his right on the Lauter. The success of these operations, was in large measure due to the excellent understanding that existed between de Monsabert and Brooks, the commander of VI U.S. Corps.

The take-off for the Rhine jump had now been secured, but the frontage was small, and there were few places suitable for a crossing. Fortune, however, again smiled on de Lattre. To the north, George Patton, with his 3rd U.S. Army, had advanced with such rapidity that Devers was able to cross the Rhine near Worms. Devers' centre of gravity therefore suddenly shifted north, and it suited the plans of all to extend de Lattre's front to include Spire.

The day of the engineers was now approaching. Months before, when du Vigier was crossing the Rhône at Avignon, de Lattre had impressed upon Dromond, his Chief Engineer, that he should be looking ahead, so as to ensure that there would be no delay in crossing the Rhine through lack of bridging equipment. Dromond did not fail him. In assessing the achievements of the First French Army during this campaign, it should be stressed that, although their American neighbours were often generous in meeting their needs, the French themselves lacked much of the equipment needed by a modern army, and also the means to carry it forward. During the past few months Dromond had been improvising in the grand manner of his chief, and with the aid of material manufactured at Châlons-sur-Saône after its liberation, and with other material hidden by a French engineer officer during the occupation, he had collected enough material for a ten-ton bridge, 300 yards in length.

With other bridging equipment, including assault bridging, the First French Army was not well provided. VI U.S. Corps promised to help, but de Lattre was in a hurry, and the equipment promised could hardly reach him in time. He feared that the Seventh U.S. Army might exploit their bridgehead at Worms by sweeping south. Although such a move would assist his own crossing by the threat it would create against the northern flank of the enemy opposed to him, he was haunted by the thought of his American friends sweeping into Germany ahead of him. Once again it had become a race.

To launch an army prematurely against a river obstacle more than 300 yards wide, and with insufficient time for detailed reconnaissance, was a serious risk to take, and on this occasion it was difficult to justify; and yet the very speed at which this difficult operation was mounted may have contributed to its success. The unfortunate de Monsabert was ordered to cross more than twenty-four hours before he had initially planned to do so, and before all the bridging equipment promised would be available.

Well might he have urged for the extra time to be given him, but the Chief's mind had been made up. Not for the first time, the impossible had got to be achieved.

Three crossing places had been envisaged, Leimersheim for the 9th Colonial Division, now commanded by Valluy, Germersheim for the 2nd Moroccan Division, and Spire for the 3rd Algerian Division.

On the night of the 31st March, the 2nd Moroccan and 3rd Algerian Divisions set forth to cross the Rhine. The 9th Colonial Division on the right was not to cross until two days later. For Carpentier, commanding the 2nd Moroccan Division at Germersheim, the ensuing struggle was to prove most arduous. Two crossing places north of the village, had been selected, and at 4.45 in the morning, twenty artillery groups brought down their deluge on the enemy defences across the river. But the price now had to be paid for the insufficient time allowed for reconnaissance. The men were too late embarking in their assault boats to take full advantage of the supporting artillery and of the remaining hours of darkness. As they approached the far bank, dawn was already breaking, their own bombardment had lifted, and a murderous fire greeted them. It was only their supreme bravery that enabled a foothold to be established on the far bank. One battalion, which until a few days before had been a unit of the F.F.I., lost eighty-eight killed. But the infantry would be the first to give full credit to the engineers. Of the ninety valiant technicians of one Engineer Regiment, fifty-four became casualties.

The crossing at Spire by the 3rd Algerian Division proved easier. De Lattre himself took the unorthodox step of telephoning Agostini, commanding the 3rd Algerian Regiment, on the evening before, and telling him he had got to get across that night. The divisional commander might well have resented this exhortation over his own head to one of his regimental commanders, but, with de Lattre, everything was permissible. Although his first assault boats had only just reached him, Agostini surprised the enemy, and established his bridgehead behind which, that same night, work was begun on the construction of Dromond's bridge, which was to have been used at Germersheim.

As soon as the bridgehead had been established, on the 1st April de Lattre issued what he called an "Orientation Directive" for subsequent operations. The gist of this was that II Corps was to capture Karlsruhe; at the same time it was to capture Stuttgart to the north, and to establish contact with the Americans to the east towards Heilbronn. After the capture of Karlsruhe, 9th Colonial Division was to come directly under Army with a view to enveloping the Black Forest to the north. But if Stuttgart was de Lattre's immediate objective for II Corps, he already had in mind the subsequent advance of that corps to the Danube—at Sigmaringen and Ulm, covered to the south by I Corps, which by then would have been brought across the Rhine, and to the north by the Americans. The spirit of Napoleon urged him on, but the directive from the Army Group, which had not yet reached him, contained no such ambitious plans for exploitation. Indeed, it only envisaged a modest bridgehead not more than fifty miles deep.

Valluy had no easy task in crossing the Rhine with his 9th Colonial Division at Leimersheim on the 2nd, but the Americans allowed him to use the Mannheim bridge, over which he sent an armoured group with orders to descend south along the east bank of the Rhine, and to threaten the right flank of the enemy opposing him. Valluy rapidly exploited success towards Karlsruhe, and, co-operating with other elements of II Corps, he captured that place on the 4th April.

By the same evening, de Lattre had three infantry divisions and one armoured division east of the Rhine, and his bridgehead ran approximately along the line Karlsruhe–north of the Black Forest–Eppingen–Spire. If it had not been for its commander, and the comprehension of Devers, the whole of the First French Army might still have been strung out along the west bank of the Rhine; but it was now to play its full part in the final phase that was so soon to lead to victory.

The beginning of April found de Lattre with his II Corps across the Rhine and progressing beyond Pforzheim, which had been captured on the 8th. But to the south his I Corps was still on the west bank, facing the Siegfried defences between the river and the Black Forest. In view of the progress of II Corps, de Lattre might well have been tempted to exploit success on the front of that corps and to give de Monsabert his head. But he decided to get I Corps across the Rhine also, before continuing the advance with his whole army united. In his own words "de Monsabert might well have swelled like a soap bubble, but be liable to burst at the slightest pressure". Moreover, the two corps of his army would have become dangerously divided, and, on his left, Seventh U.S. Army was meeting strong opposition. He therefore retained under his own wing Valluy's 9th Colonial Division, and ordered it to sweep south along the east bank of the Rhine, with a view to capturing Kehl and enabling I Corps to cross the river by the bridge which linked that place with Strasbourg. De Monsabert, for the moment, was ordered to shift the weight of his effort to the right, in order to help Valluy, and in compliance with that order he directed the 2nd Moroccan Division, now under command of de Linares, to co-operate closely with Valluy.

Although his immediate intention was to get I Corps across the Rhine, de Lattre was already turning over in his mind the outlines of what he called the "Freudenstadt Manœuvre". Freudenstadt which lay east of the Black Forest, commanded a network of communications, the capture of which would not only embarrass the enemy, but secure for himself a jumping-off place for a subsequent advance on lake Constance and the Danube. The essence of of the manœuvre was for I Corps moving through the Black Forest and for the right flank of II Corps moving south along the east side of the Forest, to converge on Freudenstadt.

In his southward advance along the east bank of the Rhine, Valluy met strong opposition at Rastatt, for the enemy opposite I Corps had not neglected his vulnerable northern flank. By skilful manœuvre by night in the western slopes of the Black Forest, Valluy outflanked Rastatt and by the 16th had captured Baden-Baden and Kehl. The capture of the latter meant the final freedom of Strasbourg, and the tolling of the cathedral bells gave expression to the relief and rejoicing of its citizens. During the long weeks that had elapsed since the end of January, when the timely action of de Lattre had saved the city from reoccupation by a vindictive enemy, it had been continually pounded by the German artillery.

Bethouart lost no time in crossing the Rhine and linking up with Valluy, who now came under his command, and he was soon fully engaged with the enemy on the plain of Baden. He had not been fully acquainted with the intentions of the Army Commander as regards Freudenstadt, but, on the evening of the 17th de Lattre decided to accelerate the manœuvre and to direct Bethouart the next day on Freudenstadt. As so often, on the occasions when he made a rapid decision, the first impulse of de Lattre was to send for the subordinates mainly concerned. The hour of the night did not matter, nor did the length of the journey, nor the state of the roads, nor the fact that the subordinates themselves might be heavily committed to battle. And so, shortly before midnight on the 17th, Bethouart, who was trying to snatch a little sleep, was called to the telephone. "Is that you, Bethouart?" rang out the familiar voice. "I want you to come along at once and bring de Hesdin with you." De Hesdin commanded the 4th Moroccan Mounted Division in Bethouart's Corps.

Bethouart has vividly described that midnight drive to de Lattre's headquarters at Karlsruhe. The roads were badly damaged, many bridges were destroyed and many deviations inevitable. Even when they reached Karlsruhe, they spent a long time trying to find headquarters. It was nearly five o'clock in the morning before Bethouart eventually found de Lattre and was informed that II Corps had outflanked the Black Forest to the north, and that he was to take advantage of this by crossing the Forest himself that very day. "Tomorrow at midday you will be in Freudenstadt with the bulk of your corps," said de Lattre. "Then you will exploit southward, encircle the Black Forest from the east, cross the Danube on the 22nd, take Constance with your right, Ulm with your left, and then push on to Austria." Such were the brief and ambitious instructions which Bethouart, almost dropping with sleep, received at dawn on the 18th April. "Magnificent!" he commented later. "But to me they came as a complete surprise." These instructions were in fact more than ambitious. They exceeded the orders which de Lattre had received from 6th Army Group and which virtually limited his rôle to clearing up the east bank of the Rhine on his front. He was also warned against any "premature advance on the part of the First French Army".

Bethouart, who was already engaged in battle facing south, ventured to point out the difficulties of modifying his dispositions and transferring his centre of gravity to the other side of the Forest, all within a few hours, but he knew it was useless. He knew also that it would be insufficient to say he would try. It had got to be done, and it would be done. "Fighting against sleep," wrote Bethouart later, "in the car which took us back to my headquarters, de Hesdin drafted the orders to his own division, while I drafted those I would send to the other divisions."

The confidence of the Army Commander was not misplaced. Bethouart reached Freudenstadt during the 18th and made contact with II Corps. That evening de Lattre himself went forward to Freudenstadt, where he held a conference to lay down the general lines for the next phase of the operations. Briefly this involved a southward advance by Bethouart to complete the mopping up of the Black Forest and an eastward advance by de Monsabert to capture Stuttgart.

The task before Bethouart was less simple than it appeared. Merely to encircle the Forest by moving south along both sides towards the Swiss frontier could not suffice, for on both sides he would have to place "stops" to prevent the XVIII German S.S. Corps from trying to escape after his advance.

On the 19th Bethouart was on the move southward, and by the 21st he had made such progress that de Lattre already considered the mopping up of the Black Forest as complete and was urging Bethouart, who now had the 1st and 5th Armoured Divisions under his command, to push on to Ulm. Once again, while still engaged in battle facing south, Bethouart was ordered to shift his centre of gravity eastward. Rarely has a commander demanded such flexibility on the part of his subordinates. "The real point of the manœuvre," he stressed to Bethouart, "is to reach Ulm, drums beating, by the 25th. And Ulm was in the American sector! But apart from the glamour of Ulm, de Lattre was anxious to outflank to the south the Swabian Jura, which lay between Ulm and Stuttgart and in which were trying to rally the remnants of the Nineteenth German Army.

Bethouart was again quick off the mark, and on the 21st a brilliant dash by the 1st Armoured Division resulted in the Danube being crossed at Mulheim on that day. But so long as 30,000 Germans, including the fanatical XVIII S.S. Corps, threatened his rear in the Black Forest Bethouart could not give his undivided attention to the advance on Ulm and beyond. Indeed, between the 25th and 27th, repeated efforts were made by the enemy to debouch from the eastern exits of the Forest. Only on the 27th were their efforts finally frustrated.

Meanwhile, on the 21st de Monsabert had captured Stuttgart which was strongly held by the remnants of LXIV German Corps. De Monsabert had directed Guillaume with his 3rd Algerian Division against the north of the city, while to the south he directed his 5th Armoured and 2nd Moroccan Division. It was the wide and rapid outflanking move of the 5th Armoured Division and its "action brutale" against the southern defences of the city which mainly contributed to its early capture; 28,000 prisoners were taken and the LXIV Corps virtually ceased to exist.

The question of his boundary with the Americans on his left was beginning to cause de Lattre a little anxiety. He knew that he was on the verge of trespassing on their preserves, but at least he was able to get Patch, the Commander of the Seventh U.S. Army to agree to a limited modification of the boundary in favour of the First French Army. Impressing his wishes on Patch, de Lattre wrote: "I am happy, General, that our two Armies, side by side, should be delivering the final *coup de grâce*. The little flowers gathered in August have brought luck to our armies. I still keep them."

The 1st Armoured Division now headed hard for Ulm. Just to the west it bumped into the 10th U.S. Armoured Division, which seemed surprised to find the French in its area. But the divisional commander made no difficulties. "We cavalrymen," he chivalrously remarked, "will always understand each other."

The 1st French Armoured Division was the first to reach the suburbs of Ulm on the evening of the 23rd, and, on the 24th, French and Americans together entered the city. Mr. Churchill, with his constant sense of the historical, sent the following telegram to General de Gaulle. "Please accept my congratulations on the capture of Ulm by French arms. I should be grateful if you would convey to General de Lattre de Tassigny and his brave soldiers my admiration for their prowess and success."

Meanwhile, to the north, de Monsabert had completed the encirclement of the Swabian Jura. Between the 22nd and the 27th of April his corps captured nearly 30,000 prisoners, among whom was young Manfred Rommel, who at once revealed the conditions in which Hitler had forced his father to poison himself.

When victory was so close, it was unfortunate that there should have been a serious setback in the relations between de Lattre and Devers. Although Stuttgart had been captured by French troops, Devers ordered de Lattre to vacate the town as it was in the American Zone, and he sent in his own Military Government Teams to take over from the French. De Lattre would not move. De Gaulle supported him and Supreme Headquarters eventually gave their agreement to the French viewpoint.

For the incident at Stuttgart there was much to be said for de Lattre's attitude, but almost simultaneously there was a more serious difference of opinion in regard to Ulm, which was unquestionably in the American Zone. Although de Lattre might argue that by moving on Ulm he was helping the advance of his American neighbours, he knew that he was exceeding the orders of his superior. In a personal letter to Bethouart on the 20th April he had said, "I hear you have crossed the Danube at Mulheim. Bravo! Put your foot on the accelerator and press on to Sigmaringen, and from Sigmaringen fly on, south of the Danube, to Ulm. Perhaps the Americans will turn us out. But the French flag will have flown there and it will help our advance on Binnerach and Kempten." The rebellious subordinate had gone too far. The understanding Devers was furious. He ordered de Lattre to send his Chief of Staff at once to Army Group Headquarters. It fell to the lot of Demetz, who had succeeded de Linares, to bear the full force of Devers' anger. Describing the incident later, Demetz said, "Devers—that good and upright Devers—was angrier than I had ever seen him." He would listen to no arguments about the associations of Ulm with Napoleon. His job was to win the war as quickly as possible. But Devers never bore malice. On the 13th May, a few days after the German surrender, Devers took the first opportunity to bury the hatchet. The festival of Joan of Arc was being celebrated at Stuttgart, and Devers expressed a wish to be present. In a spontaneous and chivalrous tribute to de Lattre, which was not without humour, he said, "For many months we have fought together—often on the same side!" For all his rebellious conduct de Lattre had profound respect for Devers, and of de Lattre Devers wrote later, "General de Lattre was a great student of Napoleon, and although times, people and weapons have changed, the names of rivers and towns are more or less the same. This caused General de Lattre to be naughty. He was the same about Stuttgart, and he had a feeling—not justified—that I gave him rôles sometimes which were not in keeping with the French tradition. None of these affairs turned out to be serious, because my system was to handle them directly and personally—not by written order or command or through the staff. Because of this procedure, we learned to trust and admire each other. I am a great admirer of General de Lattre de Tassigny. He was a great soldier—hard on all who served under him, and equally hard on those over him; but he was loyal, and would fight with everything he had, when the die was cast."

To de Lattre a name meant much. He had never liked the name "Army B", and the name which took its place "First French Army" was only a little better. He wanted a name that would inspire, and almost before the Danube was within sight he had decided that his army should become "L'Armée Rhin et Danube". This indeed was a name that savoured of grandeur and glory. Now that the enemy resistance in the Black Forest and in the Swabian Jura had been overcome the way was clear for exploitation into Austria, and the main difficulties that were now to confront the Rhine and Danube Army were administrative and geographical. The 6th Army Group had outrun its supplies, and Devers had to organize an air lift to ensure its maintenance. The Alps also loomed ahead and the exceptional severity of the winter had left later snow than usual.

Orders for the advance into Austria had reached Bethouart as early as the evening of the 25th when he was still engaged with the XVIII S.S. Corps in the eastern exits of the Black Forest. As Bethouart's corps was the better placed and the roads into Austria were few, de Lattre had decided to continue the advance on a one-corps front, leaving to de Monsabert's corps the less spectacular rôle of clearing up the rear. Bethouart now put forward two long thin arms to embrace his immediate objective, which was the Vorarlberg Massif in Western Austria. His right arm, comprising the 5th Armoured Division followed by the 4th Moroccan Mountain Division, was directed along the northern shores of Lake Constance on Bregenz and the Vorarlberg Pass. His left arm, comprising the 1st Armoured Division followed by the 2nd Moroccan Division, which was transferred from II Corps, was directed on the Inn Valley in Western Tyrol. The armour of both arms was to progress as far as it could, until the mountain barriers should compel the infantry to take over.

Schlesser, whose love of *panache* matched that of his Chief, and Durosoy, later to become Military Attaché in London, commanded the leading combat commands on each wing. Despite the threat to their extended communications by isolated enemy detachments, continually closing in behind them, these two first-class cavalry leaders pushed on at full gallop. Here and there, resistance and obstacles were encountered, but quickly brushed aside or surmounted, and by the beginning of May both wings were wending their way up the Alps.

On the right, at a station west of the Vorarlberg Pass, Schlesser came across a partially armoured train. This was quickly set in motion and Schlesser was delighted with this novel spearhead—train and tanks advancing abreast up the Pass. Before the Vorarlberg Tunnel was reached stronger opposition was encountered, but with Schlesser was the incomparable Gambiez with his "Choc" battalion. This indomitable unit, manœuvring off the road in deep snow, quickly cleared the way. At the mouth of the tunnel, a surprising message reached Gambiez. It had come by telephone from the far end of the tunnel and informed him that a detachment of the 2nd Moroccan Division had reached Saint Anton. How had this happened?

Bethouart's left wing had in fact been equally enterprising. When the armour could progress no further, and de Linares with his 2nd Moroccan Division took over, the road was found to be badly cut and further progress for the moment seemed impossible. At Toulon, in command of a detachment, de Linares had already shown his ability to get across seemingly impassable country. Now he was to do so again. He at once organized a mountain detachment, including Chasseurs Alpins on skis, which by dint of exceptional perseverance through a heavy snowstorm, found its way across the mountains to Zurs and down to Saint Anton. The "piper cub" aircraft which was intended to keep touch with it, lost all trace of its tracks. This was the detachment which telephoned to Gambiez at the other end of the tunnel.

For nine months, from the Mediterranean to the Vorarlberg, de Lattre had driven his army hard, and nobly had it responded to the most exacting of his demands. The final scene that he had envisaged was to be the junction of his army with the Allied armies in Italy, but that was not to be. It was at Saint Anton that the "Cease fire" sounded and the drama drew to its close. There in that grandiose Alpine setting the victorious army could reflect with pride on the greatness of its achievements. Proudly also could it claim that glory and honour had been restored to the arms of France.

25. RETROSPECT

DE LATTRE was now entitled to his place in history as a great commander. Some would belittle his achievement by contending that the strength of his opponent had been already spent; but, even if such a contention could be substantiated, they would do well to recall that in 1940, when the power of the enemy was at its height, de Lattre had proved a leader of uncommon merit. In the campaign which had just ended, whatever the disadvantages from which the Germans suffered, the evidence leaves little doubt that at times they fought with undiminished tenacity. In Toulon, in Marseilles, in the Vosges, in the Colmar Pocket, and on the Rhine, the exhortations of the Führer to resist to the last man had not been in vain. It was only when the Rhine had been crossed that there was any real weakening, and even then the fanatical S.S. Corps proved no mean opponent. There were, however, many handicaps that weakened the enemy. In the air he was hopelessly inferior, as indeed he was on every battle-front at this stage of the war; the growing strength of the French Resistance Movement began to take serious toll of his strength; and in the first few weeks of the campaign the advance of Eisenhower from Normandy compelled the commander of the Nineteenth German Army to look over his shoulder. These were great weaknesses, but a more cautious commander than de Lattre might never have exploited them with such resolute daring and speed.

In measuring the stature of de Lattre, it would be more

profitable to consider the handicaps from which he himself was suffering, than to consider those of the enemy. When nations are engaged in mortal combat invention succeeds invention with startling rapidity. Since last de Lattre had seen the battlefield in 1940, the technique of battle had been wholly transformed. But not only did the commander of the First French Army find himself face to face with new and unfamiliar engines of war; he found himself compelled also to learn a new military language. Since the establishment of Allied Force Headquarters, English had become the official military language, and, despite his stay at Brighton in the days of his youth, de Lattre in 1944 was by no means conversant with the English language. It was only his outstanding adaptability that enabled him to dominate such handicaps.

But not only had he to bring himself up to date. Some units in his army had fought and gained experience in North Africa and Italy, but the rest had to be trained anew. All these difficulties were overcome in a remarkably short time, and against a background that did not lighten the burden. In the period of training that preceded the campaign, and throughout the campaign itself, de Lattre was in the position of the poor relation. For almost everything he was dependent upon the Americans, and all their generosity could not compensate for the weakness of such a position. But it was not only in the material sense that he was the poor relation. The tragic events of 1940 had left in the minds of some of the Allies a lack of confidence in the French that was understandable, if not justified. Much of de Lattre's inexhaustible energy was expended in a constant fight to restore confidence on the part of the Allies in the capabilities of the French Army; and in its Commander, that Army had the most stalwart of champions. At times he was provocative and impatient beyond measure, and if a humbler attitude might have made him more popular with his allied superiors, it would never have enabled his army to play so spectacular a part in the final struggle.

When the campaign was launched this poor relationship remained a constant handicap. De Lattre could never give his undivided attention to the conduct of the battle itself, for he was engaged simultaneously in an unending struggle to put forward some French viewpoint that might be unpopular or unwelcome. Only the most robust commander could have shouldered so heavy a burden, and to the comprehension and patience of Devers is due not a little of the credit for the happy outcome of those difficult months.

Of all the qualities which de Lattre displayed in the campaign, it was his unyielding determination in the face of difficulty that was the most outstanding. To persist in carrying through an attack, despite heavy casualties, fatigue, doubting subordinates and arctic weather conditions, demands uncommon courage. Such were the conditions that prevailed both in the Vosges and before Colmar, and in which the impact of his dynamic will upon the whole army carried it forward to success.

During the years that followed the war, de Lattre was constantly preaching the need to develop the taste for risk (le goût du risque). No preacher had ever himself practised more assiduously or effectively what he preached. The decision to launch an army, that was only half concentrated, simultaneously on Toulon and Marseilles was a great risk. Principles that had stood the test of time were broken. But the risk was calculated, for it was the element of surprise that provided the margin in favour of success. Rich indeed was the reward for such a decision. It brought the First French Army to the Rhine ahead of its immediate neighbours. But in the process, the limit of exhaustion had almost been reached. The view, therefore, which had prevailed at Supreme Headquarters, that, if the Colmar pocket had been liquidated sooner, the crisis at Strasbourg would never have arisen, was hardly a fair reflection on the achievements of de Lattre's men. In the event, it was the readiness of their Commander to accept risk and his infectious determination which helped to save the city.

The forcing of the Belfort Gap to the south after failure in the north was an example of flexibility and masterly tactics, in which infantry, artillery, commando, and "choc" units were all employed to the best advantage. His flexibility and tactical ability were further exemplified by the manner in which he switched formations and units from one corps to another in accordance with their suitability, or that of their commander, for the task in hand. When he decided to make his main initial attempt against Belfort with II Corps to the north, he at once transferred Guillaume, whose ability he had so well assessed, to that corps. It was Guillaume's Algerians again to whom de Lattre allotted the daring rôle of saving Strasbourg. When he wanted to clear the east bank of the Rhine opposite Strasbourg he took Valluy's division under his own wing for the task, for, until a few weeks before, Valluy had been on his staff and was completely in his mind. Gambiez, with his "choc" unit, and commando units also were always available in the right area when required.

In other spheres also the flexibility of de Lattre was carried almost to extremes. In exploitation this was particularly marked. As the situation changed, brainwave succeeded brainwave until the far-flung units of his army were spread out over the map without any meaning pattern. A glance at the map showing the movements of his army after the crossing of the Rhine cannot fail to excite admiration for the ability of its commander to retain control. It was only what de Lattre called the "intellectual discipline" of his subordinates that made it possible. They were expected, minute by minute, to be in the mind of their commander.

An indispensable component of de Lattre's headquarters was what he called his "Brains Trust". It included men in all walks of life. At the head was Ludovic Tron, an inspector of finance, who later was to be succeeded by Bernard's Squadron Commander in the 2nd Dragoons, René Bondoux, a lawyer. There were also Roland Cadet, a Councillor of State, Jacques Monod, a biologist, Raoul de Lamazière, the General's brother-in-law, who was a lawyer, and Bernard Simiot, a journalist. Finally there were four charming girls, Mesdemoiselles Monique Vuillemin, Edmonde Charles-Roux, Christiane Lesieur, and Solenge Troisier. The functions of the Brains Trust were unlimited. Primarily it provided the mind of the Chief with that intellectual stimulant that it needed. Intelligence and beauty were his indispensable companions. The men belonged to every extreme of political persuasion and they formed an invaluable liaison link with the heterogeneous elements of which his army was composed. Indeed, they provided a kind of advisory staff on welfare and morale. But that was not the end of their duties. They looked after the unending stream of visitors, soldiers, and civilians that always flooded headquarters. Frequently they had to appease them, for the Chief was often late. Press and publicity were their responsibility, and special missions also often came their way. At all times of the day or night they had to be ready to accompany the Chief when he went forward. They listened to the daily explosions of wrath, and sometimes they were able to pour oil upon troubled waters. "Sometimes, too," wrote Monsieur Simiot later, "we used to ask the 'patron' to go forward again so that we might get a little rest!" Among the many tasks that were performed by the lady members of the Brains Trust were visits to the sick and wounded in hospital.

A visit therefore to the headquarters of the First French Army was never dull. Often it might mean hours of waiting, but there was always charming company. If the Chief was in form he was the most genial of hosts, and if the form was bad the scene might be enlivened by an eloquent outburst of anger.

Throughout the whole campaign de Lattre had an eye on the future. Never did he allow his attention to be absorbed wholly by the immediate battle. Indeed it was the mobility of his mind, among other factors, that rendered so exhausting the work of his staff. Few commanders can have been harder to serve. His successive Chiefs of Staff, Carpentier, Valluy, de Linares, and Demetz had to accustom themselves to irregular hours, short sleep, and the possibility of being sent for at any hour of the night. De Lattre was not content with the company of his own thoughts. If a brainwave occurred in the middle of the night, he would not hesitate to summon a member of his staff or a subordinate commander. Such methods of command imposed upon his staff a strain that was almost intolerable. But with de Lattre nothing was quite normal. It was a part of his technique to accustom all to drive themselves to the limit of endurance. In the hands of another commander such methods would have proved disastrous. In the hands of de Lattre they achieved miracles. To those hard-pressed officers on his staff is due no small measure of credit for the success of the campaign. De Le Boisse, head of his 3rd Bureau (Operations) was indefatigable, and Allard, head of his 4th Bureau (Supply and Transport), with few resources was never at a loss to improvise and make possible the most ambitious projects of his exacting Chief. Hard as he drove them, and despite all those disconcerting and unreasonable outbursts of temper, there were few whom he did not imspire with a deep affection and a readiness to slave for him to the very limit of their capacity.

The trials and strains which Bethouard and de Monsabert had to endure were no less severe than those of his staff. Men of smaller stature would have collapsed under the weight. If they themselves were not summoned by de Lattre at all hours of the night, the probability was that de Lattre would visit them. They never knew what would be the unpredictable mood of their temperamental Chief. At times he would curse them unjustly, at others he would flatter them with honeyed words and an irresistible smile. Recalling those days later, Bethouard said that "with a man of de Lattre's passionate nature, everything was vehement, and everyone who was able to approach him at this period will remember the nights—for everything took place at night, when all decisions were made, sometimes small and sometimes great. I recall some great decisions that were made during those memorable nights, lightning decisions which dazzled and marked this great leader as a genius." Those late hours imposed upon his subordinates the greatest strain of all. General Guisan, Chief of the General Staff of the Swiss Army, who came to know de Lattre well, presented him one day with an alarm clock, not, he made clear, to wake him, but to remind him when it was time to retire.

De Lattre had no reason to be modest about the achievements of his army, but, more than all his victories, it was the welding together of so many diverse elements into one army with one spirit that gave him the deepest satisfaction. Many might wonder whether the resistance groups in France, themselves divided in outlook, would ever work in harness with the armies that came from overseas. Among many, particularly the F.T.P. (Franc tireurs partisans), who represented the left wing of the resistance movement, there was an inborn suspicion and dislike of the army. The problem for de Lattre was to incorporate these elements in the First French Army without destroying the traditions which had been built up with the Maquis, and which were so very different from those of the regular army.

Apart from the need to swell the ranks of the First French Army, the future good relationship between the Army and the nation made it essential that the young men of France should play their full part with the soldiers of the French Empire and those of the Allies in the liberation of their country. With that object in view, de Lattre created a special branch of his staff under Manhes d'Angény, a survivor of the 14th Infantry Divisional staff in 1940, whose main function was to clothe and equip the resistance groups, and generally to incorporate them in his army. With an exceptional comprehension of his compatriots and the divergent political motives which actuated them, he was able, during the months of September and October 1944, to transform suspicion and even hatred of his army into an enthusiastic and widespread desire to fight in its ranks. Communists and indeed all comers were welcome, but he was careful to ensure that the resistance groups to which they had formerly belonged were not broken up. They thereby retained their own traditions and individuality. The successful incorporation of these men into his army was not accomplished without a struggle. Prejudices within the ranks of the resistance movement itself and prejudices among de Lattre's own subordinate commanders, all had to be broken down. Over these and other obstacles de Lattre triumphed in his battle to achieve what he called the "Amalgam". He achieved more. Into the Rhine and Danube Army he instilled as proud a spirit as animated the greatest armies of France, and it reflected his own belief in the continued grandeur of his country.

PART VI

Aftermath

1945–1950

26. A MISSION CUT SHORT

WHEN the fight ceased on the 7th May, headquarters of the First French Army were at Lindau, on the northern shores of Lake Constance. That evening de Lattre invited his corps commanders and most of his divisional commanders to dine with him at the local hotel. Hardly had they sat down to dinner, when he was informed of the arrival of many distinguished French personalities, who had been deported by the Germans. De Lattre at once got up in order to offer them the welcome that he considered to be their due. As he got up, he was handed a telegram from Paris, instructing him to place under arrest any of the individuals then arriving who had occupied any post whatever in the Vichy Government. The telegram particularly specified the name of Weygand. "Whatever might be his own personal feelings towards him", he was to send Weygand to Paris under escort.

It was a disturbing message to receive at the moment he was about to celebrate the victory of his army. To Weygand he owed not a little for that early advancement which had set him on the road to fame, and throughout the dark days from 1940 until 1942, when the invasion of unoccupied France brought separation, he had remained loyal and devoted to his former chief. But in the hour of victory, passions in France ran high, and bitter was the hatred of de Gaulle and his followers against many who had served in the Vichy Government. Weygand himself, for all his hatred of the Germans, could not escape from the wrath of his malevolent compatriots. For de Lattre to disregard the instructions, which he had now received from the Provisional Government in Paris, might well have compromised his future. But he was the last man to desert a friend in the hour of adversity.

A few moments later, in the hall of the hotel, the reunion took place. Weygand, with whom was Madame Weygand, threw himself into the arms of de Lattre and congratulated him with moving warmth on his victory. De Lattre then took Weygand to his room, where for the moment he left him, making no mention of the instructions he had received from Paris.

At one o'clock in the morning de Lattre received a further message from Paris, informing him that he was to go to Berlin and be a witness to the act of capitulation of the enemy. It was not until two o'clock in the morning that he knocked at Weygand's door and informed him of the instructions which he had received about his arrest and transfer to Paris. "Come, de Lattre, you know me," said Weygand, "Not for one day since the armistice, have I ceased to struggle with all my heart against Germany; Germany at any rate did not doubt this and acted accordingly. And this is how I am treated, at the moment when at long last I have the joy of returning to a victorious France."

De Lattre reassured Weygand and told him that not one gendarme of the First French Army would obey the order to escort him to Paris. "Tomorrow," he added, "at whatever hour you decide, the 'Choc' Battalion, with its colours, will parade in your honour. Then my A.D.C., Commandant Borie, will be at your disposal, together with my own car as far as Paris."

At three o'clock in the morning, de Lattre returned to his headquarters, but failed to sleep, and at five-thirty his A.D.C. entered his room with instructions for the General to proceed, by air, at once to Berlin. Three "Piper Cub" aircraft conveyed him, Demetz, and Bondoux to Mengen, forty miles away, where they were due to be picked up at nine o'clock by a Dakota. Leaving Mengen soon after ten, they reached Magdeburg at midday. They were to complete the sixty miles to the Tempelhof airport at Berlin in fighter aircraft, but these had already left with the American and British delegations. De Lattre refused to follow the advice of a Russian officer to await the return of these aircraft. He must not be late, and so the Dakota continued to Tempelhof. The runways had been badly cut up by bombing; moreover, they were so covered with concrete pillboxes and the debris of wrecked aircraft that they resembled the surface of the moon. Only with great difficulty was the landing effected.

The impressionable de Lattre, tired and hungry though he was, retained vivid memories of the final stages of that journey from the airport, by car, to the outskirts of Berlin. He was impressed by the "massive monolithic block" of soldiers of the Russian battalion, drawn up in twelve ranks to do him honour. He was impressed by the grim and sorry spectacle that Berlin then presented. It seemed as if he wandered endlessly through some devastated Babylon, and he was impressed also by the young Russian women, in their simple uniforms, with knees showing bare above their high boots, whom he saw at every cross-road directing traffic, with small red and yellow flags.

In the suburbs of Berlin, the car drew up at Marshal Zhukov's headquarters. But it was some time before they could find any officers and, feeling more hungry than ever, de Lattre and his staff tried to explain by gesticulation that they would like something to eat. A few minutes later one of the well-intentioned Russian soldiers produced a gramophone!

Eventually, de Lattre got in touch with Vassiliev, who had been Soviet Military Attaché in Algiers and was now on Zhukov's staff. Vassiliev conducted de Lattre to Zhukov's villa, and with Zhukov were Tedder, Eisenhower's British deputy, Spaatz, the American Air Commander, and Burrough, the British Admiral. De Lattre always formed hasty likes and dislikes and on this occasion the warmth of Tedder's greeting gained his immediate and firm friendship. Zhukov was wearing a great white cape, thrown over his shoulders like the mantle of some Knight Templar. It was a present from Eisenhower, and on it were boldly emblazoned the insignia of S.H.A.E.F. Zhukov also impressed de Lattre by what he called his metallic glance, his massive countenance, and, indeed, by his whole being, which gave forth an impression of singular power and humanity.

Although Zhukov was pleasant, he did not appear to have been warned that de Lattre would be present. Shortly after this initial contact with the allied commanders, de Lattre and Bondoux went to inspect the room in which the Act of Capitulation was to be signed. Drama impended. On the wall, at the back of the room which he now entered, de Lattre's ever-observant eye noticed that three flags had been hung: the Stars and Stripes, the Union Jack, and the Red Flag. There was no Tricolour; France, whose grandeur, lost for a moment, had been restored by the valour of his men, had been insulted. In a moment, for he was tired and hungry, de Lattre flew into one of those fits of anger, when he became as a man possessed. Upon the unfortunate Russian interpreter, who had only just been attached to him, burst the full fury of his anger. In his account of the incident, de Lattre refers to the "surprise" of the interpreter. It would be amusing to know what the interpreter himself really felt, at the strange behaviour of this foreign General, whom he had only just met and who now shouted orders to him, to see that a French flag was immediately hung beside the other three. While the Russian interpreter scurried off to try to give effect to de Lattre's orders, Bondoux was instructed not to leave the room, until they had been carried out. This was but one of countless little dramas that so coloured the life of this unusual soldier.

Comedy succeeded drama. The Russians agreed to place the Tricolour beside the other three. But nowhere could a flag of France be found. Eventually, a few young Russian girls, with some red material taken from a Nazi flag, a white sheet and some blue serge from a mechanic's boiler-suit, produced the flag of Holland, and so the work had to be started again. By the late evening, the flag of France hung beside those of the United States, Great Britain, and Russia, and de Lattre's humour returned.

The incident of the Tricolour was not the only difficulty that preceded the signing of the Act of Capitulation. At one moment it looked as though there would be opposition to de Lattre signing at all, but in Tedder de Lattre found a great ally. "I shall deserve to be hung," said de Lattre to Tedder, "if I return to France without having signed." Thanks largely to the ingenuity of Tedder and an unusually compromising attitude on the part of Vyshinsky, who had arrived from Moscow, an amiable, if complex, agreement was reached. Zhukov and Tedder, in the name of Eisenhower, were to sign as the two contracting parties, while Spaatz and de Lattre were to sign as witnesses. But in order that everyone should be satisfied, there were to be eighteen copies. On nine copies Zhukov signed first, and on the other nine Tedder signed first. On the copies which Zhukov signed first, de Lattre signed as first witness, and on the other copies, which Tedder signed first, Spaatz signed as first witness.

By a quarter to one in the morning of the 9th May, the formalities were over. Perhaps for de Lattre, more than for any of the others present, the moment was one of exceptional emotion. When, in 1940, he had seen his country trampled ruthlessly underfoot, little could he have imagined that he would live to witness the scene that had just been enacted before his eyes. But there was to be one more drama before he left Berlin. Within an hour of the signing of the Act of Capitulation, the room had been cleared and a banquet spread. It was now past one in the morning. Soon after they had sat down, Zhukov rose to his feet and paid tribute to the glory of Stalin, to Roosevelt, and to Churchill. There was no mention of France. De Lattre refused to eat or drink. The others thought he must be ill. Eventually de Lattre succeeded in conveying to Zhukov the reason for his abstention. A few moments later there came a message from Zhukov which was interpreted to de Lattre. "Marshal Zhukov wishes you to know that soon you will be able to eat and drink." Zhukov then got up again and paid a special tribute to France. The band struck up the Marseillaise and all stood up, there was much enthusiasm, and de Lattre was happy.

He was never at a loss, when it was a question of speaking, and he too now rose to his feet and paid a warm tribute to Stalin and to the Red Army, and, referring to the need for preventing a new tragedy overwhelming the world, he concluded, "France will always be needed." No jarring notes remained to mar the midnight symphony. The vodka flowed, and revelry was unrestrained. Nearly thirty toasts were drunk before the party dispersed at seven o'clock in the morning.

After barely one hour's sleep, de Lattre was up again and on the way to Tempelhof airport. But, in that moment of elation, it was difficult to feel fatigue. As the aircraft sped westward, and the ruins of Berlin faded in the distance, de Lattre's thoughts turned towards those valiant men whose exertions and sacrifices had enabled him to live those last few hours. He drafted his Victory Order of the Day, which concluded thus: "By your exertions, your fervour, and your heroism, you have restored to our country her rank and her grandeur." Above all else it was the restoration of his country's grandeur that absorbed his mind.

The successful commander in the field now found himself in

command of an army of occupation. It was not a rôle that promised to provide sufficient outlet for his insatiable energy, but the task of the moment was again to become an absorbing passion. His first aim was to inspire in the Germans a due respect for the French Army. Still impregnated with Nazi propaganda, they believed that, in so far as the French were concerned, only a handful of "Gaullist Brigands" had participated in the final victory. By its conduct and bearing, he would prove that it was a disciplined and spirited French Army that had contributed to their defeat.

But this was only the prelude to what he conceived to be his most important mission. In his own words, the French Army in Germany was there to "throw forward a bridgehead towards German youth". With his lively imagination, he saw his army in Germany as an educational force that might transform the youth of Germany. By an appeal to their hearts, he would raise them from the depths of Nazi materialism to the higher peaks of the spirit. But these idealistic conceptions did not always receive from Paris the encouragement that he expected.

In the early days of the occupation, there was another task that preoccupied the allied commanders in Germany. It was the care of those countless deportees whom the army had liberated in the final stages of the campaign. Thousands were on the point of death, and they could not be repatriated without weeks of loving care on the part of the armies. De Lattre gave this tragic problem his full and comprehending attention, and the care which the Rhine and Danube Army bestowed upon these unfortunate people was not the least of its achievements.

At the same time, de Lattre redoubled his efforts to make his army the worthy ambassador of France. Parades and inspections followed each other with unremitting frequency, and the standard of drill soared ever higher. But it was his own headquarters at Lindau that must set the example, and within a few weeks, an army of builders, gardeners, and craftsmen was set in motion in order to produce something that would worthily represent the dignity of the occupying power. Lindau soon came to rival in splendour the glittering palace of some oriental satrap, and more and more the Army Commander came to be known as "Le Roi Jean". Of all his nicknames it was the one he preferred. On the roads, a high-powered car conveyed him from unit to unit, while the motor-cyclist escort proudly heralded his approach; and on the waters of Lake Constance, he flew his flag in a stately craft of dazzling white.

The beauty of the lake, against its background of mountains, provided a perfect setting for those spectacular displays that he loved. Many distinguished men—French and Allied—will remember the splendour of de Lattre's receptions at Lindau. But the most splendid of all was that which he reserved for General Devers, to whose understanding and patience he owed so much. To the organization of that reception, therefore, he applied every ounce of his imagination. It lasted for more than twelve hours. During the day there was a review, and in the evening, by the shores of the lake, General Devers walked through an avenue of torches formed by 2,000 Goums, while music came forth from the woods. But of all the displays that marked that memorable evening, the most fantastic of all was the appearance of a mighty raft, which had been specially constructed to carry the band of the Spahis. Impressive and moving also was that closing scene, when the beams of many searchlights converged upon the lake; and there, upon a raft, two gigantic flags—the Stars and Stripes and the Tricolour—floated proudly side by side. Then out across the waters, towed by two invisible craft, they began to move away, and in the fading beams of the searchlights they were gradually lost to view. It was a happy and symbolic conclusion to the ups and downs of that singular partnership between Devers and de Lattre. Lyautey himself could have staged nothing better, and Father Bardier would have been proud of his former pupil at Poitiers. The superb showmanship was to earn for de Lattre yet another nickname—"Le Général du Théâtre de Marigny". Not only was he a showman, he was also a great actor. Ever since the days when he and his troop, on the hill above Pont-à-Mousson, would salute the distant Metz, his sense of the theatrical had continued to develop. "Third-rate actor" (*Cabotin*) said the smaller-minded critics. But a talent for acting can often serve a commander, and he who best contrives to look and act the part is most likely to inspire.

His subordinates also were expected to conform. On the occasion of his official entry into Constance, he set out by boat from Lindau with a large staff, escorted by a flotilla of small craft. At the quay at Constance, only a small guard of honour was drawn up to welcome him. Upon the Military Governor broke a storm, "You don't begin to understand the meaning of our victory or the duty of our army here. You are not fit to be a victor. You have not a speck of imagination. I shall come back in a week and I shall expect to be received here by a battalion, the regimental band, the colours of all the units stationed here, the burgomaster, and all the local authorities. The whole town must be bedecked with flags."

In dull and dreary days, the dazzling scene at Lindau brought lively and refreshing contrast. But de Lattre was not without enemies, and murmurings of these displays and of the extravagance at his headquarters began to reach Paris in exaggerated form, and to provide cheap ammunition for those who wished him ill. Extravagance there was, but it would be wrong to think, as some supposed, that de Lattre himself feasted like Lucullus. His appreciation of good food and wine was markedly less than that of most of his compatriots, and his fare was generally of the simplest. That form of extravagance he never adopted. Moreover, the underlying motive behind all that he did at Lindau was his determination that the flag of France should float proudly and worthily above his headquarters.

On the 5th June de Lattre attended at Berlin the first meeting of the four Allied Commanders-in-Chief to inaugurate the work of the Control Commission in Germany. During the meeting, it was announced on the wireless that de Lattre's position was essentially of a temporary character. It was not a tactful moment for such an announcement, and it tended to diminish his authority at the meeting; but it was a warning that he was not likely to be left long enough in Germany to complete those plans for German youth which he had so deeply at heart. Indeed, youth had then become an obsession with him. However obvious it might be that the future of the world was in its hands, there were few who were clear in their minds as to what was wanted, or ready to take the bold and active steps that were required. De Lattre was perfectly clear, and had been ready to devote all his energy to the realization of his ideas. But he was not to be given the time, even to lay the foundations of that great edifice which he had in mind.

On the 24th July, the First French Army was dissolved, and General Koenig was appointed Commander-in-Chief of the Army of Occupation. Bethouart became commander of the French Troops in Austria, and in Germany only de Monsabert remained of the three senior commanders who had led the Rhine and Danube Army to victory. On the 27th July, de Lattre welcomed his successor and issued his last Order of the Day. Grandeur and fervour were ever the theme. It ended thus: "Preserve intact the memory of our struggles, our victories, and the brotherhood of our ranks. The spirit of the Rhine and Danube Army will survive in each one of you; and tomorrow, in your new duties, may you be the fervent and uncompromising artisans of the grandeur of France." On the 4th August came the day to take leave of those who had served him so well. On the banks of the Rhine at Kehl, colour parties from every unit in his army were drawn up. Slowly, sadly, but proudly, he walked down to the bridge that led to Strasbourg, giving to each colour, as he passed, a salute that conveyed the full depth of his gratitude. It was his last glimpse of that great army, which on the morrow was to break up and pass into history.

27. PARIS

In the autumn of 1945 Paris was only just beginning to shake off the effects of a long occupation by the enemy. The Place de la Concorde and other places still bore traces of the final struggle before the Germans left. Most of the big hotels were still requisitioned by Supreme Headquarters. Maxim's was a British club. The black market flourished. Allied troops still thronged the boulevards, along which rumbled army lorries, and where large forbidding signboards were still in place to warn the drivers that "Death was so permanent". Civilian cars in numbers were only just beginning to return, and to enliven the scene with the impatient hooting of their horns. But, here and there, the heart would be gladdened, as gay and graceful creatures sped by on their bicycles. Neither the years of occupation nor the austerity that resulted could impair their chic or charm! In short it was still the Paris of the Liberation, and Leclerc and his 2nd Armoured Division, who had been the first to enter the city, were its heroes. De Gaulle was still head of the Provisional Government.

Such was the unusual Paris to which de Lattre now returned. He felt a stranger, lonely and unhappy. Only with some difficulty was he able to regain possession of the small flat which he had taken, just before the war, in the Avenue de Breteuil. He resented the somewhat abrupt manner of his recall. A few days before he had commanded a great army. Now he had not even a headquarters. In the bosom of the Rhine and Danube Army and amid the acclamations of a grateful Alsace, he had been constantly aware that the achievements of his army had been recognized. In Paris he sensed no such recognition. Neither he nor his army seemed known. There—so it seemed to him—it was only of Leclerc and his 2nd Armoured Division that men were aware. Sensitive, as ever, he was deeply mortified.

The clash of temperaments and views between de Lattre and de Gaulle precluded a relationship that was entirely happy. But, although affection might have no place, there was no one among his near contemporaries whom de Lattre respected as he respected de Gaulle. The resentment that he felt at his removal from Germany found no expression in the letter which he wrote to de Gaulle at the time. "At the moment of leaving the First Army," he wrote, "I want to repeat to you my gratitude for having appointed me a year ago to its command. It will always remain the proudest honour of my life."

De Gaulle may have been difficult with de Lattre, but he knew his worth. Indeed, it was he who gave him command of the only army which France then had, and who personally decorated him with the highest honours which France could give, the Grand Croix de la Légion d'Honneur, the Croix de la Libération and the Médaille Militaire. It was he also who deputed him to represent France at Berlin. Referring later to his relations with de Lattre, de Gaulle wrote as follows: "De Lattre was older than me and was my senior at Saint-Cyr. I had always known him. He was not easy, and I fear that I too am not easy. But I never ceased to regard him and to treat him as a 'Grand Monsieur.'" However incomprehensible de Gaulle may sometimes have been, he is as sincere and honest a patriot as France has ever known. "I am convinced," said a British Admiral, who worked closely with de Gaulle at a difficult moment in the General's career, "that de Gaulle had no thought of self. It was always France that he placed first, second, third and fourth." The views, therefore, which de Gaulle expressed in regard to his relations with de Lattre, may be regarded as wholly sincere. He now offered de Lattre the post of Inspector-General of the Army. But de Lattre could see no attraction in the offer. In his view the post would be merely honorific, unless it carried with it also the post of Chief of the General Staff. Only as Chief of the General Staff would he be able to build anew an army after his own fashion. For the moment de Gaulle could not agree.

While his future remained under consideration de Lattre found plenty to occupy his mind. He did not forget the men who had brought him fame. There now was formed in Paris an Old Comrades' Association to be known as "L'Association Rhin et Danube". Very soon it acquired the same vitality which had animated the First Army, and, in its ambitious schemes of welfare, once again Madame de Lattre was to prove her husband's devoted and untiring supporter.

At this time de Lattre used the office of the Association as his own headquarters. It was not only the welfare of its members that claimed his attention; he was determined also that their achievements should now be fully recognized. He therefore embarked upon a vast campaign of publicity to achieve his purpose. Soon the office became alive with that familiar stir and bustle that always characterized the headquarters of de Lattre. Soldiers, politicians, journalists, lawyers, and a host of others came and went throughout the day. Already, also, he was formulating his own ideas about the organization of the new army, and he was anxious that men in all walks of life should come to share his views. The critics have not been backward in condemning his love of publicity, but, whatever strain of vanity there may have been, the publicity that he set in motion was not always in his own interests.

It was not until the end of November that he ceased to be officially unemployed. Then, at last, he was appointed Inspector-General of the Army and Chief of the General Staff. Already he was clear in his own mind as to what he intended to accomplish. There was little on which to build. Perhaps it was better that he should have to start afresh. Nine divisions had been formed by the end of the war, but these were about to disintegrate. Since 1940 the vast majority of the officers had languished in German prison camps. Others had seen no service since then. "Les naphtalinés" they were unkindly christened, since their uniforms had been in mothball. Excepting those who had served with the Free French or in the First French Army, all were out of date. No class had been called up since 1940, and the machinery for doing so was rusty. But these and other difficulties were insignificant beside that insidious malaise and lack of confidence which had gripped the nation after its momentary defeat and occupation by the enemy. The restoration of morale therefore transcended all other aims. It was a task that demanded all those qualities with which de Lattre had been so richly endowed.

In the paper which he now submitted to the Government, embodying his ideas, he stressed at the outset that the efficiency of an army depended as much upon its political cohesion as upon anything else. The traditional links between the Army and the nation must be forged anew. For that reason he advocated a national and not a small professional army, for national service would provide the one opportunity in a lifetime when men of all sorts and kinds would be thrown together, learn to understand each other, and, above all, learn to live together as a team working for the common good, and not, as so often in France, as individualists. The whole conception of military service should be changed. By the substitution of open-air camps for the dismal and insanitary barracks of old, an opportunity would be provided for the development both of mind and body to the best advantage. In short, in the new army de Lattre visualized not only an instrument of war, but an indispensable instrument for the regeneration of the whole nation, by the restoration of confidence to its disillusioned youth.

The essence of this visionary conception was to be provided by the new "Light Camps," as they came to be called, which were soon to spring up all over the country. They were appropriate to a period when there was virtually no equipment, no capacity for its production, and no money. Moreover, the future form which the organization of national defence would take was not yet known. It would be premature, he argued, even to think of rearming, before there was a clearer notion as to what would be the best weapons and equipment for the future. He refrained therefore from building up at once what his critics called "an effective army". The special conditions obtaining at the time dictated concentration on moral rather than material factors. In the Light Camp, the soldier would regain physical and moral well-being. He would be given a working knowledge of all the weapons and equipment, French and Allied, then in existence. By constantly taking them to pieces and reassembling them, he would acquire such a broad and practical knowledge that he would with ease be able to adapt himself to whatever new inventions should drop from the skies in the future. Such a system would at least ensure that there would be built up immediately a reserve of men with a morale that had been wholly revitalized; but the conception went further; the nation would be provided with the healthy and high-minded citizens that it needed.

The fervour which de Lattre displayed in the realization of these grandiose projects knew no bounds. Never had that office in the "Corridor of the Generals", as it was called, at the Ministry of War in the Boulevard Saint-Germain, witnessed so animated a scene. Along that corridor now flowed that stream of visitors which had previously flooded the headquarters of the "Association Rhin et Danube". There were few things that de Lattre loved more than beautifully made models. Just as his home was filled with model ships, so now his office was filled with perfect scale models of the huts, and other components, that went to make the Light Camps. As a showman he was unequalled. To enter that office and to see him displaying his wares with his bewitching smile and his infectious enthusiasm was to be converted. He now occupied a large house at Saint-Cloud, made available by Princess Marie Bonaparte of Greece. There, too, dining late, night after night, a throng of guests would listen and sometimes advise, as their host unfolded his plans.

Meanwhile, as the war receded, Paris was beginning to shed her winter garments. Official ceremonies, receptions, and cocktail parties began to succeed each other with bewildering frequency. With all his activities, even if it was for a moment, de Lattre tried to put in an appearance. He would never shut himself up within the confines of his military life. It was as the breath of life to him to see all and to hear all that was happening in the outside world. Moreover, an ever larger public would become acquainted with his views and projects. And so Paris came to know him. He was an imposing figure. Even in battledress, faultlessly cut, he contrived to look smart, and his trousers were pressed as those of a British guardsman. Not a few of his shirts and ties came from London. On his left sleeve he wore the emblem of the Rhine and Danube Army. Above it was the emblem of the American "Rangers", and below it the honorary stripes of a "caporal chef" in the "choc" battalions. Only a few of the more valued ribbons adorned his breast Among them was the British Military Cross, presented to him by the Duke of Connaught in the First World War. On his right breast was the badge of the Parachute Regiment. He never wore the colourful "kepi" of pre-war days. It savoured too much of all those outmoded things that he was trying to abolish. His was always khaki. It adorned a head that was unusually imposing with the aquiline nose and firm chin. The brisk walk and the stick and gloves, his inseparable companions, completed the picture.

Difficulties were soon to be encountered. All the Allied Governments, with their depleted exchequers, were anxious to reduce military expenditure. At the beginning of 1946, before the budget had been voted, it was decided to reduce the Army, including the Gendarmerie, to a total strength of 300,000. The proposed reduction would have the most unfortunate effect upon the Army, which, now that it had been almost demobilized, was entirely composed of professional soldiers. The annual contingent to be called up represented alone about 200,000 men. If, therefore, the total strength of the Army, including the Gendarmerie, was to be reduced to 300,000, many professional soldiers, French and native, who had deserved well of their country in the war would have to be discharged. Among the officers so to suffer would be many who had served in the resistance movement, and whom politically it was expedient to retain.

De Lattre now had to embark upon a hard struggle to prevent the complete implementation of such a decision. He was no mean advocate. He pointed out the vast peace-time commitments of the

Army which seemed to have been forgotten. Apart from its essential rôle of defence, there was the occupation of Germany and Austria, and there were the innumerable tasks to be performed in the French Empire or Union, as it now came to be called. Moreover, more than ever before, the Army was the indispensable organ for reviving the virility of the nation. His pleading was not unavailing. The figure of 340,000 excluding the Gendarmerie, was agreed; 60,000 men had been saved by the efforts of de Lattre.

Bernard de Lattre had now himself joined the Army. Early in 1945 he had recovered from his wound, and with his youthful enthusiasm had tried to rejoin his regiment before he had been passed fit. For this he was punished, but he was able to participate in the crossing of the Rhine, and his regiment was the first to cross the Danube and to reach Constance. In August he went to the military school of Coetquidan, in Brittany. It had replaced Saint-Cyr, which had been destroyed by allied bombing. His knowledge of his father's ideas on reform and his own experiences at the training centres of Opme and Douera, made him disgusted with the antiquated methods that still obtained at Coetquidan and he did not hesitate to write the most critical letters. In December, just as his father had become Chief of the General Staff, he was able at last to spend a few weeks at home before going on to Saumur, which had now become the school for officers destined for the armour. There he found a completely different atmosphere, for it was commanded by Durosoy, who had commanded the 1st Combat Command in de Lattre's army, and was wholly impregnated with the ideas of his former chief. "I am delighted here," he wrote to his mother. "The buildings are clean, everyone is happy, and all are working keenly and learning to love their profession. . . . The instructors are interesting, the future seems rosy and the whole atmosphere is conducive to work."

The atmosphere which obtained under Durosoy at Saumur was that which de Lattre was now determined to create throughout the Light Camps. These had to be constructed in record time, for the new Chief had only taken over at the end of November 1945, and in May 1946 the first contingent of the new class was due to be called up. Of the prodigious activity which marked the opening months of 1946, few will retain more vivid memories than those officers in the Engineers and the administrative services, who were called upon to meet the impossible demands of de Lattre. But, lashed by his whip or coaxed by the irresistible charm of his smile, they performed miracles. Hardly a day passed when de Lattre did not leave Paris, by car or by air, to supervise personally the work in hand. Often, during the night, he would have had a new brainwave, and work already completed would have to be pulled down and started afresh. To raise technical difficulties, financial objections, or restrictions imposed by regulations were of no avail. His will was adamant, and in three months almost twelve camps had been completed and were ready to receive their recruits.

One of the major problems involved in the calling up of the class was the shortage of instructors, for the majority of regular non-commissioned officers were in North Africa or Indo-China. De Lattre devised a solution of fortune. The national service men would provide their own instructors. The period of service was one year. The annual contingent, therefore, would be called up in two halves, at six months' interval. After four months' service only, potential non-commissioned officers would be selected, and would then undergo an intensive two months' course at a training centre. Thus, after only six months' service, they would be available to instruct the second half of the contingent which was called up six months after themselves. It was a remarkable example of improvisation, and if it did not produce perfection, it achieved a surprising degree of success.

The most important function of the Light Camp was the infusion of high morale, and to achieve that object de Lattre, as usual, set great store by the site to be chosen. If the Camp were situated amid beautiful scenery, and, above all, on high ground commanding extensive views, it would at the outset, so he contended, elevate the spirit to a higher plane. There were many sites, therefore, which he selected himself, and the apple of his eye was Mutzig. Situated high upon a hill that once had been a fort, it dominated the whole plain of Alsace. In that grandiose scenery, with its historical associations, the mind could not fail to be inspired.

The Light Camp itself resembled a vast garden in which clustered a series of independent hamlets, represented by the platoons. The basis of the system was family life within the platoon. The platoon commander was to be the father of his men, and more than ever before was he to devote his life to their well-being. But in no sense was he to molly-coddle them; rather was he to harden them. Although food was centrally cooked, the platoon fed in its own area. Indeed, it had its own small kitchen, in which men were encouraged to supplement or improve the ordinary diet by their own ingenuity. Each platoon also had its own workshop, for there were few things upon which de Lattre insisted more than the encouragement of craftsmanship. In the workshop, every man could put his hand to something in accordance with the capacity of the individual. Moreover, the workshop enabled each platoon to improve the amenities of its area. Some of the results were worthy of the finest interior decorators in Paris.

Each platoon also had its own small assault course, parade ground, and basket-ball court. It was, therefore, almost wholly self-contained. If more varied facilities and amenities were needed, they would be found with the company or the battalion.

Arms drill was perfected as rarely before in the French Army. But the instantaneous and automatic obedience to orders must not produce automatons. In order that men might still be free to think for themselves, arms drill could be carried out in three times, quick, medium, and slow; and sometimes the cautionary word of command might be: "On the command slope arms, the front rank will do so in quick time, the centre rank in medium time and the rear rank in slow time." It was a procedure that lent itself to infinite variations and to the most comic confusion. But the men had to think.

Technical military instruction was reduced to its simplest elements. Weapons and equipment were collected from scrap-heaps of France. Sometimes under supervision and sometimes on their own, the men would take to pieces and assemble this assortment of material until automatically they developed what de Lattre called "that feeling for material," which would enable men later to handle new weapons and new equipment after the briefest instruction.

Long hours were devoted to physical training, but the high-light of every camp was the assault course. On the "parcours du risque", as it was called, was developed that taste for danger, which would enable men to discover their latent courage and to develop the full strength of their powers. In a few weeks, the most timid of men could surmount the most forbidding obstacles, many of which were due to the fertility of de Lattre's own imagination; for at every camp, the battalion assault course claimed his special attention.

At British and American battle-schools the realities of the battlefield had already been faithfully reproduced. De Lattre would go one better. A few weeks after joining, every recruit was put through what became known as the "chicken run". It was a sort of miniature range in the open, enclosed by rabbit wire. Each section would be made to advance towards an objective. From their departure base, two machine guns would pour live ammunition, a few feet over their heads, into the objective. The advance would be still further enlivened by detonations and thunderflashes to the front and to the rear. The platoon officer would supervise from a sort of bridge, half-way between the point of departure and the objective, and parallel to the line of advance. On the bridge, with bullets passing a few feet from his head, the officer was supposed to walk up and down with his arms folded, imperturbable as the captain on the bridge of his ship in time of danger. This was a little refinement which de Lattre himself added, to create, as he said, mutual confidence between the platoon commander and his men!

To enumerate all the activities at one of de Lattre's Light Camps would be impossible, but mention should be made of one daily ceremony, to which de Lattre attached the greatest importance. It was the hoisting of the Tricolour in the morning and its lowering at Retreat in the evening. This ceremony, insisted de Lattre, must be performed with extreme solemnity and dignity, for in the morning it represented the oath of the soldier, that he would dedicate the day to the service of his country, and in the service of his country, and in the evening it symbolized the examination of his conscience. It was not surprising that these unusual methods should invite criticism. "He is a 'fantaisiste'," said some: "He is turning our Army into Boy Scouts," said others. But there is little doubt that, by such devices, he succeeded in implanting a nobler sense of duty and service.

28. INSECURE SEAT

NOW that the Light Camps had been completed, an ever-bubbling stream of energy must be poured into them; and so those endless visits of de Lattre continued. His inspections became legendary. Through the camps he would sweep like a whirlwind, uprooting without mercy all that was mediocre or out-moded. Things were never wholly as he wished, and if he could find nothing else with which to find fault, he would pick on a hut in which some trivial adornment was deficient. Many will remember the scene at one camp when an electric bulb in one of the wash-houses was deficient. Officers and non-commissioned officers, however remotely connected with the affair, were sent doubling from every corner of the camp to listen to the inimitable flow of abuse.

De Lattre wanted the whole nation to see his handiwork, and he rarely carried out an inspection without a trail of spectators following in his wake. Politicians, mayors, journalists, military attachés, and others, were treated to an exhilarating if exhausting experience; for the pace was quick and the hours were long. Indeed, in his enthusiasm, all sense of time seemed lost, and, as dusk fell, the indefatigable showman would still be seen leading the straggling spectators along the assault course, gleefully expounding the horrors of each obstacle. Throughout the day he would be expounding with a clarity and vigour that was unique. He was happy speaking. Words seemed to come easily to him; and sometimes more easily still if he closed his eyes. His more felicitous little speeches would generally be prefaced by a familiar shrug of the shoulders, while his hands were folded in front of him. The unending theme was youth—the fervour of youth and the need for its total dedication to the service of France. Later, there might be a theatrical or similar performance produced by the troops, preferably in the open. Few things stirred and inspired him as these midnight performances under a clear and star-lit sky; and at the end, if the *mise en scène* had been perfect, all would gather round him to hear uplifting words.

It was the camp of Mutzig, in the heart of Alsace, that claimed most of his time. The mystique of Alsace had always drawn him, and since his victory at Colmar, Alsace and its people had acquired a place in his heart that vied with that of La Vendée. Moreover, he now had a house in Strasbourg, and although he never relaxed, it was there that he spent some of the happiest week-ends of his life. Madame de Lattre was there, patiently providing for the continuous stream of guests. Mutzig was but a short distance by car, and lively must be the memories of a host of distinguished visitors who were privileged to visit that camp. An arduous morning would be broken by a gay and festive luncheon. Charming waitresses, in Alsatian dress, would welcome the General with a becoming smile, and fragrant wine would flow to the accompaniment of martial music. But not all the visitors were in training for the strenuous hours that followed.

There was one inspection of Mutzig that was more than usually exhausting. In the late evening at last it came to an end, and de Lattre, with the spectators who had accompanied him, moved off to the airport to embark in the two aircraft which were to convey them back to Paris. Rarely have weary men been so glad to sit back and relax. But all was not yet over. There must be a final glimpse of the camp, and so the pilot was instructed, before heading for Paris, to fly over Mutzig. The nature of the hill on which it stood enabled the aircraft to encircle the camp at its own level. Then, for fully five minutes, it twirled and twisted over the area, inducing in the passengers a disturbing giddiness, as skies, parade grounds, trees and assault courses flashed past their bewildered eyes. The efforts of the accompanying aircraft to conform, at close quarters, to the antics of its companion, did little to soothe the mind. And meanwhile, unmoved and untiring, de Lattre continued his dissertation on the features of the camp.

Throughout 1946 and the early part of the following year, the tempo increased. Sometimes two camps would be inspected in the same day, but it was rare for de Lattre to reach the second camp until night was almost falling. To avoid long hours of waiting, the more cunning commanding officers established posts at the airport, or on the roads, to give warning of his approach. Some were bold enough to tackle him on his unpunctuality. "Officers must learn to be flexible," would be his invariable reply.

Those "bourgeois" habits of set routine and fixed time-tables must be cast aside.

The pace left little time for leisure, but, in February 1947, he was able to accept an invitation to attend the wedding of Mr. Churchill's daughter Mary to Captain Christopher Soames. On the following day, Mr. Churchill invited him to luncheon at his house in Hyde Park Gate. De Lattre was staying at Claridges, and his staff did everything to ensure that he should be punctual. Even so, they had anxious moments. In the morning he went on one of those shopping expeditions in Bond Street, which he came so much to enjoy, and he only returned to his hotel just before he was due to leave for Mr. Churchill's house. He actually reached Hyde Park Gate a few minutes ahead of time. Stepping out of the car, and raising his arms in the most theatrical manner, he laughingly exclaimed to those who waited, "You see, it is all a legend, this unpunctuality of mine." There must have been few luncheon parties which De Lattre enjoyed more. In his inimitable French, his host plunged fearlessly into the widest range of topics. After luncheon, de Lattre had to catch the boat train. As he embarked, he was still smoking the voluminous cigar which he had started at Hyde Park Gate.

Meanwhile, with the resignation of de Gaulle at the beginning of 1946, the provisional French Government had given place to the old system, and Monsieur Vincent Auriol was elected as the first post-war President of the Republic. De Lattre was now called upon to serve a succession of ministers of contrasting views and temperaments. Adaptable and flexible as he was, his efforts to keep in the saddle were not going to be easy. In no country have politicians feared the acquisition of too much power or popularity by a soldier more than in France, where memories of General Boulanger in the last century still linger. De Lattre was to prove no exception. The very enthusiasm with which he applied himself to the revitalization of French youth was enough to make him suspect. Moreover, his continued love of contacts with men in all walks of life earned for him again the reputation of an intriguer and a political soldier.

There is no definition that is clear as to what is meant by a political soldier. If the professional head of the Army is aflame with ideas of reform, it would be strange indeed if he did not strive to carry his minister with him. It is not surprising, therefore, that with the advent of each succeeding Government, de Lattre should exclaim to the more intimate members of his entourage "Est-ce bon pour notre affair?" "Notre affaire" was nothing more than his own plans for the reorganization of the Army and the betterment of French youth. If that was political soldiering, it was hardly a crime; nor could it fairly be ascribed to ambition, for he had already reached the summit.

It is probable that de Lattre, despite all assertions to the contrary, had no politics of his own. Indeed, at various times in his career he was assailed both by the right and the left. He had a profound faith in the fundamental good sense and qualities of every Frenchman, whatever his politics; and he longed to see them united in the service of a new and better France. If the achievement of such an ideal was not strictly within the province of a soldier, at least he could contribute his part.

De Lattre might make use of all and sundry in his determination to reach his goal, but although often in his life he had been pursued by hatred and jealousy, he never intrigued to pull men down. Indeed, he had a capacity to forgive, which was not the least of his more amiable traits. When the Second World War was over, he even agreed to receive a senior officer who, in 1942, had helped to betray him. But to many officers his unusual methods and the alternate application of charm and violence proved most distasteful. "Il fait valser les officiers," deplored the critics. For some officers a little waltzing was quite salutary; but there were others whose age and dignity did not befit them to waltz in public. It was not surprising, therefore, that among the senior officers his enemies grew; and it was among the more junior officers, and among the troops, that de Lattre sought that indispensable affection that he needed. It was easy for the critics to call him a demagogue, but few commanders have more wholly merited the affection of the troops than de Lattre. Their welfare was his constant care.

But statesmen, too, began to mistrust their ability to resist the charmer. Some of the ministers whom de Lattre served gave him their full and fervent support; some were lukewarm and others were hostile; and with every change of Government the prospects of de Lattre began to ebb and flow. In messes, and in the bars and salons of Paris, he provided a constant topic of conversation. The gossips thrived. "De Lattre is out", "de Lattre is remaining", came the alternate whispers. Twice before in his life, in 1934 and again at Montpellier in 1942, senior officers had played him false. The bitter memories which these events had left behind might in part account for the less pleasing traits in his character which now began to assert themselves. As hostility increased, he became more than ever suspicious, and from the pangs of jealousy he suffered acutely and unreasonably. But on he rode.

Mottoes de Lattre had always liked and one which he now enjoyed to quote was "Ibat" (Latin: He continued on his way). He had learnt it from Canon Kir, the remarkable Deputy and Mayor of Dijon, whose conduct during the occupation had been outstandingly courageous. A few years before, at a dinner in Dijon, the General had overheard someone criticizing his training methods. For all his strength of character, his extreme sensitiveness made him unusually resentful of criticism. To Canon Kir, who was next to him, he poured out his heart, not only then, but on the next day also, when they travelled together by air to Paris. The Canon, seeking to restore in his companion a more serene state of mind, referred to the many great men in history, who in their life-time had been criticized, and whose achievements had failed to earn due recognition. Years ago he himself had decided to ignore criticism, and "Ibat" was the motto he had chosen. A few days later, de Lattre wrote to the Canon, informing him that he also had decided to adopt "Ibat" as his motto.

But the intrepid horseman could not ride on for ever. Even his friends could not help him to surmount that formidable obstacle of credits. Despite the lack of money, and the warnings of those whose business it was to safeguard the exchequer, the building of the Light Camps had continued at an unabated pace. To de Lattre, like to many with an imaginative and generous nature, figures meant little. A nought or two at the end made no difference; and yet he could argue most plausibly that his camps were not extravagant. But his enemies lay in wait.

One day in March 1947, he was suddenly informed that he was no longer to combine the functions of Chief of Staff with those of Inspector-General of the Army. He was to be Inspector-General only. General Revers became Chief of the

General Staff. De Lattre did not hide his anger. To be removed in mid-ocean from the bridge of the ship which he himself had built and launched, and of which he was so intensely proud, was a blow that he felt more deeply than he allowed to appear. The Boulevard Saint-Germain was now bereft of that unusual light which for more than a year had shed its warming rays on the cold dark "Corridor of the Generals". His office activities were now confined to 4 Bis, Boulevard des Invalides, where Foch and Weygand had reigned before him. Although, a few weeks later, the Government appointed him Vice President of the Conseil Supérieur de la Guerre, which meant that he was the Commander-in-Chief designate in the event of war, he had lost effective control of the Army.

In September 1947, a new and unusual field was found for his activities. The Government appointed him as head of an economic mission that was to visit the Argentine, Chili, Uruguay, and Brazil. But apart from its economic aspect, which included negotiations for the purchase of wheat, the Mission was intended also to re-establish the prestige of France. On learning of his appointment, one of de Lattre's main problems was to find a suitable staff, and, above all, an intellectual companion for the voyage. It was to René Bondoux, who had been head of his "Brains Trust" at the end of the War, that his mind first turned. Bondoux was now a successful lawyer. He had only just returned to Paris after the holidays, and his office was flooded with work. One morning, while he was buried in a mass of papers, the General telephoned him. "Hallo! Hallo! Is that you Bondoux? I want you to come to the Argentine with me." "But, General," hesitated Bondoux, "I——" He was not allowed to say much more. "You are on the reserve of officers, aren't you?" interrupted de Lattre. "Then it may be necessary to call you up!" Le Roi Jean had commanded, and so Bondoux went. With him the General also took, as his A.D.Cs., the indefatigable Costa de Beauregard and Bernard, who was now in the 4th Cuirassiers and had just finished a glider course.

It was in October that de Lattre and his Mission landed at the airport of Buenos Aires. On the whole, the reception was frigid, but within two weeks, mustering all his charm, he had broken through the ice. General Peron was President and his legendary wife, Señora Eva Peron, was at the height of her powers. René Bondoux recounts how de Lattre broke the ice with the President on the occasion of their first meeting. The latter, having offered de Lattre a cigarette, tried to light it with his lighter. When it would not work he was full of apologies, but with a disarming smile, de Lattre said, "Please don't apologize, Mr. President, in France, too, we know this unhappy situation—No dollars, no petrol." The President was delighted, and the warm and genial atmosphere in which the discussions were conducted was due in part to the incident of the lighter.

The Señora devoted a whole day to conducting him round the youth organizations of the capital. Apart from the glamour of his guide, de Lattre was on his own ground, and for him it was one of the most enjoyable days of the visit. On his return from Chili, he broke his journey at Mendoza, the town at the foot of the Andes, from which the Argentine national hero, General San Martin, had set out with his army to cross the Andes and to liberate Chili. On landing, the aircraft crashed, and, although badly shaken, de Lattre emerged unmoved and proceeded to inspect the guard of honour. His prestige had been greatly enhanced. He himself was delighted when, later, a detachment of soldiers sang the "Marseillaise" in French. General Peron placed his own aircraft at his disposal for the rest of his stay.

Shortly before the work of the mission had been completed, the President told de Lattre that before he left he would like to make him a present of something that he would really like. A few days before, de Lattre had visited a school at which two boys of fourteen had recited Molière in impeccable French. "Nothing would give me greater pleasure," he said to the President, "than the presence of those two boys with me, together with their French teacher, at the Opera and at the remaining ceremonies which you have so kindly organized in my honour." No single incident during the stay of the Mission contributed more to its success, and when he left for France he could look back on one of the greatest personal triumphs of his life.

Rarely had de Lattre been happier than he was on his return to Paris. Even his enemies could not deny that he had proved a representative and most worthy ambassador. But, apart from the satisfaction of his success, the complete change had proved a most salubrious tonic. When he wished, he was the best of raconteurs, and the wealth of anecdotes which he brought back from South America provided an entertaining addition to the repertoire with which he regaled his guests. His official residence was now 4 Place Rio de Janeiro, near the Parc Monceau, and there at last he was able to gather round him his model ships and other treasured possessions.

In the spring of 1948 de Lattre was elevated to the post of Inspector-General of the Armed Forces. Although he still regretted the loss of effective control of the Army, his new appointment provided a more spacious field for the deployment of his energies. Moreover, it enabled him to renew contact with his old and original love, the Navy. The staffs of the Admiralty, Ministry of War, and Air Ministry were soon busy with the preparation of a combined exercise, in which for the first time since the War were studied the major problems of European defence.

But dark and threatening clouds began to gather in Eastern Europe, and the nations of the West, who had been anxious to disarm with such unseemly haste, began slowly to stir and to shake off their naïve torpor. France and Great Britain were the first to take common action, and in March 1947 they signed the Treaty of Dunkirk, pledging mutual aid in the event of a renewal of German aggression. A little later, Belgium, The Netherlands, and Luxembourg, soon to be known as "Benelux", took counsel also with France and Great Britain, and in March 1948 was signed the Treaty of Brussels. Not only did these nations feel the need to work together for their common defence, but they began also to be imbued with a desire to collaborate in other fields. Indeed, the seeds of the Council of Europe were already being sown. It was therefore a comprehensive Treaty that was signed at Brussels, of economic, social, and cultural collaboration, and collective self-defence. A chiefs of staff committee was formed, with the official title of the "Chiefs of Staff, Brussels Treaty Defence Organization". Such was the foundation of the alliance which came generally to be known as Western Union, and soon de Lattre was to be withdrawn from the stage of France, to play his part with other stars on the stage of Western Europe.

29. THE STAGE OF WESTERN EUROPE

THE Chairman of the Chiefs of Staff set up by the Brussels Treaty was Field-Marshal Lord Montgomery. And, at the outset, de Lattre was a member. Even in war-time, when allies are united by the common danger which threatens them, co-operation is not achieved without friction. In peace-time, with no such incentive to unity, the likelihood that co-operation would be easy was remote. Moreover, a committee is not the perfect machinery for effective command, and when two of its members happen to have such strong personalities as those of Montgomery and de Lattre, the danger of friction was almost inevitable.

Montgomery and de Lattre did not know each other well. In the concluding stages of the war, the one had commanded the Twenty-First Army Group on the Allied northern flank, while the other had commanded the First French Army, away to the south. They had met in Berlin at the end of the war and at infrequent intervals in the year that followed. They were not well matched to run in harness. Apart from their strong wills and a legitimate pride in their achievements, which some might call vanity, there were few characteristics which they shared in common. Indeed, the difference in outlook, in temperament, and in method did little to smooth the path of their chariot. "At times", wrote Montgomery, "we were in complete disagreement."

Montgomery had defeated the most brilliant of the enemy commanders, Rommel. Moreover, he had commanded the most stupendous amphibian operation in history. It was not surprising, therefore, that he should feel doubt about the ability of the unusual and temperamental partner with whom he now had to work. Even if he had been aware of his skilful handling of the 14th Infantry Division in 1940, and of the First French Army at the end of the war, he felt that de Lattre had been out of touch, for a long period, with the transformation of modern war. At first, therefore, he was disinclined to regard him as a practical or modern soldier.

De Lattre, at the outset, regarded Montgomery, quite wrongly, as too obsessed by the battle technique, which had brought victory at El Alamein and in North-West Europe, and which, in his view, might soon be out of date. In 1940, it had been a too rigid adherence to the lessons of the First World War which had largely contributed to the downfall of his country. This he was determined to avoid in the future. Moreover, even if he appreciated the necessity for that detailed planning which had been the prelude to the landings in Normandy and the Mediterranean, he disliked the rigidity of what he called "Anglo-Saxon planning". He himself had never been called upon to plan so vast an operation, but the success which had attended his acceleration of the time-table after the landing in Southern France convinced him that in the planning there had been over-rigidity.

In the early days of their journey in harness, de Lattre was still Inspector-General of the Armed Forces of France, and, as their spokesman, he felt that he had a special mission to redeem the prestige of the French Army abroad. He realized that, after the events of 1940, the views of France would carry little weight in the military councils of Europe, unless expressed with unusual force and vigour; and the world-wide reputation of Montgomery accentuated the weakness of his position and made him react the more violently. If at times he may have failed to treat the Field-Marshal with the deference that was his due, it could in part be excused by a fear that if, in his presence, he always "stood to attention", as he put it, he might incur the disapproval of his compatriots. The tenacity with which he pleaded the cause of his country might sometimes be excessive, but France never had a greater advocate.

Of all the factors that impeded harmony, the difference in temperament was the greatest. The unpredictable outbursts of de Lattre, baffling even to his own countrymen, were bound to perplex Montgomery; and, to de Lattre, the manner and speech of Montgomery, disconcertingly brief and direct, seemed sometimes overbearing. Dissimilar too were their methods of work. Montgomery enjoyed the relative quiet and solitude of a small headquarters, where he could reflect in peace. To de Lattre solitude was abhorrent. He liked to think aloud, and it was in an atmosphere of provocative argument that he best developed his plans. He worked late into the night. Montgomery, like Foch, retired early to bed.

For Montgomery, punctuality was essential. With de Lattre the flexible time-table had become an obsession. "Souplesse d'horaire", he called it. At the beginning, de Lattre did not know that the Field-Marshal always carried two wrist-watches, nor was he yet aware of the important part which they played in his life. Later the two watches were to become a frequent source of badinage between them.

Despite the difficulties, which some enjoyed to exaggerate, the efforts of Montgomery and de Lattre to understand each other were genuine and patient. In little ways, whether it was to help in the search for a château for the Field-Marshal, or to cater for his simple tastes, de Lattre would take infinite trouble. But, from time to time, the harmonious partnership was disturbed. On one occasion, when de Lattre had been particularly difficult with the Field-Marshal, a British friend of the General expressed disappointment with this unhappy turn of events. De Lattre was distressed, and he wrote to his friend on the next day:

> "It is not always easy for us to understand each other. There are so many interests and problems involved. Apart from the question of our temperaments, the duties which fall on our shoulders are very heavy. But we are going to succeed, because we intend to succeed, and I pray that those who are watching our efforts may give us the support of their faith. In the accomplishment of our task, there is in each one of us a fund of goodwill, and a fund of frankness and faith. The difficulties and the inevitable disagreements we are going to overcome. At Fontainebleau we shall be together and things will be better. And finally, there is, as Foch said, 'Loyalty to the Alliance'. That was his secret. It will be ours also; and, whatever the world may say or think, we are going to succeed."

It was away from Fontainebleau, in the more peaceful atmosphere of Montgomery's Château at Courance, a few miles away, or in de Lattre's home, in the Place Rio de Janeiro, that the two came nearest to understanding each other. Indeed, as the months passed, understanding merged almost into affection. On Montgomery's sixty-third birthday, he invited de Lattre and his wife to lunch with him at Courance. At the end of luncheon, Montgomery cut his birthday cake. He cut a slice for each one present.

Then he remembered Bernard de Lattre, who was now in Indo-China, and he cut an extra slice for him, asking de Lattre if he would send it to Bernard with his best wishes. Of all the gestures of friendship which Montgomery made to de Lattre, nothing moved him as did that cutting of the cake. It was Montgomery at his simplest and best, and, for the rest of his life, de Lattre constantly referred to that birthday luncheon at Courance. De Lattre, on another occasion, invited Montgomery to the Basses-Pyrénees, and, during the visit, the Field-Marshal accompanied Madame de Lattre to Lourdes. In such an atmosphere, it was a very different de Lattre whom Montgomery came to know.

When destiny dissolved the partnership, and de Lattre set forth to accomplish his final mission in Indo-China, letters continued to pass between them. When he died, few men paid him a more generous tribute than Montgomery. "The Marshal was a very good friend", he concluded, "to those whom he trusted, and I like to think I was included in this category. I salute his memory. He was a great soldier, a good comrade, and a very lovable man." Throughout his life, de Lattre had thrived on affection. How pleased he would have been to know that, in his final tribute, Montgomery had written of him, "a very lovable man". It was the epitaph he would have preferred above all others.

In October 1948, Monsieur Ramadier offered de Lattre the post of Commander-in-Chief of the Land Forces of Western Europe. Although the acceptance of this post would, so he thought, give him greater independence than he enjoyed as a member of a committee, he was fully aware of the pitfalls. He realized, above all, that under the conditions then obtaining, it was a mission of sacrifice that he would be undertaking; for the forces that he would be commanding would be negligible. But he accepted without conditions. "I accept", he wrote to Ramadier, "as a matter of duty and discipline, and I do so as an act of faith towards my country and the Allied Nations. The essence of my task is to place this faith at the service of the cause, for which I shall now work, with the ardent determination of participating in the common effort, which must hasten the moment when the safety of Western Europe may be regarded as valid and assured."

In theory, de Lattre had now to forget that he was a Frenchman, and become a Western European. But, in practice, so complete a transformation would have been difficult for any Frenchman of his generation. The memory of two invasions induced a conception of strategy, which at all costs must spare the soil of France the ordeal of a third invasion. Inevitably, de Lattre shared that conception, and to that extent he remained, first and foremost, a Frenchman.

Difficulties between de Lattre and Montgomery continued, but the brutal frankness that sometimes marked their talks produced in the end a comprehension of each other's viewpoint that precluded ambiguity. But it was away from Fontainebleau that de Lattre was happiest. Flying from capital to capital, he was able to make contact with the politicians and soldiers of other lands, and to regale them with his persuasive and provocative eloquence. They might not all agree with him, but none could be indifferent. Every minute of these visits to the countries of Western Europe was fully occupied. He enjoyed the privilege of inspecting Allied troops and, in his own way, he made the fullest use of these inspections to make himself known to those whom he commanded. For him an inspection was a serious business. He fervently believed that by staring into the eyes of every single man whom he inspected, he could impart a measure of his own determination and faith. Rarely, therefore, as he walked down the ranks did he commit the common error of turning too frequently to address a word to the officer accompanying him. But it was not only troops and military establishments that he wanted to see. The education of youth continued to obsess him, and he derived especial pleasure from visits to the educational establishments of other countries. In England he was able to see schools of every category, and one, at least, of the public schools that he visited would not have been flattered by the order of merit in which he placed it. After one such visit he wrote: "Mon passage parmi vous m'a laissé l'impression durable d'une jeunesse ardente et sympathique."

The arrivals and departures of de Lattre would generally be accompanied by a little commotion. He liked to be met and seen off at the airport by an appropriate gathering, and the absence of anyone, whom he expected to be there, would give rise to the familiar expression of his displeasure. On one occasion, when he was leaving London for Brussels, he had been seen off at the airport with fitting ceremony by members of the Embassy staff. There was a feeling of relief that the visit had passed off without mishap. But a few hours later, a junior member of the Embassy answered the telephone. At the other end was de Lattre. Fog over Brussels had necessitated a return to London; but there was no one to meet him at the airport. "Inadmissible," roared the angry voice. Minute by minute, the Embassy was expected to have kept touch with the movements of the aircraft.

Meanwhile the rumble of threats beyond the Iron Curtain became louder. In the Balkans and in Central Europe, more countries came under the sway of Moscow; and in Berlin, the other occupying powers, despite the most earnest and patient efforts to co-operate, were frustrated in increasing measure by the attitude of the Russians. The blockading of Berlin, and the resultant necessity on the part of the other interested powers to organize an air-lift, brought matters to a head. The gravity of these events, and the efforts which Western Europe was already making to put her own house in order, combined to bring a welcome wave of sympathy from across the Atlantic, and Western Union was reinforced by the North Atlantic Treaty. In it, the United States, the Brussels Treaty Powers, and other countries took concerted action "to safeguard the freedom, common heritage, and civilization of their peoples, founded on principles of democracy, individual liberty, and the rule of law."

The North Atlantic Treaty Organization (N.A.T.O.) which now got under way, began gradually to take over the responsibilities which formerly had been shouldered by Western Union. In due course, General Eisenhower became Supreme Commander of the more imposing forces which were now arrayed to meet the growing danger. Montgomery became his deputy, while de Lattre retained command of the land forces.

By the autumn of 1950, the labours of Montgomery and de Lattre had begun to bear fruit. They had triumphed over every difficulty, and in the blending of their integrated allied staff into an efficient and harmonious machine, the part played by the Chief of Staff, General Blanc, and his successor, General Navreau, was beyond measure. In August, in the presence of the Defence Ministers of Western Union, there took place at Fontainebleau a major exercise. In a brilliant and lucid exposition, de Lattre summarized the work which had been completed. It was to be almost his final appearance on the stage of Western Europe. A few months later, Indo-China claimed him. But the foundations of a coalition, unique in time of peace, had been well and firmly laid, and to disillusioned millions came strength and hope again.

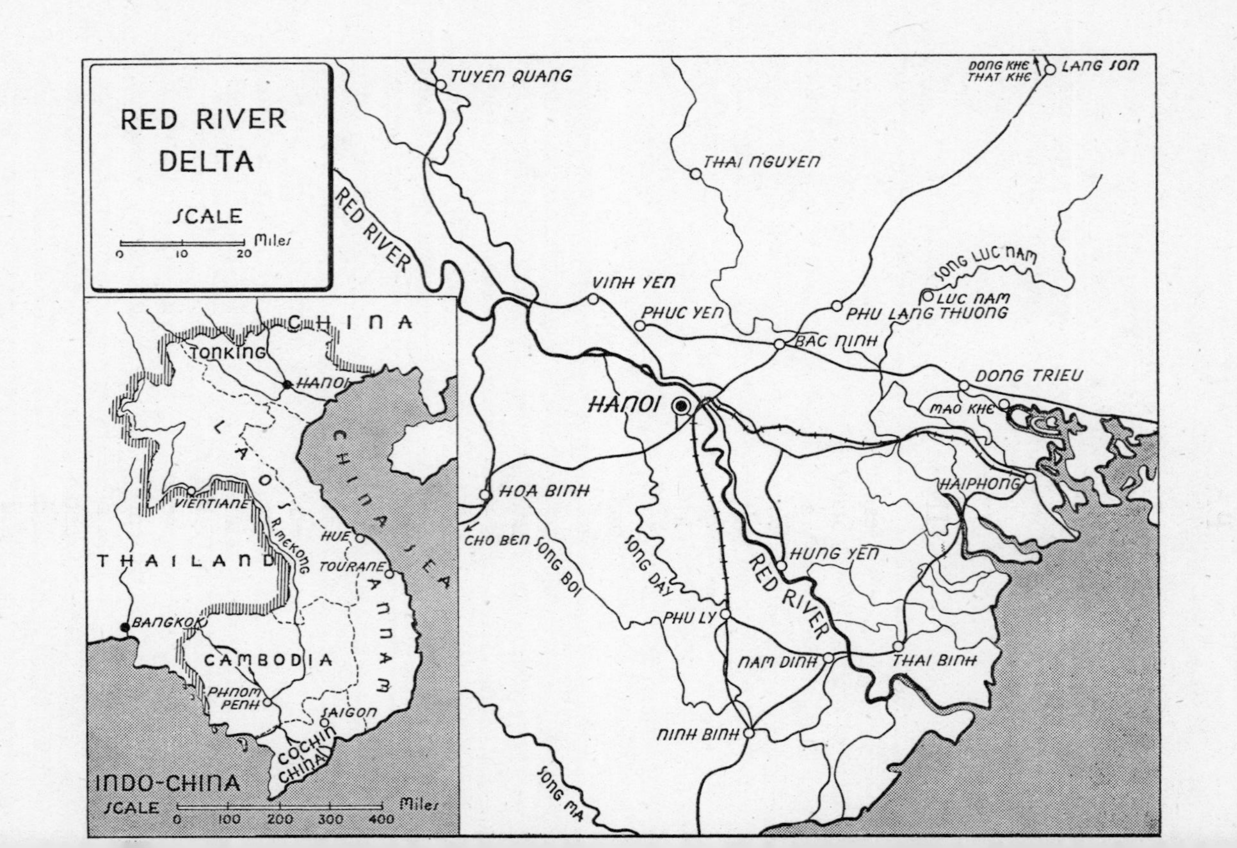
RED RIVER
DELTA
SCALE
0 10 20 Miles
TUYEN QUANG
THAI NGUYEN
DONG KHE
THAT KHE
LANG SON
RED RIVER
VINH YEN
PHUC YEN
SONG LUC NAM
LUC NAM
PHU LANG THUONG
BAC NINH
DONG TRIEU
HANOI
MAO KHE
HAIPHONG
HOA BINH
CHO BEN SONG BOI
SONG DAY
HUNG YEN
RED RIVER
PHU LY
NAM DINH
THAI BINH
NINH BINH
SONG MA
CHINA
TONKING
HANOI
LAOS
VIENTIANE
R. MEKONG
CHINA SEA
HUE
TOURANE
THAILAND
ANNAM
BANGKOK
CAMBODIA
PHNOM PENH
SAIGON
COCHIN CHINA
INDO-CHINA
SCALE 0 100 200 300 400 Miles

PART VII

The Last Mission

1950–1952

30. INDO-CHINESE BACKGROUND

INDO-CHINA comprises the former French Colony of Cochin-China and the protectorates of Annam, Tonking, Cambodia, and Laos (see map on p. 240). Vietnam is the new independent state comprising Cochin-China, Annam, and Tonking, and remains within the French Union. It is an old name revised, meaning "the country to the South". In olden times, the Vietnamese mainly inhabited the Red River Delta, and the Emperor of China regarded their country as a vassal, sometimes referring to it as "An-nam", meaning "the pacified South".

Long before the impact of European civilization, successive conquerors, sometimes from the north, and sometimes from the west, have dominated these lands, and between the seventeenth and eighteenth centuries the Vietnamese themselves gradually extended their power to the south, and might well have been regarded as imperialists. In due course, Portuguese and, later, French missionaries began to reach these shores. In their frequent struggles against invaders from the interior, it was natural that the Vietnamese should look for help from overseas, and the treatment which they accorded to the missionaries depended largely upon their ability to provide such help. If they succeeded, the highest honours were lavished upon them; but if they failed, cruel persecution might well be the penalty.

No record of the achievements of France in Indo-China would be complete without mention of that great French missionary, Monseigneur Pigneau de Béhaine, Bishop of Adran, who at the end of the eighteenth century became a legendary local figure. At that time, usurpers had driven Nguyen Anh from his domaines in Annam, and he appealed to the Bishop for help. Such was his faith in Monseigneur Pigneau, that he entrusted to his care his four-year-old son. The subsequent voyage of the Bishop to France, his organization of an expedition, and the success which crowned his efforts provide a story of unusual perseverance and courage. While in Paris, the Bishop had successfully negotiated a treaty by which, in return for her efforts, France should have sovereignty over the port of Tourane, and enjoy special trading facilities to the exclusion of other European nations.

In July 1799, a great victory at Qui Nhon settled the fate of the usurpers, and Nguyen Anh was restored to his throne. A few months later Monseigneur Pigneau succumbed to fatigue. The Emperor, soon to be known as the Emperor Gia Long, ordered a magnificent funeral, and on the temple near Saigon, which was his tomb, he had inscribed in Chinese characters the following epitaph, which he himself had composed: "When our Kingdom was a prey to diverse troubles, the Master came to our help. He took upon himself the heavy task of finding foreign ships to come to our succour, and he was able to bring them to us only after crossing mountains and seas where perils abounded. For more than twenty years he gave of his best, devising ways and means of recovering our provinces and restoring peace. The high state of perfection which our Kingdom has achieved is due above all else to the ability and exertions of the Prelate."

At a time when so many in Europe seem ashamed to refer to the bygone achievements of intrepid patriots, it is good to record that time was when the work of pioneers was appreciated, not only by the land which bred them, but also by those distant lands to whom they gave such devoted service.

But the successors of Gia Long soon forgot their debt to Monseigneur Pigneau. Persecutions followed, and it was not until the time of Napoleon III that France sought seriously to build upon the foundations which the Bishop had laid more than fifty years before. Internal divisions and suffering made the moment propitious for intervention. Anxious for the support of the catholic party, Napoleon III decided upon a policy of active support for the missionaries in China. As a result of a series of massacres, a joint Anglo-French expedition seized Peking, and, later, French forces disembarked at Tourane in Annam, to secure for France the rights which Monseigneur Pigneau had acquired in the previous century. This led, in 1862, to the establishment of the French colony of Cochin-China.

Originally there had been no intention on the part of the French to incur additional commitments. But, as history so often records, pioneer traders tend unwittingly to commit their countries to protective military expeditions, and so it was that France gradually came to acquire protectorates over Annam, Cambodia, Tonking, and Laos, until eventually was formed the Indo-Chinese Union. Until the outbreak of the Second World War, the Union had continued to prosper, agriculturally, industrially, and intellectually, to the mutual benefit of Indo-China and France, For it was not only Frenchmen who grew rich. Rice is the life-blood of these lands, and between 1880 and 1937 the area in Cochin-China under rice-cultivation increased from a million to nearly five million acres.

But, in the meantime, the victory of Japan over Russia had profoundly stirred the world. Throughout the Far East, nationalist aspirations had been awakened by the revelation that an Eastern Power could triumph against the West. The awakening was accentuated by the events of 1940, which isolated Indo-China from France. General Catroux, the Governor-General, appealed both to Great Britain and to the United States for help, but neither was then in a position to give it. At the end of 1940, the country was occupied by the Japanese. Although, until 1945, outwardly they respected French sovereignty, surreptitiously they encouraged nationalist aspirations, and gradually undermined the French position. In March 1945, they threw all pretence to the winds. The French were given an ultimatum to hand over the army, the navy, the banks, and the administration. Admiral Decoux, who had succeeded Catroux as Governor-General, refused to comply, whereupon 80,000 Japanese attacked 7,000 Frenchmen and the 30,000 Vietnamese who fought with them. There was little hope, and only 6,000 men made good their escape and joined the Americans in China.

The Japanese at once proclaimed the independence of Vietnam, upholding the authority of the Emperor Bao Dai. Five months later, on the eve of capitulation, they completed their sinister work of destruction, by handing over to the rebellious elements in the country the modern weapons which they themselves had taken from the French in March. Conditions, therefore, were perfect for the movement of emancipation which now sprang up under the name of "Viet-minh", a corruption of "Viet-nam Doc Lap Dong Minh", which means the "League for the Independence of Vietnam". It comprised members of several nationalist parties, of which the most active was the Indo-Chinese Communist party, founded in 1925 by the future President Ho-Chi-Minh. They had awaited their chance in Southern China, and upon the capitulation of Japan they entered Tonking and Bao Dai abdicated.

Such, briefly, was the situation which the French were called upon to retrieve. In October 1945, General Leclerc, with an armoured division, reached Saigon, where the French residents had been living under the protection of a company of French colonial infantry and a battalion of Gurkhas sent by the British. Later, Admiral Thierry d'Argenlieu, who had retired from the Navy and joined a monastic order, arrived at Saigon with instructions from de Gaulle to "re-establish French sovereignty in the territories of the Indo-Chinese Union". There was something ironical in the simplicity of General de Gaulle's instructions, for the task before Thierry d'Argenlieu was anything but simple. In a few months the Japanese had brought to almost nought the devoted efforts of generations of great Frenchmen. In Cochin-China the French had only an insecure footing, and from their compatriots in Tonking they were completely cut off, for at Hanoi, Ho-Chi-Minh, now self-styled President of the Democratic Republic of Vietnam, was securely established.

In March 1946, the French were able to negotiate with Ho-Chi-Minh, and they recognized his position, subject to his remaining within the Indo-Chinese Union. Their troops were therefore able to enter Hanoi and to establish contact with the 14,000 Frenchmen who had suffered unspeakable hardships under the Japanese, Chinese, and then rebel occupation. Ho-Chi-Minh was then invited to Paris and accorded the treatment due to a Head of State, but the negotiations which ensued, with a view to finding a *modus vivendi*, came to nought. He returned to Indo-China, and the French found themselves face to face with a full-scale rebellion. But not all Vietnamese nationalists were prepared to follow Ho-Chi-Minh, and the French decided to support Bao Dai, who was then living in exile in Hong Kong. Bao Dai was the direct descendant of Gia Long, the friend of Monseigneur Pigneau. The French, therefore, had reason to hope that the happy partnership of old might be renewed.

Meanwhile, the rebellion gained ground, and by November 1950 the situation had become critical. Despite courage and tenacity of a high order, one by one, French posts near the frontier had fallen or been withdrawn. Dong-Khe, That-Khe, and Lang-son were occupied in turn by the hordes of Ho-Chi-Minh. Soon, the French retained only a precarious grip on the Red River Delta round Hanoi and Haifong. The fall of Hanoi seemed inevitable.

31. LIFT UP YOUR HEARTS

IN France, where enthusiasm for the war in Indo-China had never been great, the news of continued reverses caused even patriotic Frenchmen to wonder whether further sacrifices were justified. Moreover, they felt that France was alone and unsupported in her struggle, for in the United States there was little sympathy for a war which to the average American was a continuation of outmoded European imperialism. Few Americans at the time were ready to believe that Frenchmen in Indo-China were dying for the same cause as their own sons in Korea. Echoes of these misgivings could not fail to reach the hard-pressed French Army in Indo-China. That its morale was not more seriously impaired by so severe a test was a great tribute to its younger leaders. But breaking-point had almost been reached, and, if disaster was to be averted, drastic and immediate action was required.

In the hour of peril, it was to General de Lattre, now over sixty, that the French Government turned. For a commander who already held the highest military post in Europe, the prospect was hardly attractive. Ten years before, his friend Weygand had taken over command when the battle was already lost. The warning was clear, and age alone would have given de Lattre the excuse for declining. But he was the last man to turn aside from a situation in which there was an element of risk. Moreover, he had always been a gambler, and for years he had trained the young French Army to acquire a taste for taking risks. Indo-China was a challenge; he must prove true to his teaching. To M. Pleven, the President of the Council, who asked him whether he would be prepared to go to Indo-China to restore the situation, the reply of de Lattre was characteristic: "I have nothing to gain and doubtless much to lose. All the more reason for accepting, and, as a good soldier, I shall do so without hesitation". De Lattre did not lack a sense of humour, and he must have derived a measure of amusement from the trick which fate now played him. In his struggle to rebuild the French Army at home, it had been Indo-China that had always baulked him; Indo-China, with her insatiable demands for men, for money, and for material, had deprived him of everything that he needed most for his purpose. He must have come to curse the very name, and now it was the cause of Indo-China that he must champion. But champion it he would, with all the fervour that was his.

It was not the French Government only that accorded to de Lattre its full confidence. A few days after his appointment as High Commissioner and Commander-in-Chief in Indo-China, a friend of de Lattre came across Field-Marshal Montgomery in London. "De Lattre is the one man," said the Field-Marshal with conviction, "who can clean up things in Indo-China." This spontaneous expression of confidence was a most genuine tribute from one who once had doubted his ability. In language less generous, the enemies of de Lattre, too, paid their tribute. "It needed a fool," commented one in New York, "for a foolish enterprise. They have found him, and he is quite capable of succeeding."

At midnight on the 13th December, de Lattre set out from Orly Airport. Two thousand old comrades of the First French Army had assembled from all corners of France to speed him on his way. With dramatic effect, the lights of the cameramen shone upon their banners, fluttering in the midnight breeze. It was a most moving send-off, to which de Lattre was not insensitive. The spirit of the First French Army still lived, and "les gars", as he called his men, still trusted him. Again he must prove worthy of their trust. "I shall give of the best that is left in me," he told them. He was to give all.

Bernard had already been in Indo-China for more than a year. For months he had commanded a post about twenty miles south-east of Hanoi, which involved also the responsibility for the security of the surrounding area. An account written by his superior at the time gives him credit for accomplishing his task in a manner that was fully worthy of his father. "He is one of the few officers", he wrote, "who has really given thought to the problem of our presence here, and he has resolved it in a concrete manner. In the area round his post, he has captured the hearts of the local population. They are confident, and they salute him with a cheer when he passes. Moreover, they smile, and this is a rare event in this unhappy country. The local militia are alert and trustworthy . . . and are comfortably installed in their solid towers. There is an animated market, a clean dispensary that is fully used, and a small maternity home. There are also active youth organizations, and a sports ground is in process of being established." The first-hand experience which these responsibilities gave to Bernard fully entitled him to write with authority on the local situation, and the full and intensely interesting letters which he wrote home had given his father a most valuable picture of the situation, which supplemented the information obtained from official sources. Already, in October 1950, he had written to his mother: "Tell Father we need him here; otherwise things will go badly." In November, he had written a depressing account of the morale, particularly that of the civilian population in Hanoi: "There is a kind of fear-psychosis," he wrote, "everyone is pulling in different ways; nothing is done; there is no leader; all is hesitation; civilians are going away . . . there are even soldiers who spread rumours, contaminating that which is still good . . . there is no official information . . . there are only rumours . . . the local paper says nothing. . . . It is curious how the French will not be honest with each other. The result is panic and terror . . .". But, apart from Hanoi, the state of morale elsewhere seemed still healthy. "Morale is all right," wrote Bernard in another letter, "we need no one to come out and report on that; we are prepared to accept any discomfort, but we want to know what we are driving at; we want to be commanded."

We can only surmise what passed through de Lattre's mind as he sped through the air to render his last and most difficult service to his country; but the letters of Bernard had clearly indicated that the essence of the problem was morale. It is difficult to think of that momentous flight, and of all to which it was the prelude, without recalling the picture of Montgomery, flying over the Mediterranean in the autumn of 1942, on his way to take over command of the British Eighth Army. Both were flying to redress a situation in which morale had been compromised. Each had his own technique for restoring it. With de Lattre it would be shock action. It was rare for him to arrive anywhere unnoticed; but on this occasion something more spectacular than usual was required to mark the event. As he neared Saigon, therefore, he was probably already turning over in his mind how best to produce on arrival some drama that would shake the land. The most trivial shortcoming might have to serve his purpose.

It was on the 17th December, 1950, that he stepped from his aircraft at Saigon. The Guard of Honour presented arms, and the band struck up the "Marseillaise"; but someone was out of tune. Here was the opportunity. The delinquency of a bandsman or the faultiness of an instrument must be made the occasion for the drama. In a flash, he unleashed that torrent of abuse that had no equal, and which, once again, was out of all proportion to the seriousness of the offence. Everyone was sent for to listen to the tirade. Although de Lattre preferred to be loved than to be hated, experience had taught him that, if quick results were required, it was the exercise of violence rather than charm that was most effective. Echoes of the incident with the band reverberated throughout Indo-China—"Le Roi Jean" had arrived. Already the mere announcement of his appointment had revived hopes, and now that he had arrived, there was an instantaneous feeling in the army that it was commanded; and if those who were insecure in the saddle began to tremble, all were on their toes.

Along the deserted avenues, he drove from the airport to the Residency. Clouds of gloom hung heavily over a city that seemed lifeless. But he was not disconcerted; rather was he the more determined that the sun should break through, for it was for that purpose he had come. "In a few months' time," he said, "crowds will be here to welcome me along this same route."

De Lattre did not dally long in Saigon. Two days sufficed for the present. Already the clouds had begun to disperse; the idle began to stir, and the useless were on their way back to France. After paying his respects to the Emperor Bao Dai, on the 19th December, he flew north to Tonking, for it was there that the need of his presence was imperative; moreover, Ho-Chi-Minh had himself declared that he would be in Hanoi by the feast of Tet, just after Christmas. De Lattre would be there first. At the airport, to ensure once again that his arrival had been duly noted, there was to be a further application of shock tactics. De Lattre was a Five Star General, but on the aircraft that had been placed at his disposal four stars only had been painted. The Air Officer Commanding, himself a Four Star General, was present at the airport. It was upon him that the storm broke. "What the devil do you take me for? A . . ." There was more to come. The unfortunate second pilot had a beard. "I give you five minutes to remove that beard," roared the General. When he landed at Hanoi, men with paint and brushes were standing by, and in a moment the fifth star was added. To a member of his staff de Lattre later confided that he had to abuse those whom he liked best. Much as he admired the Air Force, they must turn themselves out properly.

In Hanoi the arrival would be just as spectacular, but the method would be varied. Although the enemy was almost at the gates of the city, and although most of the available troops were committed to the defence of the contracting perimeter, there would be a review. De Lattre relied more than anything else upon the establishment of personal contact with those whom he commanded, to infuse that all-conquering confidence that burned within him. All must see him; and so, on the very day of his arrival, as night was falling, every available man was made to parade. Some had come straight from battle, and most were still at short notice to move. In the fading light they marched past that legendary figure, which now became known to them. Few can have failed to fall under the spell, and, as the sun set upon that unusual scene, most must have felt an infusion of strength.

At the end of the parade, officers of all ranks were assembled. De Lattre addressed them all; but it was for the younger officers that his words were intended. "Messieurs les Capitaines et Messieurs les Lieutenants," he said, "it is because of you that I have agreed to take on this heavy task. I promise you that from today you will be commanded." To the senior officers present, the words seemed pointed; and some must have felt that their days had been numbered.

It was not for the army only that de Lattre had conceived the Hanoi review. The army, as Bernard had written, despite its reverses, had retained a degree of morale; but it was to lift up the hearts of the civilians too that the review had been ordered. As the fall of Hanoi seemed imminent, plans for the evacuation of the civil population were already well under way. Indeed, hardly had de Lattre returned to Saigon when, in the face of further attacks, the local commander in Tonking was requesting permission for the plans for evacuation to be put into effect. De Lattre was furious. Against such a background how could the morale of the civil population ever be restored? Seizing a piece of paper, he drafted the following message to the Commissioner of the Republic in Tonking:

1. All instructions previous to my arrival cancelled.
2. Hold on.
3. General Salan arrives by air at 1400 hours and will assume command Tonking.
4. Arriving myself.

Not even the women were to be evacuated. The contracting perimeter did not matter; war was not a question of positions, but a conflict of wills. "I shall overwhelm Tonking," boasted Ho-Chi-Minh. "Tonking shall be held," affirmed de Lattre.

The Commander-in-Chief gave characteristic emphasis to these decisions. He telegraphed to his wife in Paris, saying that she must come at once herself to Hanoi. Together they must set the example. Throughout their married life Madame de Lattre, with undue modesty, had played an immeasurable part behind the scenes, and the whirlwind speed at which her husband galloped did not make things easy. Often de Lattre would speak to his friends of her exemplary patience, and of the difficulties that she so cheerfully endured. Within a few days Madame de Lattre was again at his side.

Only a few days had elapsed since de Lattre had touched down at Saigon. The full magnitude of the problem, and of all its ramifications, was already clear to him, but it was the root that mattered; and the root was morale. The battle for morale was the first to be won, and into that battle he threw all that he had; and from it, too, he withdrew all that was useless. The purge was intensified. The "order of the steamship ticket", as dismissal came to be called, was distributed with a lavishness that caused inevitable miscarriages of justice. But ruthless though de Lattre could and had to be, he was not insensitive; indeed, he often suffered deep remorse. "Have I been too hard?" he would say later to his Chief of Staff, and sometimes, if not too late, the damage would be repaired. But it was a situation that demanded those extreme measures, which results were so fully to justify.

Rarely can a commander so quickly or so wholly have inspired others with his dynamic faith and courage. Doubt and gloom were dispelled by rays of hope; the timid found courage, and the brave became braver. If, in some isolated post, a commander showed hesitation or doubt as to his rôle, he would receive a message that was a model of brevity: "J'arrive". That simple message contained a wealth of meaning which only those who received it could explain; and when, a few hours later, the Chief himself arrived, the effect was complete.

32. A TIMELY GAMBLE

THE arrival of the new High Commissioner could not have been better timed. In the middle of January Ho-Chi-Minh launched a major offensive against Hanoi. Although a revitalized army gave him a warmer reception than he had expected, the situation soon became critical. On the 13th January there had been clashes with the enemy along the whole of the seventy-mile front between Luc Nam and Vinh-Yen, and on the 15th this developed into a major attack against Vinh-Yen itself, which is only twenty-five miles north-west of Hanoi. This was the first occasion on which the enemy had concentrated his forces, and risked battle in the open country. Although the exact number engaged is not easy to estimate, it seems evident that Ho Chi Minh had committed a very large force to the battle, for he was determined to capture Hanoi. In the face of strong artillery opposition and bombing from the air, by very weight of numbers he forced the Franco-Vietnamese to give ground. For four days the French Air Force, with little time for maintenance, was giving continuous support to the army, and it was only with great difficulty that the enemy was held.

It was not likely, at such a critical juncture, that de Lattre would remain at his headquarters. To Vinh-Yen he must fly to see for himself; the pilots of the three "Moranes" attached to his headquarters were sent for, and briefly informed that in an hour's time he would take off. Anxious for his safety, they warned him that there was fog. The warning was unheeded. They tried again; Vinh-Yen, they argued, might well by now be in enemy hands. "Is there any report to confirm that?" said de Lattre. There was no confirmation, and further hesitation was useless. Into the fog, therefore, they took off for Vinh-Yen. Their misgivings in part had been justified. When the aircraft touched down on the airstrip of Vinh-Yen, the enemy was barely 1,000 yards away. Rarely had de Lattre's presence on the battlefield been more opportune or effective. The sight of their Commander-in-Chief stepping from his aircraft, in the very heat of the battle, and himself under fire, had an incalculable effect on the will to resist. His parting words, as he boarded the aircraft to fly back to Hanoi, were just what were wanted: "Tenez bon, les petits gars," he said. "Je reviendrai bientôt." When he spoke to them thus, there was nothing they would not do for him.

Although the situation was just in hand, de Lattre was fully aware of its gravity. Indeed, there were no reserves immediately available. Returning to Hanoi in the evening, he went straight to the office of the local commander, General Salan. Going up to the map, he pointed to Vinh-Yen. "It is there, at this moment," he said, "that the fate of Tonking is being decided, and Tonking has got to be saved. I must have every available battalion here at once, not only from Tonking, but also from Cochin-China, which for the moment must get on as best it can. I want every civil aircraft in the country requisitioned." He had decided on a great gamble. Although even in Cochin-China, a thousand miles to the south, the situation was by no manner quiet, the risk must be taken. It must be denuded of troops.

Allard, his Chief of Staff, who had served him so well as head of his 4th Bureau in the First Army, was present, and during these momentous discussions was already busy working out how the many and intricate moves could be effected. Apart from the problem of the battalions coming by air, those coming by road from other parts of Tonking would have to traverse country in which at that time mines and ambushes abounded. But if anyone could produce troops out of a hat, it was Allard.

At ten o'clock, after one of the most exhausting and worrying days of his life, de Lattre returned to his own house, where an anxious party of journalists awaited him. Lesser men would have been too tired or too busy to receive them. But he always had time for the Press. He appreciated to the full the rôle it could play in sustaining the morale, not only of the public at home, but of the troops in the field, where Press accounts and broadcasts quickly reach them. In a brief interview, and in jocular mood, he addressed them. "It's a great battle—you must go up and have a look."

Throughout the night, wireless messages between Hanoi and Saigon flowed without ceasing. The decision to establish an air-bridge between Cochin-China and Tonking had only been taken at eight o'clock in the evening. At four o'clock on the following morning, the first aircraft, laden with troops, had taken off. The motley procession of Skymasters, D.C.3's, three-motored Junkers, and others was reminiscent of a similar crisis thirty-five years earlier on the Marne, when the taxis of Paris, requisitioned in haste, had rushed troops to the battle.

It was a triumph of staff work. Within a matter of hours, and in the middle of the night, some of the troops were withdrawn from forward posts, issued with new clothing and equipment, and rushed to the airfield. For three nights and days the fifteen aircraft—there were no more—plied to and from Saigon to Hanoi. Imagination, determination, and the whole-hearted co-operation of all gave de Lattre his battalions.

Throughout the battle, which lasted four days, Hanoi saw

little of de Lattre. He was always forward. Where to be, in a moment of crisis, is a problem that will always confront commanders. There can be no rule. More than anything else, it is a matter of intuition. The mobility of de Lattre at such moments must have heavily taxed the ingenuity and forethought of his signals and liaison staff. But there is little doubt that his continual absence from his headquarters was fully justified, for his influence upon every corner of the battlefield was profound.

By the 19th January it was estimated that the attackers had lost 5,000 killed, and at the end of the day the remnants withdrew to the mountains. The first major victory of the Franco-Vietnamese forces had been won. Whatever the future of the conflict may be, and as these lines are written it still rages, the victory of Vinh-Yen marked a turning-point in the war. Among his own people, the reputation of de Lattre was now firmly established, and in the hearts of the enemy he already inspired fear. "De Lattre the terrible", they now began to call him.

33. INTUITION

WITH the victory of Vinh-Yen, de Lattre might also claim to have won the battle for morale; but the military situation had not been radically transformed. While the Franco-Vietnamese forces were not strong enough to exploit success, those of Ho-Chi-Minh had always the mountains and valleys beyond the plains to which they could withdraw for refuge. The French, therefore, were still on the defensive, and before offensive operations could even be contemplated, the Red River Delta must be made secure. During the succeeding weeks, therefore, a perimeter of concrete defences started to spring up to the north, and north-west of Hanoi. It was not continuous but took the form of a series of defensive works designed to cover the four main approaches from China. The scene of prodigious activity which marked their construction was reminiscent of the creation, a few years earlier, of the Light Camps in France, in which some of the engineer officers then serving in Indo-China had themselves been concerned. They well knew, therefore, what was expected of them, and the work proceeded at that phenomenal pace which was the only pace which de Lattre knew. To raise technical difficulties was "inadmissible". "Only de Lattre", wrote Colonel Clement, "could have ensured the completion of so gigantic an enterprise. Nearly every day his aircraft came circling over the block-houses. Orders rained down on us, criticizing the siting of a post or the emplacement of a weapon. He harassed us without ceasing, and made us redouble our efforts. The enthusiasm and energy of this man of iron was superhuman. He was everywhere at the same time . . . we admired him profoundly, and the Vietnamese venerated him as a national hero."

In six months, 600 concrete works, of varying sizes, had been constructed, armed, and equipped. While that work was proceeding, de Lattre was already planning the next phase—the formation within the perimeter of mobile groups, which in increasing measure would be able to assume the offensive. A quarter of a century earlier he had been concerned with the organization of mobile groups in Morocco, and although times and conditions had changed, and armoured cars had taken the place of the mounted North African Spahis, the essence of the problem was still a matter of mobility. Strategic mobility he had, and the air had already served him well in transporting troops from Cochin-China to Tonking; but tactical mobility was less easy to acquire. Mobility on the roads was easy enough, but it was off the roads, in the low-lying and often flooded paddy fields that the enemy, with his lighter equipment and knowledge of the country, had the advantage. It was for infantry, therefore, as ever, that the need was mostly felt, and for infantry that was lightly equipped. At the outset there were seven mobile groups of approximately brigade strength; and commando units were included as soon as they became available. The commanders of these groups, de Lattre called his "Marshals", and even if a divisional organization was interposed, more often than not, he liked to direct their operations himself. He gave them a hard time, but they were well provided with wireless sets and always had aircraft at direct call. On one occasion, one of their commanders protested that his group had been reduced to one battalion and one battery of artillery. "Have you enough men to carry out your mission?" said de Lattre. "Oui, mon General," replied the group commander. "Then stop grousing, or I will take away your last battalion and you will carry on with what is left."

Although the Commander-in-Chief spent so many hours away from his headquarters, he found time on most days to hold a conference. His conferences at that time had a character all their own. General Chassin, commanding the Air Force in Indo-China, has vividly protrayed them. In the corridor, outside the Chief's room, all would be waiting for the bell that denoted he was ready. Into the room they would then troop, looking anxiously at his face to see what sort of a mood he was in. He himself, seated firmly behind his desk, presented an imposing figure, with his aquiline nose, his chin held high, and that imperious gaze which greeted all who entered. The timid began to behave like schoolboys, manœuvring so as not to be in the front row, and to escape being questioned by the master.

"Sit down, gentlemen," came the signal to begin; and according to the tone of his voice, tension would increase or diminish. Although at times there were heated scenes, generally these conferences passed off fairly quietly. The great thing was not to oppose the "Patron" in public. In private he would always listen, even if he disagreed. The subsequent procedure was unlike that at the usual conference, where heads of branches spoke and were then questioned by commanders concerned in the operations under consideration. De Lattre did most of the talking, and he broadened the scope of the discussions to include every variety of topic, from world affairs to public opinion in foreign countries. Often, too, he would read out telegrams that had passed between himself and Paris, and speak of his own preoccupations. In fact, he liked to create an atmosphere of mutual confidence, and such was his power of speech and persuasion that few would leave the conference without a better and a wider knowledge of what was wanted, and, above all, a greater determination to carry on the fight.

By March, the situation had been gripped by a master hand, but it was clear that nothing in the nature of far-reaching results could be achieved without substantial additions to his resources, particularly in manpower. Paris must help, and so to Paris he must go, to plead the very cause which had so hindered and baffled him when he had been struggling to rebuild the French Army in Europe. But with remarkable suppleness he developed once again an almost fanatical enthusiasm for the cause in hand. In the middle of March, he set out for Paris, armed with enthusiasm and faith, the gift of persuasive eloquence, and substantial successes to his credit. No advocate could have been better equipped to plead so unpopular a cause. He did not fail.

Within two weeks de Lattre was back at his post. His return was opportune, for at the end of March Ho-Chi-Minh resumed the offensive. Haifong was now the objective, and it was in the Dong-Trieu area that he struck. It was not often that de Lattre showed fatigue, but on his return from Paris he was tired and sick, and although a high temperature compelled him to stay in bed, it did not prevent him from immediately assuming control of operations. He seemed obsessed by the conviction that Mao-Khe would prove to be the critical point of the battle then being waged and that, at all costs, Mao-Khe must be held. Under the command of a brilliant soldier, Colonel Sizaire, a force was hastily improvised and despatched at night, by boat, to Mao-Khe. Before embarking, Sizaire was sent for by de Lattre and given verbal instructions for his task. Recounting the events later, Sizaire recalled the vision that he had of de Lattre that night, still feverish, pushing him with an imperious gesture to the top of the stairs and repeating mechanically, as if in a dream, "Mao-Khe, Mao-Khe, Mao-Khe."

Sizaire and his men had an adventurous night, for some of the boats went aground and Sizaire himself spent most of the night splashing about in water and mud. When Mao-Khe was reached the enemy was in possession of the northern suburbs, but Sizaire was in time to stem the tide, and when that night the attack was resumed the enemy was driven off.

On the same night de Lattre ordered an air reconnaissance over the area. It was the first time during these operations that the Air Force had been employed on night reconnaissance. The Air Force reported that the hills north of Dong-Trieu were dotted with the lights of enemy fires, that gave the impression of a camp of barbarians. Presumably they were awaiting the order to push on and exploit success at Mao-Khe. On the next night another air reconnaissance over the area showed it to be in complete darkness, and, with some justification, de Lattre's intelligence staff concluded that, as a result of their failure at Mao-Khe, the enemy had decided to cut his losses and withdraw. Reports from other sources confirmed this belief.

The operations branch had therefore accepted this appreciation, and had put forward a plan to denude the posts at Mao-Khe and to incorporate their garrisons in a mobile force that was to be launched northward, with a view to cutting off the supposed retreat of the enemy.

De Lattre was present while the staff deliberated, and he listened to what seemed to be a sound enough appreciation of the situation. But he seemed silent, uneasy, and far from convinced. Suddenly the silence was broken. "You're a poor lot of chaps," said de Lattre. "The Viet-minh are still occupying those hills. The only difference is that they have now been ordered to camouflage their presence. Not one post at Mao-Khe is to be withdrawn." The next night, the equivalent of four enemy brigades was hurled against Mao-Khe, which, thanks to de Lattre, was firmly held by alert and determined troops. With heavy losses the attackers were driven back. The faith of de Lattre in his own intuition, and his failure to regard the advice of his staff had not only ensured success, but probably averted misfortune. Intuition he undoubtedly possessed to an uncanny degree; indeed, he prided himself that he could "smell things out", and some may recall, on the occasion of an inspection, a sudden raising of the head, two or three sniffs, and, after a pause, the exclamation: "It smells bad." He was generally right. Although not apparent to others either the morale of the unit, or something else was radically wrong. For a commander the gift was invaluable, but for his intelligence staff it could be most disconcerting.

34. MORTAL BLOW

THE second major success against the Viet-minh at Mao-Khe, and the promise of reinforcements from France, made it now possible to think of limited offensive action against the enemy.

But de Lattre rightly appreciated that the problem could never be solved by French troops alone; moreover, it was unfair that the burden of the operations now contemplated should fall upon French soldiers alone. The time had come for the Vietnamese themselves to play a full part in the struggle for their independence. De Lattre, therefore, devoted much of his seemingly unlimited energy to the creation of a Vietnamese Army. It was an ambitious project, for it postulated in the first instance the recruiting and training of Vietnamese officers and non-commissioned officers, and this in turn demanded time. However, the first Vietnamese units were quickly formed and led by French officers, most of whom volunteered for this service.

There was much of the Grand Seigneur in de Lattre, and a full consciousness of the obligation in his position to set the example. If the young Vietnamese Army was to flourish, it must be officered by the best officers that France could produce. No one was better qualified to give a lead than his own son Bernard. It is unlikely that Bernard needed any encouragement on the part of his father. He was now only twenty-three, and his record already had been remarkable. At the age of sixteen, he had been the youngest soldier serving in the First French Army to be decorated with the Médaille Militaire. The taste for taking risks, which his father had so assiduously striven to implant in the new French Army, was his in full measure. He had always volunteered for the seemingly most exciting jobs; commandos, airborne troops, and then Indo-China, in turn had claimed his service. Now, happy though he was in a first-class armoured-car regiment, the Ier Régiment de Chasseurs, he did not hesitate to follow the strange and untried path, whither duty seemed to call. Family history was repeating itself. Thirty-six years earlier, his father had followed a similar path. Then it had been the Infantry that had called for volunteers. Cruel losses had thinned its ranks, and it was to the Cavalry that France had called to provide infantry officers. De Lattre had been among the first to volunteer. The son was not found wanting when it became his turn to follow the example that had been set by his father.

By the middle of April, preparations were sufficiently advanced to embark upon the first of the offensive operations that had been planned. It was known as "Medusa". As often in this campaign, it was the factor of rice that dictated the character of the operations. The possession of the richest rice fields was equally important to both sides. The first crop was due to be harvested in June, and operation Medusa was designed to deny to the enemy the rice fields situated in the Delta south of Haifong. Meanwhile, Bernard de Lattre had been intensively training his Vietnamese recruits at Hanoi, and the battalion in which he was serving was able to play its part in the protracted operations that were eventually crowned with success. He and his untried men acquitted themselves with conspicuous success, and on the 11th May at Phu-Ly the proud father decorated his son with the Croix de Guerre. Two days later, at the invitation of Sir Malcolm MacDonald, the General set out to attend a conference at Singapore.

Meanwhile the problem of rice was also exercising the mind of Ho-Chi-Minh. The very existence of his Army, apart from its ability to fight, depended upon rice, and the sources from which he could draw were limited. Thus it was that on the 28th May, he launched a very large force against the south-west corner of the delta in the area of the River Day, with a view to securing the rice fields that covered the area. De Lattre had now returned from Singapore and Bernard again was in the forefront of the battle.

On the 30th May, de Lattre gave an interview at his headquarters at Hanoi to a Belgian journalist. With his customary clarity and enthusiasm, he discussed the operation then in progress,and he referred with particular pride and affection to the part being played by his son, at the head of his Vietnamese troops. While he was speaking, Allard came into the office. His face, usually bronzed, at that moment seemed almost white. He had no need to speak. Hardly had he entered the office, when de Lattre said: "Bernard is dead!"

Bernard had in fact been killed in the very early hours of that morning on the banks of the River Day near Nam-Dinh. The flat country on either side of the river is dotted with rocky hillocks, and it was one of these which a platoon of Bernard's company had been ordered to hold. Bernard himself had installed himself during the night on the summit of this rock. Beside him were a Lieutenant Mercier and a Vietnamese corporal. About one o'clock in the morning the silence of the night was broken by the outbreak of small-arms fire, and, soon after, the corporal was wounded. Bernard saw to it that the first-aid dressing was applied, and shortly afterwards the enemy could be seen advancing in the plain below. Soon after three, mortar shells began to fall round the rock, and it was one of these that caused Bernard's instantaneous death. Mercier also was wounded and died later. The Vietnamese corporal, although himself wounded, was able with the help of others to carry Bernard's body to a cave at the foot of the rock. He returned to his post and played a gallant part in repelling the attack.

For a moment, perhaps for the only moment in his life, the giant, who had stood so valiant against all disaster, was prostrated. Of all the memories which came floating through his mind, that of the fifteen-year-old Bernard outside the prison wall of Riom must surely have been amongst the most painful. It would have been so easy, and there would have been every excuse, for giving Bernard a period of rest. Since the age of sixteen, he had seen his fair share of fighting, and was entitled to a rest, and in the hour of grief, there seems no doubt that such were the thoughts that tormented the mind of the distracted father. To his wife, then in Paris, he telegraphed: "Pardonne moi de n'avoir pas su te le sauver." But whatever the father had wished, never would Bernard have consented to privileged treatment. To his mother he had written: "For a year and a half I have tried to do my job decently, like all my friends. I am very happy that father should be here, but I want to carry on with my job just as before." And in another letter he had written: "Until the very last day of my campaign in Indo-China, I intend to do a job which none can say was given me through influence."

Whether de Lattre ever felt tempted—and it would have been only human if he had been—to find Bernard a more sheltered job, never for one moment did he yield; rather was he more spartan in regard to his own son than to anyone else. But now that Bernard was dead, he felt entitled to grant him one privilege; and so he flew back to Paris, taking with him in the aircraft the bodies of Bernard, of Mercier, and of Corporal Mellot who had been killed with him. A funeral service for Bernard and his companions was held in the Chapel Saint-Louis, at the Invalides, and, at the special request of Madame de Lattre, the service was also to be in memory of all those who had fallen in Indo-China. On the following day, Bernard was buried at Mouilleron-en-Pareds, his father's birthplace in La Vendée.

It was understandable that, at first, some should criticize the action of de Lattre in flying back to Paris, but one who was present at the service at the Invalides, wrote later of the "transcending impression" which it made. To the people of France, nothing could have brought home in more vivid manner the grim reality of the scene in Indo-China, and the sacrifices which the best of her sons were prepared to make.

Few young men at the age of twenty-three can have had so full and inspiring a life as Bernard de Lattre. At the age when most boys would still have been at school, he was already winning laurels on the battlefield, and at the age when many might have been still at a university, already he had given five years of devoted service to his country. Indeed, the record of Bernard was an inspiration to the youth of France. To some of the Vietnamese also, the death of the High Commissioner's son, at the head of Vietnamese troops, may have seemed symbolic of a new era, in which France was prepared to make the heaviest sacrifices in a cause that was not merely her own.

Although for de Lattre the blow had been mortal, he quickly dominated the first pangs of grief. One very near to him at the time, formed the impression that he now acquired new powers. The very cruelty of the blow had served to soften those outbursts of anger that had formed so unpleasant a trait in his character; and he seemed to develop a more philosophical and balanced outlook on life, and a clarity of vision and a soundness of judgment that were greater than before. But a few months only were to pass before his own life was to close, and France was to be deprived of these new and enhanced powers.

35. STATESMAN AND DIPLOMAT

"MARSHAL DE LATTRE was a brilliant soldier," wrote Montgomery, "but he was more than that, he was also a statesman." Breadth of vision and the ability to see beyond the difficulties of the day were among his statesmanlike qualities. In Indo-China, although the problems of the battlefield were sufficient to absorb his entire energy, they were never allowed to contract his vision. He did not forget that he was High Commissioner, as well as Commander-in-Chief. Of course the battle must be won and a degree of security and confidence re-established, and to the achievement of that object the French Army would contribute its full share. But more it could not do towards the solution of a problem that was no longer the concern of France alone. De Lattre had not come out as the servant of an imperialist France, to ensure the permanence of outmoded methods. He had come out to defend the people of Vietnam against the most ruthless form of imperialism the world had yet seen. He was in fact an anti-imperialist. But a sceptical and doubting world, in which the minds of enemies and friends alike had been poisoned by years of insidious propaganda, would not credit France or its flamboyant proconsul with motives so selfless. The sceptics must be confounded and the doubters convinced.

While, therefore, de Lattre continued personally to direct the operations of the army, he applied himself simultaneously to another twofold task. Firstly he must convince the people of Vietnam, not only that he had come to ensure their independence but also that the war now raging was their war. Secondly, he must convince both the British and the Americans that the struggle in Vietnam was but a part of that greater struggle against the forces of evil. The sons of France in Vietnam were laying down their lives for the same cause as the soldiers of the United States and Great Britain and others on the battlefields of Korea and in the jungles of Malaya.

On the 19th April, a few weeks before Bernard was killed, de Lattre had conducted Tran-van-Huu, the Prime Minister of Vietnam, and some of his ministers over the battlefield of Vinh-Yen. He chose the occasion to make a speech which would leave no doubt in the minds of his hearers as to the honesty of his intentions. At that moment work was in full progress on the block-houses round Hanoi. "Some may look upon these block-houses," said de Lattre, "as the outward sign of the permanence of a French occupation. On the contrary, Mr. Prime Minister, they are the ramparts behind which the independence of Vietnam will be built up. I have come here to bring about your independence, and not to limit it. The French Army, too, is here to defend that independence, but the protection of our arms would have little meaning, were it not for the fact that it gave Vietnam the means to become strong enough to save itself." It was a felicitously worded speech. De Lattre paid tribute also to the soldiers of Vietnam and their achievements during the recent battles. "They justify my faith," he said, "in the grandeur of Vietnam of tomorrow, for her youth, under French commanders today, tomorrow will be serving in the ranks of a Vietnamese Army." It was the familiar refrain again that ran through all his most uplifting speeches. Youth must strive for the grandeur of their country.

How would the head of the Vietnamese Government reply? Did not the uncertainty of the position and of his own future dictate caution and ambiguity rather than a clear-cut pronouncement of support for the French? His reply was crystal clear. He paid a warm tribute to what he called de Lattre's "pleasing humanism", which would create a deep impression in the hearts of his compatriots. "I am happy," he said, "to reaffirm publicly and solemnly the confidence which my Government and the people of Vietnam place in you in our struggle against the common enemy." He went on to define the common enemy. "Can they call themselves patriots, those men who deliberately place themselves under the orders of a foreigner to propagate an ideology that denies any idea of country? Vietminh is the enemy of the people, for not only does it fail to realize its aspirations, but it would submit them to the domination of a foreign dictatorship." The speech grew in vehemence. "Against those who persist in accepting money from a foreign power, in order to lead our country to ruin, the struggle will be carried on without mercy and the law applied with extreme vigour."

Whatever might be the sequel to the thoughts and intentions expressed in those memorable speeches, they marked a new phase in the relationship between France and the Government of Vietnam. On that April afternoon in Vinh-Yen, de Lattre followed up his successes on the field of battle with a triumph in the field of statesmanship. Clouds of mistrust were dispelled.

In all his planning and visions for the future, whether it was in Germany, in France, or in Vietnam, it had always been youth that was to be the main instrument for their realization. The death of Bernard seems to have accentuated de Lattre's passion to be of service to youth. Devotion to that service provided a measure of solace in his irreparable loss. Moreover, the death of Bernard in the service of their country added new strength to the appeals which de Lattre made to the youth of Vietnam.

On the 11th July, in the presence of the Prime Minister, de Lattre attended a prize-giving at the Lycée Chasseloup-Laubat. He must have been thinking more than usually of Bernard on that day, for exactly two months before he had proudly decorated him with the Croix de Guerre. The thought of his own sacrifice inspired him to speak to the youth of the Lycée with profound and moving emotion. He spoke then as if they had been his own children, and he spoke with a frankness that spared the feelings of none. He reminded them that Vietnam was at war. He reminded them that the young men of France, as well as their own, were laying down their lives for a war that was a Vietnamese war. He reminded them that they, the young intellectuals of their country, had great responsibilities. It was to them that the others looked to lead them against tyranny and to preserve their independence. "I, who have known and loved the youth of many nations," he said, "tell you that, the youth of this country can, if it so will, measure up to the demands of history. . . . Be men. If you are communists, go and join the Vietminh. There are some over there who are fighting well for a bad cause. But if you are patriots, fight for your country, for this war is your war. When there are sufficient Vietnamese Officers of the right quality, then will Vietnam have total independence. But this does not depend on France; it depends on the *élite* of Vietnam." Only the future can tell how many of those who listened to the words of that stricken parent were moved by their sincerity. They were not the words of an imperialist. Was there not, after all, a new and selfless motive that urged the youth of Europe to lay down their lives in far-away lands?

But it was not sufficient that the people of Vietnam should understand the new nature of France's mission. With the British, de Lattre was in frequent touch. Already in May he had been to Singapore. With convincing clarity he had emphasized that Vietnam was the keystone of the whole edifice which American,

British, and French were supporting in Eastern Asia. With MacDonald, the British Commissioner General in South East Asia, he was on the best of terms. But he did not feel that he had the sympathy of the Americans. He had never been to the United States, and he longed to go there and to pour out his thoughts to those in authority. With Mr. Heath, the American Minister in Vietnam, he had a good understanding, and eventually he was invited by the Chiefs of Staff Committee to visit the United States in September.

On the 23rd July, de Lattre was present at the inauguration of an american library, set up by their information service in Saigon. This little ceremony afforded him the opportunity, in the presence of the American Minister, of emphasizing the international nature of France's mission in Indo-China. "Our mission," he said, "is to stop the expansion of communism, by intensifying the war effort, and in strengthening everything that can contribute to the work of resistance." Such were the views that he was to develop later during his visit to the United States.

A few days later, Governor Dewey together with Mr. Casey, Minister for External Affairs of Australia, paid a visit to Vietnam. This provided another opportunity for de Lattre to prepare public opinion in the States for his forthcoming visit. On Dewey he made a great impression, and, before leaving Saigon, Dewey proclaimed publicly his conviction that Vietnam was struggling to safeguard the free world. In his whole experience, he added, he had never seen countries undertaking a common task with such reciprocal understanding. Asked privately, a few days later, what he thought of de Lattre, Dewey said, "He is the most stimulating personality I have met for a long time."

At the end of July de Lattre returned to France, and in August, as had become customary, he and Madame de Lattre went to Cape Vern in the Basses-Pyrénees for a cure, and to prepare for the journey to America. On the 7th September, they both embarked in the "Île de France". Once again he called upon the faithful Bondoux to accompany him.

On the 13th, the "Île de France" reached New York, and among those who came on board to greet de Lattre was Senator Cabot Lodge, who had played so conspicuous a part as liaison officer between de Lattre and Devers. His stay in the United States was to last twelve days. His object was firstly to convince the United States that the problem in Indo-China was international, and, if he could succeed in that, to accelerate the delivery of American war material. In the next twelve days his output of energy was prodigious, but the sands were fast running out. It was the last great service that he was to render to France.

The task that lay in front of him was as hard as any that he undertook. There were great prejudices to break down, not the least of which was a deep-rooted and misguided antipathy to so-called French imperialism. His knowledge of English was still only fair, and among those with whom he was to make contact, he would find fewer who understood French than in the countries of Europe. Moreover, his experience of the great American people was limited to his dealings with American soldiers. Indeed, he was committed to give battle on ground that had been barely reconnoitred. But he felt that his knowledge of the Americans was sufficient to justify his confidence in the outcome of his mission. Writing of this visit shortly before he died, and speaking of the Americans, he said: "I found them just as my great confidence in them had led me to expect: they were cordial, simple, generous, and of infinite delicacy of feeling—so much for their qualities of heart; and mentally I found them serious, ready to listen, conscious of their responsibilities, and anxious only to commit themselves with full knowledge and in a good cause."

The tenor of his arguments throughout his stay would be that war in Indo-China was not a colonial war. It was, on the contrary, an anti-colonial war, against the only form of colonialism then in existence—red colonialism. Tonking was the keystone of South East Asia. It protected Indo-China, Indonesia, Siam, and Burma, and if they fell, the communist wave would surge over India and Western Asia to the Red Sea. By then two-thirds of the Moslem world would have passed into the totalitarian camp, and North Africa would be threatened. Such were the views that he would have to put across in his halting English to soldiers, statesmen, journalists, and others.

At 2 p.m. on the 13th September the endurance test started. He was not yet ashore. The Press attacked him while still on board, and at Washington next day they delivered their second onslaught. Then in rapid succession he had to address service chiefs at the Pentagon, the Senate, the State Department and the National Press Council. At innumerable luncheons and dinners, too, he was expected to speak, but the greatest ordeal of all was before the television cameras. Many tried to dissuade him from so risky an enterprise, for with television it was hit or miss, and, with his indifferent English, the odds were on his missing. But, again, it was the element of risk that tempted him.

There was little time in which to make up his mind. On the afternoon of the 16th, only two days after his arrival in Washington, he faced the ordeal. There was a panel of four newspaper representatives—three men and one woman. There was also a lady "Moderator". Senator Cabot Lodge was to act as interpreter. Off went the first gun. "General, I know this trip of yours to the United States is not a pleasure trip. Are you seeking aid from us for your war in Indo-China?" De Lattre said he would answer that question in a minute, but he wanted first to make apologies for his English. He would have difficulty in finding his words, but whatever he said would be the truth. "I'm certain of that, General. Now will you answer the question?" came the second shot, and the barrage continued. "General, there are a great many people in this country who believe that in case of war, the French haven't the will or the capacity to fight. What do you think of that?" It was perhaps an unfortunate question to put to one who had just lost his only son in battle, and whose country had in recent years lost thousands killed on the battlefields of Indo-China. But it was a question that was exercising many in America, and the questioner should not be too harshly judged. In their quest for truth, the task of the Press-men is not always easy. But de Lattre did not allow his anger to be provoked, and he mastered a situation that might well have proved awkward.

His decision to face the television cameras was a bold gamble, and his superb triumph in this new role was the high light of the visit. If words failed, the gesture, the expression, and the sincerity carried the day. Before the cameras his hands had been free to gesticulate, for there was no paper from which to read, but when, a few days later, he had to address the National Press Club in Washington, his hands were less free, for he had to read from a paper. But his speech was clear and convincing. He prefaced it with a tribute to the amazing expansion of the United States Army in the war, from 200,000 to 12,000,000 men; then he turned again to the achievements of France in Indo-China, to the selflessness of her motives, and to the disastrous consequences to civilization, if France had chosen a less robust course of action. Again he triumphed.

The luncheons, the dinners, the speeches, the meetings, and the visits continued. The Naval College at Annapolis and the Military College at West Point were privileged also to receive him. The pace never slackened, and on the 23rd he was expected once again to face the television cameras. If it was a handsome tribute to his first performance, it was a heavy additional burden to impose upon a tired man.

On the 25th September de Lattre was in New York. It was the last day of his visit. In the morning Cardinal Spellman, in the presence of de Lattre and his wife, celebrated Mass in memory of Bernard. At a luncheon later at the Knickerbocker Club, de Lattre was assured by one of the speakers, that he had been a great source of inspiration to all. Just before midnight, de Lattre and his wife set forth by air on their return to France.

No tribute to the success of the visit could have been more genuine or eloquent than that which was paid by General Collins, when he visited Indo-China a few weeks later. "You came like a crusader to present the cause for which you were fighting in Indo-China. You pleaded it with all your incomparable ardour and conviction. Few of your campaigns have created enthusiasm that is comparable to that which you raised by your visit to America. No one has ever shown, as you showed, in such simple language, all that is at stake in Indo-China, nor made so clear the issues that are possible. To our people you have rendered a great service."

Early in 1953, a year after de Lattre died, it was agreed that the Indo-Chinese problem should be considered as one and the same as that in Korea and Malaya. The seeds which de Lattre had sown had not been unfruitful.

36. FORTITUDE SUBLIME

ON the 26th September de Lattre, with his wife and those who had accompanied him to America, touched down at Orly Airport, on the outskirts of Paris. Normally the mind of de Lattre was busy with the future, but for once, during the flight across the Atlantic, it was filled with reflections on all that he had seen in America and on all that he had striven to accomplish. In the twelve days that had just passed, he had expended in the service of his country almost the last reserves of power that yet remained to him, and he had reason to be satisfied. Uppermost in his mind seems to have been that haunting question that was put to him when he faced the television cameras: "Was there the will to fight?" De Lattre felt satisfied that he had answered that question with fitting conviction; for as he stepped out of the aircraft, and confronted the Press of his own country, almost his first words, after a generous tribute to his hosts in America, were: "The great and valiant American democracy fully recognizes the worth of the reborn French Army. Through me a tribute has been paid to our magnificent soldiers in Indo-China, who are the living proof of our will to fight."

For the next few days he was busy reporting on his mission. De Lattre spoke little of his health; indeed, he disliked it if people said he looked ill or tired. But he was already a very sick man, and on the morning of the 4th October he went to see his doctor. The doctor had no doubt as to the nature of his illness. It was cancer. Knowing also the manner of man with whom he was dealing, he knew full well that it would be useless to hide the truth, and so the truth he told. At that moment the courage of de Lattre shone forth in all its grandeur. There was a moment's hesitation, and then he said: "Eh bien! Either there is another mission for me to fulfil first, or else I shall be reunited with Bernard the sooner."

With the words of his doctor still ringing in his ears, de Lattre attended a luncheon party given by the Anglo-American Press and spoke of his visit. On the following day, he went to London at the invitation of the British Chiefs of Staff. The meetings, luncheons, and the dinners started again. One afternoon he gave the Chiefs of

Staff an exposition of the situation in Indo-China, which lasted over two hours. Despite his lack of fluency, he spoke in English, and the Chief of the British Air Staff described it as a most remarkable performance. That same evening there was a dinner at the French Embassy. After dinner de Lattre again spoke on Indo-China, and when he spoke, with that inimitable and persuasive clarity that was his, everyone would listen with rapt attention. On this occasion, many of those present were his compatriots, and, although he started in English, he spoke mostly in French. The Lord Chancellor, who was present, said afterwards that, although his own French was not fluent, it was one of the most brilliant expositions to which he had ever listened.

Only fortitude of a sublime order could have sustained de Lattre during these three days in London. It was as though the knowledge that his days were numbered brought him increasing power and determination. The eloquent and persuasive voice must be heard in the fullness of its power, before it should be silenced for ever. On the 8th October he went back to Paris, and on the 11th he had to speak at another Press luncheon.

However egocentric the complex character of de Lattre may have been, he seemed to lose all regard for self in that hour of trial. There can have been few commanders in history who, in the days of peace, devoted so assiduously their spare moments to the welfare of those who had served them and helped to make them famous. On the morning of the 9th October he underwent a small operation at the military hospital of Val de Grâce. Afterwards he was exhausted, but the Rhine and Danube Association had a reunion in the afternoon, and, after initial hesitation, he determined once again to summon strength to attend. For once he had to admit to the Secretary General of the Association that he did not know how he would be able to go through with it, and he, who normally could extemporize without difficulty, asked for some notes. He said he had not the strength to improvise.

When de Lattre reached the headquarters of the Association, now in the Rue Paul Valery, he found the entrance lined by picked members of the Association. When they sprang to attention with that snap and precision that was so dear to de Lattre, he seemed at once to revive. When a few minutes later he entered the hall, where his old warriors and their families were gathered to welcome him, a spontaneous wave of affection seemed to surge towards him. For a moment the burden of his own cares and suffering was thrown aside. The prepared notes he threw aside, and with all his old eloquence and enthusiasm he spoke of Indo-China, and of his visit to America. All were agreed that they had never seen the "patron" in such form. It was his last visit to them.

On the 18th October he and his wife left by air for Indo-China. At Rome he broke his journey for forty-eight hours, for he had a mission to fulfil at the Vatican. In Vietnam there are nearly two million Roman Catholics, and the attitude of some of them towards France had given cause for anxiety. He was anxious, therefore, to discuss the situation with the Pope, and he asked for an audience. The outcome of yet another mission was to prove successful

Vietnam, together with Laos and Cambodia, were now known as the Associated States. On the 19th October, for the last time, de Lattre touched down in Indo-China. Always ready with an appropriate and inspiring message for the Press, to those journalists who confronted him as he alighted from the aircraft he declared: "I return with increased faith in the future of the Associated States. My determination to help them in the accomplishment of their destiny has also been renewed, and to the service of their youth I am resolved to consecrate my entire being. 'Faith and determination' must be the watchwords for all."

Then he drove through Saigon to the Residency. It was ten months since he had driven through those same streets for the first time. Then they had been deserted and silent, for all seemed lost. Now they reverberated with the acclamations of its citizens. "Vive le Général de Lattre", "Vive l'Armée Vietnamienne", greeted the High Commissioner as he drove triumphantly along. De Lattre had said that one day they would greet him thus, and the warmth of this welcome must have brought a measure of gladness to the heart of the sick and sorrowing man.

On the 21st October, the Emperor Bao Dai gave a large dinner-party in his honour, and on the 22nd, General Collins, Chief of Staff of the United States Army, paid a visit to Saigon, and there were more banquets. It was on the occasion of this visit that Collins paid so generous a tribute to all that de Lattre had accomplished during his visit to Washington. Malcolm MacDonald also paid de Lattre a visit a few weeks later, and the community of their outlook was still further strengthened.

The length of de Lattre's stay in Indo-China was only to be for a month or so, for he knew he must return for consultation with the doctors. To a limited few only, was the gravity of his illness known. Among those who knew was M. Latourneau, the Minister of State for Relations with the Associated States. He arranged for the inaugural meeting of the Council of the French Union in Paris, at the end of November, to coincide with the needs of his health.

Before returning to France, de Lattre, together with his wife went to see the rock near Ninh-Binh, where Bernard had been killed. There was an element of risk in the undertaking of this sad pilgrimage, for operations were in progress within a few miles, but Madame de Lattre insisted on accompanying him.

During those last few weeks in Indo-China, de Lattre strove to throw off his own cares by devoting more than usual attention to the welfare of the troops. He was determined that they should spend Christmas in a manner that befitted the occasion. Moreover, he considered it the duty of the civil population to repay the debt they owed to the soldiers, by contributing handsomely to their Christmas celebrations. With that object in view, he invited the leading business men to a reception at the Residency. There he appealed to their generosity. He did not appeal in vain. This was one of his last acts before he left for France.

Further successes on the field of battle were to mark the last few weeks of de Lattre's presence in Indo-China, and they were to provide encouraging material for the report which he was to give before the Council of the French Union at the end of November. Although he himself directed the opening phases, it was left to General Salan to bring the operations to a successful conclusion. Hoa-Binh was the objective which de Lattre chose. Apart from the fact that it controlled communications between Annam and the Chinese frontier, it provided an area of operations in which the superiority of French fire-power could be exploited to the full, without the risk of massacring innocent civilians. Moreover, its capture would prove a serious blow to Viet-Minh prestige, and would therefore be likely to draw considerable enemy forces.

As a preliminary to this project, on the 11th November de

Lattre started offensive operations against Cho-Ben, an important line of approach into the Delta, thirty miles south-west of Hanoi. In three days Cho-Ben fell, and that gateway was closed. The resourcefulness of his admirable staff then enabled him to switch within twenty-four hours the same force which had captured Cho-Ben to Hoa-Binh. As a result of the surprise which this mobility gave him, Hoa-Binh was captured at small cost.

During the next two months, the enemy, as de Lattre had hoped, engaged about thirty regular battalions in his efforts to retrieve the situation at Hoa-Binh. But the French inflicted a series of defeats upon the enemy which cost the latter more than 20,000 casualties. Although it was Salan who was now directing the operations, he generously gave the full credit to de Lattre for the soundness of the initial conception.

On the 20th November, 1951, de Lattre and his wife boarded the regular Constellation aircraft at Haifong for Paris. It was to be farewell to Indo-China. It was also to be his last flight. De Lattre must have suspected it; moreover there were moments when he poured out his heart to his most intimate friends and confessed that the death of Bernard had left a gaping and incurable wound. At such moments he seemed to lose the will to live, but at others his will would reassert itself, and he would seem to cling to a belief that by some miracle he might yet be spared to render further service to his country.

Eleven months only had passed since de Lattre had reached Indo-China, in that critical month of December 1950. In the country itself he had barely spent seven of the eleven months that had elapsed, but the record of those months can rarely have been surpassed. By the imposition of his will, he had retrieved a situation that even the most sanguine had regarded as beyond repair. To his own troops he had restored the will and the power to achieve victory on the battlefield, and abroad he had restored a measure of confidence in French arms. With unrivalled eloquence, both in his own and in a strange tongue, he had pleaded a cause that even in his own country was hardly more popular than in America. Some at least of the people of Vietnam he convinced of the sincerity of French intentions. On that night in December 1950, when he had left Orly Airport and said to the veterans of the First French Army that he was going to give of the best that was in him, he had not spoken vain words. His only son and his own life were the measure of his sacrifice.

Although it was noticed at the meeting of the French Union that he had difficulty in going up the stairs, and seemed to be in pain, the account which he gave of the situation in Indo-China, had all his customary lucidity. It was the last occasion on which that persuasive voice was to be heard in the councils of France. The sickness gained, but his courage remained steadfast. A few days later, General Devers passed through Paris and de Lattre invited him to luncheon. The doctors had now decided to operate, and, on the afternoon of the 18th December, he entered the Clinique Maillot, in the Rue Paul Deroulède, in Neuilly. That same day he lunched for the last time at 4 Place Rio de Janeiro. His last two guests were the Archbishop of Paris and François Valentin, who had defended him in 1942. Despite the circumstances, although at moments he seemed to wince, as if in pain, his conversation sparkled.

37. THE PEACE OF MOUILLERON

THE room which de Lattre occupied in the clinic at Neuilly was characterized by extreme simplicity. Indeed, knowing how, throughout his life, he had been content with nothing but the best, Madame de Lattre had expected him to complain. But never before had he seemed so satisfied with simplicity. It had only been when the prestige of France required it, that he had sought befitting pomp. In the clinic at Neuilly, neither prestige nor dignity were at stake, and so pomp could give way to that fundamental simplicity that so few suspected.

On the 19th, the operation was carried out, and the vitality of the patient pulled him through. To the outside world there seemed no cause for alarm, but one who was with him constantly at the clinic noticed that, despite the continued clarity and alertness of his mind, there had been an alarming transformation. Although he was able to read the papers that were brought to him, even the effort of putting on his spectacles seemed too great.

At the beginning of January, his condition grew worse, and there seemed little hope. To the Abbé Badré, Chaplain General of the Army, de Lattre said that he wished to prepare himself seriously for the end. During the last days he grasped in his right hand the crucifix of his First Communion, and with his left hand he said his rosary, which from time to time would fall on the sheet. On Wednesday, the 9th January 1952, just before losing consciousness, de Lattre uttered his last words, "Where is Bernard?" At half past five on the afternoon of the 11th, in the presence of Madame de Lattre, her brother, Raoul de Lamazière, François Valentin, and the Abbé Badré, he breathed his last.

Paris was dumbfounded. Not only had it failed to realize the seriousness of his illness, but the very vitality of this dynamic figure made it difficult to realize that he was no more. Without warning, the most dazzling light which had illumined the French scene for years had been suddenly extinguished. The death of few men has so deeply stirred so many people, great and lowly, in many lands. From remote corners of the earth, and from men and women who had never known him, there came a spontaneous wave of sympathy for the valiant lady who, within so short a time, had lost all that was dear to her.

In Mouilleron-en-Pareds, the village priest gently and tactfully broke the news to his father, then in his ninety-seventh year. In a near-by cottage, overwhelmed with grief, sat Jacques Daniau, the coachman, and his wife. "Pauvre petit Jean," she kept repeating. On the eve of the state funeral, the coffin was placed upon a tank beneath the Arc de Triomphe. That noble arch has looked down on many memorable scenes, both of triumph and disaster. The scene that evening was one of peculiar grandeur, as reverent crowds filed past the coffin, while on the left bank of the Seine, behind the tomb of Napoleon, two searchlights projected a "V" into the skies. An unmistakable hush fell on the gay city, the hush that only comes when a great man has departed. Late at night, the President of the Republic conferred upon de Lattre the highest worldly honour. Placing a baton upon the tank, he raised him to the dignity of a Marshal of France.

On the following day, the people of Paris bade farewell to de

Lattre. It was difficult to believe that they were the same Parisians who a few years before had allowed him to return unnoticed and unthanked into their midst. Now from Notre Dame to the Invalides, into the Rue de Rivoli and the Champs Élysées, they flocked in their thousands to pay their belated tribute to the Marshal, and the lonely lady who followed him. On the Esplanade des Invalides, in the presence of the President of the Republic, and with Eisenhower and Montgomery among the distinguished pall-bearers, for more than an hour troops marched past the gun-carriage, saluting for the last time one who had striven so devotedly to serve their interests. It was his final parade, and its splendour was as he would have wished it. "C'est bien, les gars," would have been his comment.

On the next day, de Lattre was laid to rest at Mouilleron-en-Pareds, beside Bernard, just by the entrance to the cemetry, in the site which he himself had chosen a few months before, in the shade of two trees. Two plain white crosses mark the graves. How vivid was the contrast to the splendour of his lifetime! but in the grandeur of their simplicity they reveal the real de Lattre.

After de Lattre's death, life continued at Mouilleron, much as it had done when he was a boy. His father, now ninety-seven years old, was still Mayor. His sight was impaired, and he remained upstairs, where in an adjoining room, more than sixty years before, his son had been born. He still received his secretary every afternoon, and conscientiously applied himself to the affairs of the village. Once a week, Jacques Daniau still came in to help, and, when at home in their cottage, he and his wife would regale the passing stranger with tales of Monsieur Jean; and, in the telling, laughter would mingle with tears.

His windmill at Mouilleron is now a chapel to perpetuate the memory of a father and son, who gave all for France. It was fitting that de Lattre should rest in the shade of those windmills. They were his oldest friends. From youth they had watched over him. Even from afar he had often felt their mystic power, and in their presence his restless spirit had always found unwonted peace and calm.

EPILOGUE

"DE LATTRE was one of those people," said Canon Elchinger in Strasbourg Cathedral, shortly after his death, "whom one could never quite encompass. Every time you met him, you discovered something new. No frame would hold him; he would burst through them all. No particular school of thought or politics could claim him as its own." Indeed, there was no normal standard by which his stature could be measured. Even his most intimate collaborators never wholly comprehended their unusual chief. But of all the motives which inspired that complex and intensely human character, it was his love of France that transcended all others. To the service of his country he gave that unsparing and unquestioning devotion, that he demanded of others. In the grandeur of France he believed with the fervour of a crusader, and when her glories, for a moment, were eclipsed, he strove to restore them in all their former brilliance.

At Versailles, on one façade of the Château, may be read these words: "A toutes les gloires de la France." To de Lattre they were a challenge from a bygone century. But the glory that he sought for France, was no mere wild and foolish dream. In the hearts of a disillusioned youth, lacking in purpose and content with mediocrity, he sought to rekindle the flame of high endeavour, and to renew a pride in work well done. "Fais bien ce que tu fais," he had written to Bernard. "Fais bien ce que tu fais," was his message to France. No surer path could lead her back to glory.

BIBLIOGRAPHY

CHAIGNE, LOUIS, "Jean de Lattre", (Fernand Lanore, Paris).

CHURCHILL, WINSTON S., "The World Crisis" (Thornton Butterworth, London); "The Second World War" (Cassell, London).

DE LATTRE DE TASSIGNY, "Histoire de la Première Armée Française" (Plon, Paris).

EISENHOWER, DWIGHT, "Crusade in Europe" (Heinemann, London).

GARRIC, ROBERT, "Un Destin Héroique, Bernard de Lattre" (Plon, Paris).

GUDERIAN, "Panzer Leader" (Michael Joseph, London).

LIDDELL HART, B., "The Other Side of the Hill" (Cassell, London).

MASSON, ANDRÉ, "Histoire de l'Indo-Chine" (Presse Universitaire de France, Paris).

MAUROIS, ANDRÉ, "Lyautey" (Plon, Paris).

MICHEL-DROIT, "De Lattre, Maréchal de France" (Pierre Horay, Paris).

PALAT, "La Ruée sur Verdun" (Berger-Levrault, Paris).

LYET, PIERRE, "La Bataille de France, Mai–Juin, 1940" (Payot, Paris).

SIMIOT, BERNARD, "De Lattre" (Baudinère, Paris).

WEYGAND, "Rappelé au Service" (Flammarion, Paris).

WILSON, FIELD-MARSHAL LORD, "Eight Years Overseas" (Hutchinson, London).

MISCELLANEOUS

"Au Maréchal de Lattre, Hommages, Ordres du Jour, Discours". (Alsatia, Colmar).

"Revue Historique de l'Armée".

Index

Abdel Krim, 40–1, 43
Abetz, 102
Adran, Bishop of, 241–2, 245
Agadir, 9, 36
Agay, 138
Agostini, 191
Air Forces:
  First French Air Corps, 178
  12th Tactical Air Command (U.S.), 175
Airborne forces, 136, 139–40
Aisne, River, 14, 26, 30, 71–89
Aix-en-Provence, 142, 147, 149, 151, 155
Aix-la-Chapelle, 13
Albert, 23
Albert Canal, 60
Albord, Colonel, 105
Alexander, Field-Marshal, 129, 136
Algeciras Conference, 36
Algiers, 106, 122, 126–7, 129, 135, 209
Allard, 204, 253
Allauch, 148
Allied Forces Headquarters, 128, 130, 201
Alps, 198–9
Alsace, 10, 13, 14, 99, 154–7, 160–2, 165, 168, 170–2, 177, 189, 216, 222, 225–6
Altkirch, 165
Ambroselli, 114
Annam, 241–3, 273
Annapolis, 269
Annelles, 83
Antwerp, 161
Ardennes, 168–9, 178
Arles, 151
ARMIES:
  BRITISH
    21st Army Group, 161
  FRENCH
    Armies
      Army "B", 123–4
      First Army (1940), 68
      First Army (1944), 158 *et seq.*
      Second Army, 68, 72, 82–3
      Third Army (1914), 14
      Fourth Army (1914), 14
      Fourth Army (1940), 71, 82
      Fifth Army, 63–4

FRENCH
  Armies—cont.
    Seventh Army, 68
    Ninth Army, 68, 72, 75
  Corps
    I, 156 *et seq.*
    II, 156 *et seq.*
    VIII, 90–1
    XIII, 82
    XX, 13
    XXIII, 77
  Divisions
    1st Armoured, 138 *et seq.*
    1st Reserve Armoured (1940), 75
    1st Free French, 141 *et seq.*
    2nd, 83, 87–88
    2nd Armoured, 157–8, 165–6
    2nd Moroccan, 155 *et seq.*
    3rd Algerian, 141 *et seq.*
    4th Moroccan Mountain, 179 *et seq.*
    5th Armoured, 164 *et seq.*
    5th Light Cavalry Division, 74–6
    9th Colonial, 130 *et seq.*
    10th, 177
    14th, 64 *et seq.*
    36th, 88
  Brigades, Regiments, etc.
    1st Combat Command, 138 *et seq.*
    2nd Combat Command, 142 *et seq.*
    3rd Algerian Divisional Reconnaissance Regiment, 144 *et seq.*
    5th Hussars, 15
    12th Dragoons, 9 *et seq.*
    25th Reconnaissance Group, 64 *et seq.*
    28th Dragoons, 8
    Half-Brigade Chausseurs, 64 *et seq.*
    4th Infantry Regiment, 47
    35th Infantry Regiment, 64 *et seq.*
    49th Infantry Regiment, 34
    59th Infantry Regiment, 49
    93rd Infantry Regiment, 18 *et seq.*
    151st Infantry Regiment, 55 *et seq.*
    153rd Infantry Regiment, 64 *et seq.*

FRENCH
Armies—cont.
24th Battalion, 175
Chasseurs Alpins, 199
Commandos, 145 *et seq.*
"Choc" battalions, 132 *et seq.*
Goums, 39, 43, 101, 132, 141 *et seq.*
F.F.I. (Forces Françaises de l'Interieur), 150 *et seq.*
F.T.P. (Francs Tireurs Partisans), 205
GERMAN
Army Groups
Army Group A, 67 *et seq.*
Army Group B, 67 *et seq.*
Army Group C, 67 *et seq.*
Armies
First (1914), 14
First (1944), 137, 174
Second, 80
Twelfth, 68, 80–1, 86
Nineteenth, 137 *et seq.*
Corps
XIV, 81, 88
XVIII, 195, 198
XXXIX, 88–9
LXIII, 165, 177
LXIV, 177, 196
Divisions
1st Panzer, 70 *et seq.*
2nd Panzer, 70 *et seq.*
10th Panzer, 70 *et seq.*
11th Panzer, 149, 156
17th, 88
73rd, 88
86th, 88
244th, 147
338th, 163
UNITED STATES
Army Groups
6th, 158 *et seq.*
12th, 161, 168
Armies
Third, 161, 168
Seventh, 134 *et seq.*
Corps
VI, 136 *et seq.*
XXI, 181 *et seq.*
Divisions
10th Armoured, 196
12th Armoured, 184
UNITED STATES
Divisions—cont.
3rd, 149, 177, 179–80, 182
36th, 166, 177
Regiments
109th Infantry, 184
Arras, 28
Atlas, Middle, 37, 42
Attigny, 74, 83, 86, 87, 88
Aubagne, 147–8, 150
Aube, 91
Auberge-St.-Pierre, 15
Auriol, Vincent, 227
Autun, 157
Auxerre, 47
Avignon, 105–9, 149, 151, 155–6, 190

Baden-Baden, 193
Badre, Abbé, 276
Ballon d'Alsace, 160
Bandol, 145
Bao Dai, 243–5, 249, 272
Barcelona, 127
Bardier, Father, 6, 213
Bari, 139
Barr, General, 180–1
Bastia, 132
Bavidot, Sergeant, 15
Bayonne, 34–5, 52
Beaufre, Lieutenant-Colonel, 179
Belfort, 64, 155, 156–8, 160–5, 170, 186, 202
Belgentier, 144
Benelux, 232
Berchtesgaden, 184
Bergnicourt, 88
Berlin, 208–9, 211, 214, 216, 238
Besançon, 155, 157, 163
Bethouart, 7, 9, 156-8, 162–4, 178–9, 184–5, 193–5, 198–9, 204–6, 215
Biarritz, 33–4
Billotte, 60, 177, 182
Binnerach, 197
Bitche, 169
Bizerta, 101
Black Forest 186, 188, 192–6, 198
Blanc, General, 238
Bonaparte, Princess Marie, 219
Bondoux, René, 203, 208–10, 230–1, 266
Bordeaux, 34, 137, 142, 162

Borie, Commandant, 208
"Bouboule", 116, 118–19
Bourg, 156
Bourret, General, 61
Bousquet, Charles, 45–7, 49, 51, 54, 61
Boutancourt, 70
Bouvellemont, 75–7, 79, 80
Bouvet, 140
"Brains Trust", 203–4, 230
Bregenz, 198
Bridoux, 108
Brighton, 7, 201
Brisach, 164, 177–8, 182, 184
Brittany, 134, 137, 221
Brooke, General Sir Alan, 163
Brooks, General, 175–6, 189
Brosset, 141–2, 145–6, 149, 155
Brussels, 238
Brussels Treaty, 232–3
Buccio Isthmus, 133
Buenos Aires, 230
Bullitt, William, 146
Bureau, Father, 109
Burnhaupt, 165
Burrough, Admiral, 209
Bussang, 160

Cadet, Roland, 203
Cadolive, 147–8
Cambodia, 241, 243, 272
Cannes, 137
Cap Nègre, 140
Cap Vern, 266
Capitulation, Act of, 208–11
Carcassonne, 104
Carpentier, 179, 191, 204
Carpiagne, 147
Carthage, 101
Casablanca, 37
Casey, 266
Catroux, General, 95, 243
Cavalaire, 138
Céhin, Lieutenant, 84
Cerny, 26
Chad, Lake, 158, 184
Chagny, 77
Chalampe, 184
Chalons-sur-Marne, 83, 89–90
Chalons-sur-Saône, 190
Chamberlain, Neville, 62
Champagne, 28
Chappuis, 150
Charles-Roux, Edmonde, 203
Chasse-Loup-Laubat, Lycée, 265
Chassin, General, 256
Château Porcien, 77, 81 86–8
Chemin-des-Dames, 26, 28–30
Cho-Ben, 274
Churchill, Mary, 227
Churchill, Sir Winston, 129, 134, 160, 162–3, 173, 196, 211, 227
Clémenceau, 2, 33–4, 46, 141, 163, 186
Clement, Colonel, 255
Clermont-Ferrand, 91–2, 97, 116, 118, 120
Cochet, General, 100
Cochin-China, 241, 243–4, 252, 255
Coetquidan, 221
Cogolin, 140–1
Collins, General, 269, 272
Colmar, 64, 164–6, 168, 170, 174, 177–8, 182, 184–6, 200, 202, 226
Colmar Canal, 182, 184
Combined Chiefs of Staff, 135
Compains, 119
Conseil Supérieur de la Guerre, 230
Constance, 213–14, 221
Constance, Lake, 193, 198, 207, 213
Constans, 109
Control Commission in W. Germany 214
Corap, 72
"Corniche", 7
Corsica, 105, 124, 130, 132, 142
Coulommiers, 49
Courance, 235

Daladier, 53
Daniau, Jacques, 1, 4, 5, 34, 44, 276–7
Daniau, Mme, 276–7
Danube, River, 192–5, 197–8, 221
D'Arcy, Colonel, 130
Darlan, Admiral, 102, 104–7
Dauphiné, 138
Day, River, 260
De Beauregard, Commandant Costa, 230
De Camas, Colonel, 73, 108
De Chambrun, General, 41
Decoux, Admiral, 243
De Denant, Mlle, 3
De Gaulle, General Charles, 51, 54, 64, 95, 100, 102–3, 120, 122–3, 130, 139, 143, 146, 163, 172, 180, 185, 196–7, 207, 216–17, 227

De Gaulle, Henri, 6
De Hesdin, 194–5
De La Boisse, 204
De Lamazière, Raoul, 203, 276
De Lamazière, Simone, 46
De Larminat, 142–3, 149
De Lattre de Tassigny, Anne-Marie (Comtesse de Marcé), 142–3, 149
De Lattre de Tassigny, Bernard, 48, 84, 98–9, 101, 103, 109, 114–9, 121, 126–7, 140, 157, 203, 221, 230, 247–9, 259–63, 265, 270, 273–5, 277–8
De Lattre, Jean:
Career:
birth, 1; education 5–7; student at Saint Cyr and Saumur, 8–9; joins 12th Dragoons, 9; wounded by lance, 15; volunteers for the infantry, 17; record as infantry officer, 18–28; first staff appointment 28; appointed to Morocco, 34; rôle at Taza, 42; returns to France, 43; prepares for École de Guerre, 44–7; engagement and marriage, 46; student at École de Guerre, 47–9; appointed to Weygand's staff, 50; involved in troubles of February 1934, 53; appears before parliamentary commission, 53; appointed to command 151st Infantry Regiment, 55; appointed to Centre of Higher Military Studies, 59; appointed Chief of Staff, Strasbourg, 61; promoted Brigadier General, 61; appointed Chief of Staff Fifth Army, 63; appointed to command 14th Infantry Division, 64; rôle at Rethel May and June 1940, 70–89; appointed to Tunis, 101; recalled to France, 102; appointed to command XVI Military Division at Montpellier, 103; suspected of "Gaullist" activities, 104; ordered to oppose Allied landings, 105; defiance of Vichy, 108; trial and imprisonment, 111–17; escape and flight to London 119-121; leaves for North Africa, 123; appointed to command "Army B", 123; preparations in North Africa, 124–8; captures Elba, 130–3; lands in South of France, 140; captures Toulon and Marseilles, 140–54; advances to the Vosges, 154–9; forces Belfort Gap and advances to Rhine, 160–4; difficulties before Colmar and Strasbourg, 165–70; refuses to abandon Strasbourg, 171–7; liquidates Colmar pocket, 177–85; crosses Rhine and exploits success into Austria, 186–99; witnesses Act of Capitulation in Berlin, 208–11; mission to Germany, 211–15; appointed Inspector-General of the Army and Chief of the General Staff, 217; creates the "Light Camps", 218; difficulties, 227–9; mission to South America, 230–1; appointed Inspector-General of the Armed forces, 232; appointed commander of Land Forces Western Europe, 236; partnership with Montgomery, 233–9; appointed to Indo-China, 245; first actions to restore morale, 248–51; victory at Vinh-yen, 254; builds up Vietnamese Army, 259; death of Bernard, 260–1; confirms French intention to grant independence to Vietnam, 263–4; visits United States, 266–9; mission to Vatican, 272; last visit to Indo-China, 272; death, 276.
Characteristics:
ambition, 6, 44, 47
appearance, 7, 9, 220, 256
clothes, love of, 12, 33, 122
command, methods of, 204–5
courage, moral and physical, 4, 15, 30, 40, 90, 270–1, 275
diplomatic qualities, 230–5, 266–9
dress, importance attached to, 19, 56, 92, 136
drill, importance attached to, 56–7, 212, 223
esprit de corps, capacity to create, 57, 59, 154, 206, 215
extravagance, 50, 57, 214, 229
glory and grandeur, cult of, 6, 24, 50, 64, 97–8, 104, 198, 206, 211–13, 215 222, 264, 278
knowledge of men, 47, 75, 206

De Lattre, Jean—*cont.*
morale, capacity to raise, 11, 20, 39, 42, 65, 73–4, 166, 173–4, 218, 248–50, 252, 254, 274
physical training, importance attached to, 217, 225, 253, 267–8
religious faith, 4, 26, 108–9, 117, 276
showmanship, 11, 16, 33, 213–4
tactical ability, 152, 160–2, 175, 202
temper, 30, 41, 87, 126, 138, 162, 171, 204, 210, 214, 225, 237–8, 248–9
training methods, 11, 218, 223–4
vanity, 9, 32, 207, 233, 237
welfare, attention paid to, 19, 20, 26, 49, 57, 59, 101, 217, 223, 271, 273
De Lattre de Tassigny, Mme, 48–9, 98, 108, 111–2, 115–9, 126–7, 217, 226, 235–6, 250, 261, 266, 269, 270, 272–7
De Lattre de Tassigny, Roger, 2–4, 185, 277
De Linares, Colonel, 144–6, 180, 193, 197, 199, 204
Delmotte, General, 104, 107
Demetz, 157, 197, 204
De Monsabert, de Goislard, 42, 141–2 144–51, 155, 157–8, 160–1, 175–7, 179, 182, 184, 189–93, 195–6, 198, 204, 215
Dequenne, Charles, 73, 119
Deutch, 16
Devers, General Jacob, 123, 130, 143, 154, 158, 161–2, 166, 168–71, 174–7, 180–2, 185, 188–90 192, 197–8, 202, 213, 267, 275
De Villiers, Roger, 114
Dewey, Governor, 266
Dijon, 156–7, 229
Dinant, 67
Djebala, 37
Dody, 155
Dong-Khe, 245
Dong-Trieu, 257
Douaumont, Fort, 21, 24, 146
Doubs, 160, 162
Douera, 125–7, 221
"Dragoon", 135–6, 139
"Drôle de Guerre", 65
Dromond, 155, 190–1
Dunkirk, 85
Dunkirk, Treaty of, 232
Durosoy, 221
Du Souzy, Colonel, 168–71
Düsseldorf, 161
Du Vigier, General, 142–3, 147, 149, 151, 155–7, 163–4, 176, 180, 190

École de Guerre, 44–5, 47
Eisenhower, General, 128–9, 134–5, 143, 157–8, 165, 169–71, 185–6, 200, 209–10, 238, 277
El Alamein, 104, 234
Elba, 130–1, 133
Elchinger, 278
Ensisheim, 182, 184
Épinal, 157
Eppenghen, 192
Escault, 60
Etain, 20
Europe, Council of, 232

Faissault, 78–9
Faron, 145
Farrère, Claude, 145
Fez, 35, 40, 42
Foch, Marshal, 13, 29, 49, 50, 94, 99, 230, 234–5
Fontaine, 164
Fontainebleau, 235, 237–8
Forbach, 64
Franco-Soviet Pact, 52
French Air Force, 184, 249
French Union, Council of, 273, 275
Freudenstadt, 193–5
Frey, 173
Frot, 53

Gall, 133
Gambiez, Lieutenant-Colonel, 132, 199, 203
Gambsheim, 175
Garbay, 180
Gavotte, 151
Gemenos, 149
Georges, General, 91, 96
Gerardmer, 161
Germain, 77
Germersheim, 191
Getten, 126

Gia-Long, 242, 245
Gibraltar, 35, 43, 126–7
Giraud, General, 42–3, 56, 60, 122–3, 127, 130
Giromagny, 164
Givry, 86
Gouraud, General, 29
Grange, Forest of, 162
Grenoble, 138, 140, 154–5
Grimaud, 138
Grusenheim, 178, 182
Guderian, General, 67, 72, 75, 77, 80, 82, 85–6, 88–91
Guillaume, General, 39, 47, 141, 148–9, 151–2, 156, 160–1, 172–3, 180, 188–9, 196, 202
Guisan, 205
Gurkhas, 244

Haguenau, Forest of, 175, 189
Haifong, 245, 260, 274
Hanoi, 245, 247, 249–54, 260, 263, 274
Happy Valley, 23
Hazebrouck, 29
Heath, 266
Heilbronn, 192
Hénault, Anne-Marie (Mme Roger de Lattre), 2, 3
Hericourt, 163
Hering, General, 48, 61
Himmler, 165–6
Hitler, 51, 61, 67, 103, 129, 196
Hoa-Binh, 273–4
Ho-Chi-Minh, 244–5, 249, 251–2, 254, 257, 260
Hong Kong, 245
Huningne, 164
Hyères, 142, 145

"Île-de-France", 266
Ill, River, 180
Indo-China, 222, 236, 239, 241 *et seq.*
Indo-Chinese Communist Party, 244
Inn Valley, 199
Innaven, Wadi, 42
Istrian Peninsula, 129

Jaujard, 140
Jebsheim, 178, 182
Jesse, 44, 46
Jesuit College, Montpellier, 109
Jesuit College, Rheims, 126
Jibuti, 95
Joffre, Marshal, 14, 17
Jonval, 77
Juin, Marshal, 41, 122, 135, 163, 173, 180

Kaids, 37
Karlsruhe, 188–9, 192, 194
Kehl, 193, 215
Kempten, 197
Kilstett, 176
Kir, Canon, 229
Kleist, General, 68–9, 80
Knickerbocker Club, 269
Koenig, General, 215
Krafft, 175

La Bascule, 77
Lacordaire, Father, 114
La Fère, 28
Lamont, 74
Langres, 86, 158
Langson, 245
Laos, 243, 272
La Pomme, 147
La Poudrière, 145
La Preste, 105
Larzac, 104
Latourneau, 273
Launois, 77–8
Lauter, 188–9
Lauterbourg, 188–9
La Valette, 145
Le Blanc, 116–118
Le Cateau, 14
Le Chesne, 70
Leclerc, General, 95, 128, 157, 166, 176, 184, 244
Legentilhomme, 95
Leimersheim, 191–2
Le Muy, 138, 140
Les Corbières, 104, 106, 109
Lesieur, Christiane, 203
"Light Camps," 218–19, 221–6, 254
Lindau, 207, 212–14
List, General, 80
Livry-Level, 121
Ljubljana Gap, 129

Lodge, Cabot, 143, 169, 182, 266, 268
Lomont, Fort, 161
London, 121–2, 220, 238, 246, 270
Lorraine, 10, 13, 14, 99
Lourdes, 7, 236
Luc-Nam, 251
Lunéville, 70–1
Lyautey, Marshal, 35–6, 43, 99, 213
Lyons, 110–1, 120, 137–8, 155–6

MacDonald, Malcolm, 260, 272
Machault, 89
Mâcon, 120, 157
Magdeburg, 208
Maginot Line, 63, 67
Magnan, 131, 142, 145–6, 155
Maillot, Clinic, 275
Maison Blanche, 127
Manhes-d'Angeny, 72, 73, 205
Mannheim, 192
Mao-Khe, 257–8
Marcé, Comtesse de, see de Lattre de Tassigny, Anne-Marie
Mareth Line, 102
Marie, Father, 117
Marne, River, 20, 89–91, 253
Marrakesh, 34, 37
Marseilles, 137–8, 142, 146–54, 200, 202
Marshall, General, 133
Masevaux, 179
Massif Central, 98, 100, 139
Maubeuge, 13
Mazagran, 83, 87
"Medusa", 259–60
Meknes, 35, 37–8, 40
Mellot, 261
Mendoza, 231
Mengen, 208
Mercier, 260–1
Meriaux, 19, 20
Metz, 10, 11, 55, 213
Meuse, River, 20, 67–9, 71
Meuse, Côte de, 20
Mezières, 13, 30
Milburn, 181, 184
Mittelhauser, 95
Molsheim, 174
Monod, Jacques, 203
Mons, 14
Mont Redon, 145
Montbeliard, 162–3, 168, 172, 177
Montgomery, Field-Marshal, 102, 104, 158, 233–8, 246, 248, 262, 277
Montluc, 110, 112
Montpellier, 103, 105, 107, 109–10, 115, 137, 229
Montrieux, 144
Morlière, 179
Morocco, 32–43
Moselle, River, 9, 10, 14
Mouilleron-en-Pareds, 1, 5, 33, 44, 141, 179, 185–6, 262, 276
Moulouya, Upper, 38–9
Mourmelon, 20, 74, 89
Msila, 42
Mulaidris, 40
Mulheim, 195, 197
Mulhouse, 64, 160, 164–5, 178–9
Mutzig, 222, 225–6

Nam-Dinh, 260
Naples, 135–6
National Press Club, 268
National Press Council, 268
Navreau, 238
Neuilly, 275
New York, 246, 266, 269
Nguyen-Anh, 241–2
Ninh-Binh, 273
Nivelle, General, 26
Nogues, General, 95
Normandy, 129, 134, 137, 157–8, 200, 234
North Atlantic Treaty Organization, 238

O'Daniel, 149, 179–81
Omont, 72, 75–7
Opme, 98–9, 221
Oran, 139
Orly, 246, 270, 274

Palatinate, 188–9
Palewski, 163
Paris, 14, 33, 86, 119, 126, 158, 160, 172, 207–8, 214–24, 226, 230–1, 253, 261–2, 270–1, 273–7
Paris, Archbishop of, 275
Patch, General Alexander, 135–6, 138, 140, 142–4, 147, 151–2, 154, 158, 161, 196

Patton, General George, 154, 157, 169, 190
Peron, 230–1
Peron, Eva, 231
Pershing, General, 41
Pétain, Marshal, 21, 95, 104, 112
Petit, Claudius, 120–1
Pforzheim, 188, 192
Phu-Ly, 260
Pigneau de Béhaine, see Adran
Pléven, 246
Po, River, 166
Poeymireau, General, 37, 39 40
Poincaré, President, 12
Poitiers, 5, 213
Poix-Terron, 70, 75–7, 79
Pommier, 73
Pont-à-Musson, 9–11, 15, 17, 58, 213
Pont-de-Vaux, 120
Pont Mirabeau, 46
Provence, Théâtre d'Opération de, 105–6
Puntous, 110
Puy-de-Dôme, 98, 119–20
Pyrenees, 124, 126

Qui Nhon, 241
Quinche, 108

Rabat, 37
Ramadier, 236
Rastadt, 193
Ravin de la Dame, 22
Realtor Reservoir, 149
Red River Delta, 241, 245, 254
Requin, 91
Resistance Movement, 136–9, 205–6, 220
Rethel, 30
Retourne, River, 83
Revers, 107, 229
Rheims, 71, 126
Rhine, River, 157, 162, 164–6, 177–8, 184, 186, 188, 200, 202–3, 215, 221
Rhine and Danube Association, 217, 219, 271–2
Rhône, River, 137, 154, 190
Rhône Valley, 107, 138, 140
Ribeauville, 180, 182
Ricard, Captain, 47
Rif, 37, 40, 43
Riom, 112, 114, 116–7, 261
Roetsch, Louis, 116, 118–19
Rome, 139
Rommel, General, 233
Rommel, Manfred, 196
Roosevelt, President, 211
Rouffach, 184–5
Rougemont, 164

Saigon, 244, 248–51, 253, 266, 272
Saint-Anton, 199–200
Saint-Aygulf, 140
Saint-Cloud, 219
Saint-Cyr, 216, 221
Saint-Joseph, College of, 5, 6
Saint-Joseph Prison, 112
Saint-Laurence, 44
Saint-Louis, 99
Saint-Pons, 109–10
Saint-Raphael, 140, 142, 147
Salammbo, 101
Salan, 250, 252, 273–4
Salon, 120
Saône, River, 120
Sarreguemines, 64, 181
Saumur, 221
Saverne, 63, 165, 170–1
Savoy, 138
Schaeffer, 151
Schlesser, 199
Schlieffen Plan, 13
Schmeltz, 15, 16
Sedan, 67, 71
S.H.A.E.F. 166, 209, 215
Siegfried Line, 186, 188–9, 192
Sigmaringen, 192, 197
Signy-L'Abbaye, 75–6
Simiot, Bernard, 203–4
Singapore, 260, 265
Sizaire, 257
Soames, Christopher, 227
Soissons, 26
Sollies, 142, 145
Somme, River, 23, 85
Soppe-le-bas, 179
Spaatz, General, 209–10
Spahis, 255
Spanish-Moroccan border, 41
Spellman, Cardinal, 269
Spire, 190–2
Stalin, 129, 211
Stonne, 80

Strasbourg, 157, 165, 170–8, 180, 186, 193, 202, 215, 278
Stuttgart, 192, 195–8
Sudre, 147–8, 150
Suippes, 83
Sultan of Morocco, 35–6
Swabian Jura, 195–6, 198

Tabouis, 109–10
Tafiliat, 37
Taranto, 140
Tarascon, 151
Taza, 39, 41–2
Tedder, Air-Marshal, 209–10
That-Khe, 245
Thiancourt, 14
Thiaumont, 22
Thierry d'Argenlieu, 244
Thionville, 13
Thugny-Trugny, 86–7
Tonking, 241, 243–4, 250, 252–3, 267
Touar, 145
Touchon, 72, 75–7
Toul, 9
Toulon, 137–8, 141–9, 151–2, 154, 199, 200, 202
Toulouse, 106, 110–11, 114, 126
Touraine, 241
Tran-Van-Huu, 263
Troisier, Solange, 203
Tron, Ludovic, 203
Troubridge, Admiral Sir Thomas, 130, 132–3
Truscott, 157
Turenne, 99, 177
Tyrol, 199

Ulm, 192, 194–7
United States, 245, 266–9

Valentin, François, 110–1, 126, 275–6
Valluy, 173, 191–3, 203–4
Vanves, 126
Vassiliev, 209
Vaugirard, College of, 6
Vaux, Fort, 21, 146
Vaux-Champagne, 83
Vendée La, 1–4, 18, 46, 54, 226, 262
Verdun, 20 *et seq.*, 86
Vergha, Wadi, 40–2
Verneau, General, 104–5
Versailles, 28, 168, 278
Vervins, 72
Vesoul, 158
Vichy, 91, 95, 99–100, 103–7, 111, 122 124, 207
Vietnot, 121
Viet-Nam, 241, 243–4, 255, 259, 263–6, 272, 274
Villers-le-Tilleul, 72
Vinh-Yen, 251–2, 254, 263–4
Vitry-le-François, 13, 75, 89–90
Voie Sacrée, 21
Von Bock, General, 67, 82, 85–6
Von Kluck, General, 14
Von Leeb, General, 67
Von Manstein, General, 68
Von Moltke, General, 13
Von Rundstedt, General, 67, 81–2, 85–6
Vorarlberg, 198–9
Vosges, 63, 157–8, 165–6, 170–1, 173, 177–8, 200, 292
Vuillemin, Monique, 203
Vyshinsky, 210

Waddington, 119
Wangerbourg, 63
Washington, 139, 182, 267–8, 272
West Point, 269
Weyersheim, 175–6
Weygand, General, 54–5, 94–5, 97–8, 100–2, 112–3, 245, 297–8
Weygand, Mme, 50, 208
Wiese, General, 157, 162, 165
Wilson, Field-Marshal Maitland, 128–31, 134, 138–9, 154, 158
Wissenbourg, 174
Worms, 190

Yeu, Île d', 46
Ypres, 29

Zeller, 137
Zhukov, 209–11
Zurs, 199

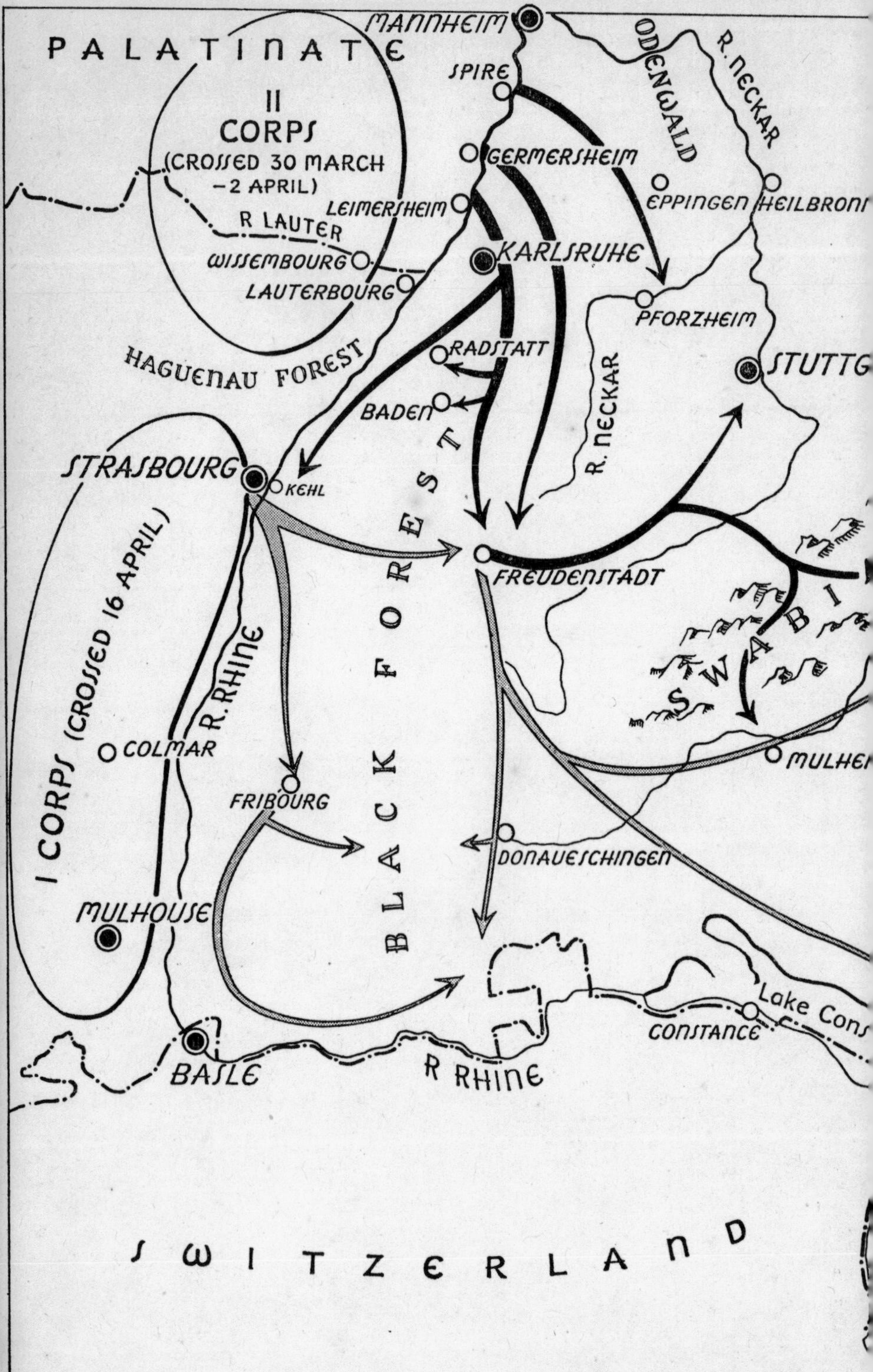

PALATINATE

II CORPS (CROSSED 30 MARCH – 2 APRIL)

MANNHEIM

SPIRE

GERMERSHEIM

ODENWALD

R. NECKAR

EPPINGEN

HEILBRON

LEIMERSHEIM

R LAUTER

WISSEMBOURG

LAUTERBOURG

KARLSRUHE

PFORZHEIM

HAGUENAU FOREST

RADSTATT

BADEN

R. NECKAR

STUTTG

STRASBOURG

KEHL

BLACK FOREST

FREUDENSTADT

I CORPS (CROSSED 16 APRIL)

R. RHINE

SWABI

COLMAR

MULHE

FRIBOURG

DONAUESCHINGEN

MULHOUSE

Lake Cons

CONSTANCE

BASLE

R RHINE

SWITZERLAND